A GUIDE
TO
BIBLICAL
PROPHECY

A GUIDE TO BIBLICAL PROPHECY

Edited by
CARL EDWIN ARMERDING
and
W. WARD GASQUE

Wipf and Stock Publishers
150 West Broadway • Eugene OR 97401
2001

A Guide to Biblical Prophecy

Edited by Gasque, W. Ward and Armerding, Carl
Copyright©1977 by Gasque, W. Ward and Armerding, Carl Edwin

Reprinted by *Wipf and Stock Publishers*
150 West Broadway • Eugene OR 97401

Previously published by Hendrickson Publishers 1977.

Contents

Foreword

I have no idea under which sign of the zodiac I was born (although, if
I were sufficiently interested, I could find out rather quickly) and,
even if I have not sufficient mathematical expertise to expound
Kepler's laws, I know that, when he discovered them, he realized
with wonder that he was thinking the Creator's thoughts after Him.
But it is one thing to track the course of the planets and quite
another to foresee the shape of things to come.

The shape of things to come is a favorite object of study in some
Christian groups. Their findings might command more confidence if
they all came to the same conclusion. But, even when they claim to
base their study on Holy Writ, they disagree widely in their findings.
The reason for this disagreement—a reason that many of them are
unwilling to admit—is that Holy Writ does not provide us with the
means of plotting the course of future events. Yet Christian faith
embraces the future in its scope, together with the present and the
past, because Christian faith is faith in Jesus Christ as Lord.

The primitive and universal Christian confession, "Jesus Christ is
Lord," acknowledges Him as the one who occupies "the highest
place that heaven affords" because of His death and resurrection.
The crucified and risen one is Lord of His people: "For to this end
Christ died and lived again, that he might be Lord both of the dead
and of the living" (Rom. 14:9). He is Lord of the universe, for it is
the Father's good pleasure "that at the name of Jesus every knee
should bow, in heaven and on earth and under the earth, and every
tongue confess that Jesus Christ is Lord" (Phil. 2:10 f.). And by the
same token He is Lord of the future. What more desirable future can
Christians contemplate than one in which their Lord is acknowledged
as Lord by all?

In the last third of the first Christian century, the prospects for the survival of the believing community were not bright. Roman law conceded it no right to exist, and the imperial power had begun to show its hostility to the Christian name. If an objective observer had been asked in those days to whom world dominion belonged, his reply would have been, "To Caesar, of course." Caesar was all-powerful, and the future was his. It took unusual faith for anyone to maintain, in the face of all the evidence to the contrary, that world dominion belonged to Jesus—that He was all-powerful, and that the future was His, so that those who were on His side were on the winning side. One man who had the necessary faith to maintain this was John, writer of the Book of the Revelation. He tells how he had a vision of heaven, and saw the celestial beings in suspense, waiting for something to happen, or rather for Someone to appear, to unleash the accomplishment of the divine purpose for the world. This purpose is recorded in a sealed scroll, held in the hand of the Almighty. Where is the conquering hero who will take the scroll, break the seals, and read the contents, so that they may be translated into fact? At last the conquering hero arrives, announced as "the Lion of the tribe of Judah," the Messiah of David's line. But when John turns to see the Lion, what he sees is "a Lamb standing, as though it had been slain." And it is this Lamb, so recently led to the slaughter, who claims the right to take the scroll and break the seals, and ever-widening concentric circles break into praise until all creation joins in the new song. In other words, Jesus' submission to suffering and death was the victory which entitled Him to world dominion. "The will of the Lord shall prosper in his hand" (Isa. 53:10). Jesus, not Caesar, is all-powerful; the future belongs not to the mailed fist but to the pierced hand. However long the conflict may last, the issue is not in doubt: the decisive battle has been fought and won on the cross. The followers of the Lamb have a share in His victory; they in their turn conquer "by the blood of the Lamb and by the word of their testimony, for they loved not their lives even unto death" (Rev. 12:11). This was the message of hope and encouragement for hard-pressed Christians toward the end of the first century A.D. The future was secure in the hands of their crucified and exalted Lord; what more did they need to know? And what more do we need to know?

Their hope remains, and will remain, the authentic Christian hope, even if future millennia look back on the first two thousand years A.D. as the primitive age of church history. What matters is the cer-

8

tainty of the final triumph, when Christ is universally confessed as Lord, not its timing. Each successive Christian generation occupies the place of that generation which will witness the dénouement, just as the first Christian generation so consciously did. For, as John Henry Newman put it,

> Though time intervene between Christ's first and second coming, it is not *recognized* (as I may say) in the Gospel scheme, but is, as it were, an accident. For so it was, that up to Christ's coming in the flesh, the course of things ran straight towards that end, nearing it by every step; but now, under the Gospel, that course has (if I may so speak) altered its direction, as regards His second coming, and runs, not towards the end, but along it, and on the brink of it; and is at all times near that great event, which, did it run towards it, it would at once run into. Christ, then, is ever at our doors; as near eighteen hundred years ago as now, and not nearer now than then, and not nearer when He comes than now.

Some contributors to the following pages find it possible to go into greater detail than this, but this is the essence of our Christian hope: Jesus Christ is Lord, and the Lord is always at hand.

F. F. Bruce

Preface

As we have visited various churches and university campuses during the six years we have been associated with Regent College, Vancouver, we have been asked by pastors, student workers, and others whether we could recommend a good book on the subject of Bible prophecy. The general concern has been for something less sensational and essentially more biblical than the runaway bestseller *The Late Great Planet Earth* and the spate of popular books on the subject which has followed its success.

Since we could not recommend anything which really met the need, we decided to produce one. And rather than writing a book by ourselves—thus running the risk of being accused of representing an eccentric approach to the subject—we decided to enlist the aid of a group of Bible teachers and scholars who would represent a wide range of Christian communities and institutions. In this way we have attempted to present not so much our own personal views but rather the mainstream evangelical Christian consensus.

It sometimes comes as a shock to certain young Christians to whom we minister to learn that the views represented by many of the popular writers on Bible prophecy are of very recent origin and do not, in fact, represent the convictions of any of the historic confessions or of most evangelical theologians. But this is a point which must be forcefully made.

However, it is not our purpose primarily to be negative, to criticize the recent popularizers. Rather, we offer this book as a positive statement of biblical teaching, as a handbook on the subject for the ordinary, intelligent reader. We do not intend it as a substitute for Bible study but rather as a challenge to return to the text of the Bible itself, which is the ultimate authority in such matters, to see whether or not we have represented its authentic teaching. If some take excep-

11

tion to our views, as will doubtlessly be the case, we will have achieved our purpose if we have caused them to rethink their positions *on the basis of Scripture.* And if we learn that this modest volume has been of positive benefit to others who have been unable to swallow the improbable speculations contained in many of the recent books but who have had difficulty in forming their own conclusions, we will be doubly happy.

Our thanks to the many who have helped in the production of this book: the fifteen contributors, whom we honor as esteemed friends and co-workers for the kingdom of God; the pastors and student workers who asked us for a "layman's guide to biblical prophecy"; Bonnie Brockett, Helen Keisler, Dal and Kit Schindell, Charles and Pam Wanamaker, Marcia Munger, Richard Browning, Susan Walker, Mary Houser, Richard Riss, and Muriel Sawatsky—friends and former students who have helped with various stages of the editing and proofreading; and Professor F. F. Bruce, Rylands Professor of Biblical Criticism, Manchester University, who wrote the foreword.

Our prayer is that this work will serve to glorify the Lord Jesus Christ, whom we serve and for whom we wait. *Maranatha!*

Carl Edwin Armerding
W. Ward Gasque

12

Contributors

Carl E. Armerding, Professor of Old Testament, Regent College, Vancouver, British Columbia, Canada (Christian Brethren)

F. F. Bruce, John Rylands Professor of Biblical Criticism and Exegesis Emeritus, University of Manchester, England (Christian Brethren)

Riley B. Case, Superintendent, Marion District of the United Methodist Church, Marion, Indiana (Methodist)

Robert G. Clouse, Professor of History, Indiana State University, Terre Haute, Indiana (Grace Brethren)

Edmund P. Clowney, President and Professor of Theology Emeritus, Westminster Theological Seminary, Chestnut Hill, Pennsylvania (Orthodox Presbyterian)

William A. Dyrness, Professor of Systematic Theology, New College Berkeley, Berkeley, California (Presbyterian)

W. W. Gasque, E. Sheppard Professor of Biblical Studies, Regent College, Vancouver, British Columbia, Canada (Christian Brethren)

Donald A. Hagner, Professor of New Testament, Fuller Theological Seminary, Pasadena, California (Presbyterian)

C. M. Kempton Hewitt, Dean and Professor of Biblical Studies, The Methodist School of Ohio, Delaware, Ohio (Methodist)

Walter C. Kaiser, Jr., Dean and Professor of Old Testament, Trinity Evangelical Divinity School, Deerfield, Illinois (Evangelical Free)

†George Eldon Ladd, former Professor of Biblical Theology, Fuller Theological Seminary, Pasadena, California (American Baptist)

Paul E. Leonard, lay theologian and consulting engineer, Milwaukee, Wisconsin (Independent)

Richard N. Longenecker, Professor of New Testament, Wycliffe College, Toronto, Ontario, Canada (Baptist Convention of Ontario, Quebec)

James P. Martin, former Principal and Professor of New Testament Emeritus, Vancouver School of Theology, Vancouver, British Columbia, Canada (United Church of Canada)

John Warwick Montgomery, theologian, apologist, lawyer, and author, Orange, California (Lutheran)

Ian S. Rennie, Academic Vice-President and Professor of Church History, Ontario Theological Seminary, Willowdale, Ontario, Canada (Presbyterian)

James Robert Ross, pastoral counselor, Lexington, Kentucky (Church of Christ)

†J. S. Wright, formerly Principal of Tyndale Hall and Canon of Bristol Cathedral, Bristol, England (Anglican)

13

About the Editors

Carl E. Armerding is Professor of Old Testament Studies at Regent College, Vancouver, British Columbia, Canada, where he has served since its inception in 1970, eleven years as principal. He holds degrees from Gordon College, Trinity Evangelical Divinity School, and Brandeis University; he has done further research in Jerusalem and Cambridge. He is the author of *The Old Testament and Criticism,* the editor of *Evangelicals and Liberation,* and has written numerous scholarly and popular articles in a wide variety of journals and symposia. A frequent speaker at conferences for students, lay and professional church leaders, and academic colleagues, he is currently at work on a major commentary on the book of Judges.

W. Ward Gasque is the E. Marshall Sheppard Professor of Biblical Studies at Regent College, Canada's largest theological school. He is a graduate of Wheaton College, Fuller Theological Seminary, and Manchester University; he has pursued further study at Basel, Cambridge, Lausanne, and Princeton. Author of *The History of the Interpretation of the Acts of the Apostles,* editor or co-editor of several collected works, including *Apostolic History and the Gospel* (in honor of F. F. Bruce), and New Testament editor of the multivolumed New International Biblical Commentary series, he has traveled to more than forty countries and has lectured on more than sixty college and university campuses. His current major project is a commentary on the Greek text of the Acts of the Apostles for the New International Greek Testament Commentary.

1

The Age of Aquarius

William Dyrness

If the pretensions of astrology are genuine, why do not men of every age devote themselves to this study? Why from our infancy do we not fix our eyes on nature and on the gods, seeing that the stars unveil themselves for us, and that we can live in the midst of the gods? Why exhaust ourselves in effort to acquire eloquence, or devote ourselves to the profession of arms?

—Aurelius Fuscus, Roman Philosopher

The Modern Interest in Astrology

Ask anyone on the street what sign of the zodiac he is born under, and he can tell you. Ask the same person to tell you Kepler's laws, and he will think you are crazy.

One of the strangest paradoxes of history is that the nation with the highest standard of living, the leading scientific and industrial technology, and one of the highest literacy rates in the world, should be experiencing a rebirth of interest in astrology and fortune telling. The same newspaper that announces space walks and advances in cancer research probably carries a daily horoscope. Every day, over fifty million Americans consult readings in twelve hundred newspapers. For that day, they can find a prediction that is determined solely by the arrangement of planets on the day of their birth.

By now, perhaps, we take this in stride and smile as we are told to "avoid unusual involvement," forgetting that this interest is a recent

15

development. Only since World War II has the popularity of astrology become prominent. As recently as 1898, the French dictionary *Nouveau Larousse Illustré* could say: "Astrology has hardly any adherents other than swindlers who play on public credulity and even these are fast disappearing." False hope!

Two world wars and economic instability have succeeded in reviving interest in predicting the future. Just after the crash in 1929, many stores vacated in New York City because of bankruptcy were taken over by gypsies who experienced no recession.

World War II quickened interest in the prophetic. Adolph Hitler had his own personal astrologer, though his example probably was not influential. Astrology had three million followers in the United States by 1946. According to *Life* magazine, horoscopes were appearing in one hundred newspapers.

After the war, attention was diverted from the stars. Things were going well enough for a while to hold our attention on earth rather than gazing toward the heavens. But the beat generations of the 1950s reminded us that all was not well, and by the late 50s and early 60s people had begun wondering and consulting their horoscopes.

It is true that many people would never admit to believing in what they find out, but that does not stop them from going to great lengths to discover their readings. By the mid-60s, astrology had become a widespread and profitable fad. By 1965, there were a score of astrological periodicals. Sales of *Horoscope* magazine's annual guidebook more than doubled from 1962 to 1966 (reaching five million). In 1966, sales of Ouija boards tripled. Abrams and Strauss department stores in New York made the news in 1969 by hiring Lloyd Cope as astrological consultant. Apparently their example was followed by others, as there are now supposed to be 10,000 full-time astrologers in America (with 175,000 working part-time). The most famous is probably Carroll Righter, Hollywood's resident astrologer, whose daily column appears in 306 newspapers and reaches forty million homes.[1]

It is also true that "astro-philosophers" claim the stars impel but do not compel. This does not, however, change the fact that astrology propounds a thinly veiled fatalism. People want to know what will happen to them more often to escape responsibility for their behavior —marred as it is with frustration and failure—than to be spurred on to great moral efforts. It is easier to seek to know what will happen to this man than to ask, "What should this man do?" What will be, will be, so let us make the most of it—this is the gospel of astrology. Prophets forecasting doom and destruction have always abounded. But during the 60s some were taken seriously and began making the news. In 1965, Ruth Montgomery's book on seer Jeane Dixon, *A Gift of Prophecy,* appeared and stayed on best-seller lists for months. Mrs. Dixon, known for her humanitarian concern, is most famous for her prediction of Kennedy's assassination, which appeared in a 1956 issue of *Parade* magazine: "A blond Democratic president will be elected in 1960 and will die in office," she had written. Rather unspecific, but not bad as prophecies go. Edgar Cayce, who died in 1945, was another prophet who came to prominence in the 1960s. No fewer than five books were published in that decade on this sleeping prophet, who had been able to diagnose and treat all kinds of illnesses while asleep. His Association for Research and Enlightenment, a hospital and a school he founded in Virginia Beach, Virginia, has attracted thousands in recent years. Last but not least, biblical prophets have been given a fresh hearing—and not only by Christians—as Hal Lindsey's *The Late Great Planet Earth* demonstrates. Published in 1970, this book sold over six million copies in less than six years.

Is pragmatic, hard-headed America turning into a nation of mystics? Can such a practical people give serious attention to prophets? Do we really believe the astrological creed that "certain vibrations inbreathed by a newly born babe endow the tendencies of character it will manifest" (Llewellyn George) and that a decisive influence on the earth is exerted by the stars? Perhaps this is a part of the current interest in Eastern thought. For in Asia, astrology is a natural corollary of the prevailing world view. There is a sense of closeness and of identification with nature. There is a feeling for the underlying harmony of all things, a harmony all men wish to share. All of this is attractive to Western man as he tries to pull together the fragmented strands of his existence. Peace and harmony are exactly what he would like, and if astrology can help, then bring it on.

Historical Background

But this Eastern influence, which cannot be denied (though one could debate whether it is cause or effect), does not account for the phenomenal recent interest in predicting the future. To understand this we must look into our own history, and take the time to reflect on some lessons it suggests. There have been two periods of history before our own when this fascination for astrology has been felt: the late Greek or Hellenistic period and the late Middle Ages and the Renaissance. The first time this essentially Eastern preoccupation came into our Western tradition was in the Hellenistic period of ancient Greece (ca. 300 to 200 B.C.).[2] It is instructive to notice the conditions under which this took place.

By the time of Plato (d. 347 B.C.), traditional religion in Greece was dying. The people had lost touch with their classical mythology. No longer were there gods to turn to who had struggled and suffered like men and who thereby lent meaning to human striving. Encouraged by the Platonic philosophy, people turned to the worship of heavenly bodies. With the rise of Macedonia the social structure of the city states disintegrated; and while the empire of Alexander was at its zenith, the social and spiritual vacuum was the most threatening. The Stoics and Epicureans bravely fought against the rise of superstition, but in vain. During the reign of Alexander (336 - 323 B.C.), the first instruction in astrology took place. Of course, the astral theology of the Platonists had prepared the way, but it was Persian influence that introduced the worship of the seven planets. By the early second century, astrological manuals abounded.

Causes of Interest in Astrology

What was happening? As E. R. Dodds explains it, empty thrones were calling out to be filled. "In default of any positive object," he argues, "the sentiment of dependence attaches itself to the purely negative idea of the unexplained and unpredictable, which is Tyche (Chance)."[3] Religion in the traditional sense still existed, but, much like Christianity (and Judaism) today, it was routine and without influence on the values of life. And as G. K. Chesterton has said, when a man ceases to believe in God (or gods), he doesn't believe in nothing, he believes in anything.

Another way of looking at this is to say that the Greeks experienced a failure of nerve, as Gilbert Murray suggests in *The Five Stages of Greek Religion.* Man saw himself alone in a world in which he had no allies. There were no more gods appreciative of human effort. It was natural that astrology, which is essentially a surrender to chance, should become popular. Murray comments in a way relevant to modern America: "It is worth remembering that the best

18

seed-ground for superstition is a society in which the fortunes of men seem to bear practically no relation to their merits and efforts."[4] Such is the feeling of man standing alone, stripped of the comfort of faith. Dodds concludes that the individual turned tail and bolted from his own freedom.

Early Christianity fought this religion of fate. It is possible that Paul's reference to the *stoicheia* (elements) in Colossians 2:8 may refer to the mystic signs of the planets.[5] Some early Christians, however, took more interest in the stars than was healthy, though the early Church Fathers inveighed against the practice. Constantine, the first Christian emperor, established December 25 as Christmas because the winter solstice had previously been the holiday of the sun, and he brought Pythia's sacred tripod from Delphi to Constantinople as a piece of plunder. Augustine denounced belief in the influence of the stars as inconsistent with the Christian view of God and man, and his views became official in the church.[6]

The church in the Middle Ages did not keep itself completely pure, however. As a result of the Barbarian invasions, the Teutonic belief in fate penetrated medieval theology.[7] In a celebrated incident occurring in 1108, the Archbishop of York was refused Christian burial because a book of astrology had been found under his pillow. Thomas Aquinas and Dante, while preserving human freedom, allowed the stars some influence over man's activities. Since much of classical antiquity was rediscovered through Arabic sources, a great deal of astrology was imported along with it. Thus, chairs of Astrology were established in all the leading universities, and strange and terrifying prophecies abounded.

That the sixteenth century marked the peak of this second great rise of astrology and prophetic speculation is not without significance. Even the most religious men included the influence of the stars in their creed. It was a day of synthesis when neo-Platonism, Greek mythology, and Christian theology were joined in uneasy alliance. The painter Dürer's famous print *Melancholia* is filled with astrological, as well as religious, allusions. Philip Melanchthon, the famous disciple of Luther, occupied the chair of Astrology in Wittenberg. How Christians could allow such superstition can be illustrated by a treatise from that period called *Astrology Theologized: The Spiritual Hermeneutics of Astrology and Holy Writ.*[8] In this treatise, astrology is equated with the light of nature that

19

belongs to our present earthly life, whereas theology is seen as a spiritual understanding, arising from within by the illumination of the Holy Spirit.

One of the most famous astrologer-prophets dates from this period. Michel Nostradamus was born in a small town south of Avignon, France in 1503. His book of prophecies, called *The Centuries*, was published in 1555, and its reception was spectacular enough for King Henry II of France to invite the author to become part of his court. Its predictions (over one hundred of which are supposed by his followers to have been fulfilled) include references to France and Europe. The following lines were seen to refer to the rise of Napoleon and his rule:

> In the deepest part of Western Europe
> A Child will be born of poor parents
> Who by his language will seduce the great army.
> His fame will increase further because of a
> government expedition toward the East.[9]

But why should this revival of prophetic interest occur in the sixteenth century? Wasn't that the period of the rebirth of learning and scholarship? The Renaissance was that, but it was more. As in ancient Greece and our own day, the outward splendor merely concealed a deep-seated spiritual crisis. Medieval man had sought and found a harmonious hierarchical system in which each part of life and the world had meaning in the grand scheme of salvation. His world view, imaginatively captured in Dante's *Divine Comedy,* was like a journey in which all the stages reassuringly fitted together. With the Renaissance and the Reformation, the unity was broken, strange new factors called for attention, and man's place in the scheme of things was no longer secure. Violent social upheavals, manifested in peasant wars and the sack of Rome in 1527, threatened the whole social structure. With the rediscovery of classical form, humanists proclaimed a new day for the individual man, but it was a solitary man facing life without traditional supports. The Christian faith, while still accepted in principle, ceased for many—as in our own day—to be a vital principle of living. In the uncertainty many more began to look to the stars.[10]

An interesting footnote is provided by the last great astronomer who believed in (and practiced) astrology, Johannes Kepler (d. 1630).

He called astrology an unbearable but necessary slavery in which he had to indulge to support his truly scientific researches. After much study he had come to doubt the horoscope's predictions of personal fate. From this date on, the science of astronomy was separated from the superstition of astrology.

Current Dilemma

The Enlightenment of the eighteenth century heralded the end of astrological speculation. Man was coming of age, comfortable in this world and unconcerned about the next. Strange, then, that in our own highly sophisticated century we should again wish to believe in the influence of the stars. Wars and economic collapses have called into question the humanistic ideals of the Enlightenment, and for a third time the question became insistent: Who am I and what am I to make of myself?

It is the Christian view that history leads somewhere and that it has an end. The Christian view proposes, moreover, that it is a personal and loving God who directs history's course, who has acted decisively in it in Jesus Christ, and who stands at its end. For the believing Christian, then, it is precisely because an all-wise God is directing history that the moral and scientific efforts of man make any sense. Because we live in a moral order that has direction, we can work for truth and goodness. Since Hegel (mediated by Marx and Darwin), our Western view of progress has been secularized. We cannot bring ourselves to believe history is going nowhere (that it is cyclical, for example, as the Greeks believed). Yet, if there is direction, either it must be implicit in the whole process (determined) or it must be provided by ourselves.

We also cannot give up believing in an end to history, whether it be an apocalypse, a final synthesis, or a classless society. What shape the "end" will take depends, of course, on one's "theology." The counter-culture of the late 1960s reminded us again and again of the end, and the vocabulary of apocalypse came into vogue once more. Theodore Roszak articulated the dream of the flower children with his hope that in those discontented elements "the innovation can be found that might transform this disoriented civilization of ours into something a human being can identify as home."[11] Not everyone gave up so completely on the technocracy as Roszak. More recently, Alvin Toffler has predicted a future of ever-increasing change and

21

transience, assuring us with the certainty that only a prophet with credentials would claim: "The nature of what can and will be done exceeds anything that man is yet psychologically and morally prepared to live with."[12] Whatever the exact shape of the future, it is coming. And Toffler, in true prophetic style, writes to help create the consciousness man will need to guide his evolution. And there are more. Charles Reich sees the dawning of "consciousness three" as the next (final?) level. George Leonard, in *The Transformation,* sees man advancing into a state of higher being, of oneness with all existence.[13]

The keynote of all these excursions into the future is inevitability. One may join the march or not, but that it has direction is sure. The last-named book is significantly subtitled "A Guide to the Inevitable Changes in Mankind." We should be grateful, I suppose, for the optimism of these prophecies, but one cannot escape the feeling that our fate is sealed and there is really very little we can do about it.

It was precisely this point that bothered poet Archibald MacLeish at the beginning of World War II. He felt himself living in a generation of prophets. They were all prophets of doom. But this bothered him far less than their fatalism. MacLeish complains: "The generation to which I belong believes . . . in a predetermined pattern of life" and they prophesied because their fate was sealed. "Our generation fled to fate," he explains, "not by opposing it . . . but by searching it out in order that we might yield to it, and by yielding then not only our responsibilities but our will."[14] Then with a perception that recalls the decline of faith in ancient Greece and our own secularism: "We fled to fate—we invented a fate of our own—to escape a world which had grown too large for us, a world too complicated to understand, too huge to know."[15] No science or education has equipped us to deal with the world's complexities, and real faith has become inoperative.

Against this background, the revival of interest in biblical prophecy is to be seen. As MacLeish was writing, many Christians were busy identifying Mussolini with the Antichrist of Revelation and the Axis powers with the revived Roman Empire. Charts of biblical events were prepared to show how God was working out His program. It is, of course, a great comfort for the believer to trust in God's direction. But great comfort can easily become a crutch or even an escape. If it is true that prophecy is concerned only with the actions of God, it can easily follow in our thinking that what we do does not really matter. The biblical view is that what God does is always vitally related to what man does. We will often have occasion in the course of these essays to reflect on the moral context of prophetic teaching. Prophecy is not merely prediction; it is judgment and it is promise.[16]

We have noticed that the rise of astrology and prophetic speculation has its origin in the feeling of helplessness. Events that occur around the individual seem to bear no relation to his efforts. Astrology offers the perfect ritual for such a "theology." But the danger is that Christians, experiencing this same sense of helplessness in face of world events, can replace astrology with biblical prophecy. Unknowingly, they may simply be giving fatalism a Christian veneer.

In 1958, when the current interest in prophecy was growing, a prominent popular magazine ran a series on biblical prophecy written by theologians of different persuasions. The evangelical contribution concluded with this paragraph: "The study of Bible prophecy is difficult but rewarding. God has revealed many facets of His plan. How thrilling it is to watch events as they unfold, and see the working of His mighty hand."[17] "Watch it coming"—an admonition very different from that of the apostle Paul: "But as to times and seasons, brethren, you have no need to have anything written to you. For you yourselves know that the day of the Lord will come like a thief in the night" (I Thess. 5:1-2).

It is no coincidence that the publication of Hal Lindsey's first book on prophecy coincided with the greatest revival of astrology in three hundred years. (It is interesting to note how often his book appears in bookstores alongside astrology manuals.) Man can escape as easily into prophecy as astrology. In either case, he is a pawn and thus relieved of moral responsibility. That this was no part of Lindsey's purpose is clear from the final pages of his book. Certainly God has used his treatment to lead many to a commitment to Christ, and for this God is to be praised. But we must be careful that our longing for Christ's return is not motivated by a desire to escape responsibility.

One writer, in castigating all prophetic, optimistic views of the future, makes a statement that Christians would do well to ponder: "Those with a vested interest in . . . Armageddon, like any devout fundamentalist, find comfort in the thought of an approaching *dies irae* (day of wrath) on which the faithful will at last be recognized when and where it really counts."[18] How often one hears: "Praise God, the end is coming soon" with just such an implication. Once

I was approached after a service at which I had preached by a member of the congregation who exclaimed: "What a joy to think Christ is coming soon and the last battle will take place!"

"Can you really say that gladly," I answered, "when you know that battle will send thousands or millions to a Christless eternity?"

"Well," he responded, in words that reflected more the spirit of his age than biblical truth, "it's inevitable, isn't it?" That, I believe, is fatalism and not Christian truth. Indeed the end is certain, and we yearn to see Christ; but we do not long for His judgment. Nor is judgment "inevitable"; one has only to recall the story of Jonah and Nineveh. Above all, the thought of Christ's coming should motivate us to compassion, to a more diligent proclamation of the gospel, and to greater efforts for righteousness, knowing that even the giving of a cup of cold water is related to the end, when Christ will remember every righteous deed.[19]

Conclusion

It is important to remember that the New Testament was written at a time when belief in fate was widespread. The geocentric view of the world led to a common acceptance of the belief that events were governed by the stars. Ralph P. Martin believes that that great passage in Philippians 2:5-11 was addressed to people living in just such an atmosphere. He writes: "It assures us that the character of the God whose will controls the universe is to be spelled out in terms of Jesus Christ. He is no arbitrary power, no capricious force, no pitiless, indifferent fate. His nature is love . . . His title to Lordship can be interpreted only in terms of self-denying service for others."[20]

This Person is the same today as when Paul wrote these words, and His continued Lordship provides meaning not only for our evangelism, but also for our moral, educational, and scientific endeavors, for all of these reflect His glory.

Clearly, the escape into prophecy and astrology reflects the identity crisis brought about by a spiritual vacuum. Never has this vacuum been more evident than today. William Braden, in his book on the cultural revolution, argues that Black Power, Eastern religion, drugs, and astrology "are all in one way or another related to the question of identity."[21]

24

The proper response to such a vacuum is not to offer an escape—even if it is into a quasi-Christian view of the future—but rather to proclaim the Christian view of man. Here, Christianity provides for a vital present relationship with the living Christ, and a day-to-day dependence on Him. Only in this context can we sincerely pray the prayer of Revelation: "Even so, come, Lord Jesus "(KJV). For the Person who offers personal fulfillment is the Lord of the future.

Notes

1. The literature on this phenomenon has become large and uneven. Some of the better surveys written from a Christian point of view are Gary A. Wilbern, *The Fortune Tellers* (Glendale, CA: Regal, 1972); *Astrology and the Bible,* William J. Petersen, ed. (Wheaton, IL: Scripture Press, 1972); and Joseph Bayly, *What About Horoscopes?* (New York: Pyramid Pubns, n.d.).

2. The author is aware that the presence of astrological symbols in Mexican pre-Colombian civilization argues for the universality of this phenomenon. Still, historically, the preoccupation entered Western tradition in the way I am about to describe.

3. *The Greeks and the Irrational* (Berkeley: U of Cal Pr, 1968), p. 242.

4. *Five Stages of Greek Religion* (New York: Anch. Doubleday, 1955), p. 127. Pliny could justly say two centuries later, "We are so much at the mercy of chance that Chance is our God" (*Natural History,* ii., 22).

5. Cf. Michael Green, *Evangelism in the Early Church* (Grand Rapids: Eerdmans, 1970), pp. 124, 125. And M. Cohen, *Myths of the Space Age* (New York: Dodd, 1967), p. 102.

6. "But to desire to predict the characters, the acts, and the fate of those who are born from such observation, is a great delusion and great madness. . . . And so these notions which have their origin in certain signs of things being arbitrarily fixed upon by the presumption of men, are to be referred to the same class as if they were leagues and covenants with devils" (*On Christian Doctrine,* Bk. II, chaps. 21-23).

7. For much of this brief historical development I am indebted to Rudolf Thiel, *And There Was Light* (New York: Knopf, 1967), pp. 56 ff.

8. See the 1649 edition reprinted in London (George Redway, 1886), Anna Bonus Kingsford, ed.

9. *Oracles of Nostradamus,* Charles A. Ward, ed. (New York: Scribner, 1940), p. 286, Century III, Quatrain 35.

10. See on this C. S. Lewis, *The Discarded Image* (Cambridge: At the University Press, 1964), and Johann Huizinga, *The Waning of the Middle Ages* (London: E. Arnold, 1927).

11. *The Making of a Counter Culture* (New York: Anch. Doubleday, 1969), p. xiii.

12. Alvin Toffler, *Future Shock* (New York: Random, 1970), p. 205.

13. *The Transformation* (New York: Delacorte, 1972). Some of the titles that embody this apocalyptic theme are: William Irwin Thompson, *At the Edge of History* (New York: Har-Row, 1971); Judson Jerome, *Culture Out of Anarchy* (New York: McGraw, 1970); and Theodore Roszak, *Where the Wasteland Ends* (New York: Anch. Doubleday, 1973). For a summary of this kind of thinking, see the astounding article by Joyce Carol Oates, "New Heaven and New Earth," *Saturday Review*, November 4, 1972, pp. 51-4.

14. Archibald MacLeish, "Prophets of Doom," *Atlantic*, October 1941, p. 478.

15. Ibid., p. 479.

16. John Baillie notes that the Old Testament prophets always pronounced judgment or gave hope in the light of the present. "It would seem that when the Word of God is brought to bear radically upon our human life, this must be the prevailing note." "Beware the Whitewash," *Christian Century*, October 31, 1951, p. 1248.

17. Allan MacRae, "Bible Prophecy," *American Mercury*, October 1958, p. 34.

18. Samuel McCracken, "Apocalyptic Thinking," *Commentary*, October 1971, p. 68.

19. That even recent evangelical interest in prophecy neglects the ethical content can be seen in *Christianity Today*'s report of the June 1971, Jerusalem Prophecy Conference. "An emphasis on the ethical significance of futuristic prophecy evidently did not fall within the conference purpose" (John H. Mulholland, "Heightened Interest in Prophecy," May 26, 1972, p. 14).

20. *Carmen Christi: Philippians 2:5-11 in Recent Interpretation and in the Setting of Early Christian Worship* (Cambridge: At the University Press, 1967), p. 311.

21. *The Age of Aquarius: Technology and the Cultural Revolution* (Chicago: Quadrangle Books, 1970), p. 8.

2

The Danger of Mistaken Hopes

Robert G. Clouse

Through the centuries, many Christians have been unable to maintain the tension of the possibility of the return of Christ in their time and have felt compelled to set the date for the Second Coming. Even Jesus' disciples wished to pinpoint this event when they asked, "When will this be?" (Mark 13:4). In answer, the Lord warned His followers that there would be trials and that signs would accompany these persecutions, but for His return He gave no date. In fact, He clearly stated, "But of that day or that hour no one knows" (Mark 13:32). At the time of the ascension, Jesus reiterated His position when the disciples asked, "Will you at this time restore the kingdom to Israel?" and He answered, "It is not for you to know times or seasons, which the Father has fixed by his own authority" (Acts 1:6-7).

Despite the clear teaching that Christians are not meant to know the time of the end of the age, many scholars have made calculations based on the mystic numbers in Daniel and Revelation and selected a date or approximate time for the Second Advent. These attempts always have led to dismal failure and the consequent discrediting of prophetic preaching. Perhaps it is possible to reverse the maxim that the only thing we learn from the past is that we learn nothing from the past. With this hope, the following illustrations of the date-setting tendency have been chosen from the major eras of church history: Montanism, which represents the danger of too dogmatic a millennial teaching from the early church; Joachim of Fiore and his followers illustrating the same tendency in medieval times; the date-setting work of Johann Heinrich Alsted, also demonstrating this habit of mind during the Reformation era; and Leonard Sale-Harrison's continuance of this current of thought in the modern period.

Montanism

The first of these examples, Montanism, grew from the teachings of Montanus in Phrygia during the latter half of the second century and eventually caused great commotion in the early church.[1] Apparently the movement was not heretical at its inception but was an exaggeration of the morality and discipline of the post-apostolic church. It emphasized an excessively supernatural, Puritanic outlook against what was considered a growing laxity on the part of most Christians. Montanus, according to some accounts, had been a priest of Cybele and had no special talents other than a fanatical zeal. He fell into trances during which he felt himself to be the special instrument of the Spirit of God. Two women who were converted to his belief, Priscilla and Maximilla, left their husbands and, joining Montanus, went out preaching the near approach of the millennial reign of Christ. According to them, this was to occur not at Jerusalem but in Pepuza, a small village in Asia Minor. This message, propagated with enthusiasm and accompanied by glossolalia and frenzied prophesying, spread to Rome and North Africa, causing turmoil in the church. The councils and bishops who had to deal with the New Prophecy (as Montanism often was called) generally denounced the movement as the work of demons and excommunicated its followers. Nevertheless, among the converts to the group we find one of the outstanding leaders of the early church, Tertullian.[2]

Montanism, despite the early and continuing opposition to it, seems in most points to be orthodox. It did, however, seek a continuance of the miraculous gifts of apostolic times which had gradually disappeared as Christianity gained acceptance. In addition to the emphasis on prophecy and speaking in tongues, the New Prophecy stressed fanatical asceticism and discipline. All the enjoyments of life were suspect and works of art were condemned. Women were not to wear attractive clothing, and virgins were to be veiled. Fasts and other disciplinary exercises were multiplied as the best preparation for the return of Christ. Martyrdom was sought, and attempts to

28

escape persecution by concealment or flight were considered sinful. Those who lapsed from the faith never were allowed to return.

These teachings put a great gulf between those who observed them and those who did not. Montanists considered themselves to be "spiritual," whereas other Christians, no matter how reverent, were "psychical." These teachings were given with the expectation that the age soon would end and the millennium would be established. The Montanists lived under the vivid expectation of the great final catastrophe and therefore looked with contempt on efforts to change the present order of things. Maximilla, the last of the three prophets to die (A.D. 179), stated: "After me there is no more prophecy, but only the end of the world."[3] This prediction failed, and the New Prophecy gradually died out.

Joachim of Fiore

The date-setting millennialism of the Montanists has reappeared again and again in Christian history. During the Middle Ages, its most interesting form was in the work of Joachim of Fiore (1132-1200) and his followers.[4] Joachim came from Calabria, and during his busy life was at times a courtier, traveler, missionary, and hermit. About 1177, he became abbot of the Cistercian Abbey at Corazzo. He developed so great an interest in Bible study that he asked to be relieved of his duties, a request that was granted in 1182. After this, Joachim produced in the short space of a year and a half three important books: *Book of the Harmony of the New and Old Testament, Exposition of the Apocalypse,* and *Psaltery of Ten Strings.* In these works he divided the history of the world into three epochs: the age of the Father (Petrine) until the time of Christ; that of the Son (Pauline) from the birth of Christ to 1260; and that of the Holy Ghost (Johannean) from 1260 onward. (The number 1260 is derived from Revelation 11:3 and 12:6.) Joachim called this the "everlasting gospel," an expression taken from Revelation 14:6, "Then I saw another angel flying in mid-heaven, with an eternal [or everlasting] gospel to proclaim to those who dwell on earth, to every nation and tribe and tongue and people." The third age, which was to begin in the year 1260, was to be a time of contemplation when all the world would become a vast monastery. His outline of the events that would lead to this age states that the papacy, which was Antichrist, was to be eliminated by the emperor. The empire would then be destroyed by

29

the Saracens, and ten kings from the east would, in turn, be destroyed by the Tartars. An order of contemplative monks would take charge of the church and institute a reform program that would usher in the sabbath of humanity, a time of rest and peace for all.

Francis of Assisi

Joachim's teaching might not have attracted much attention, for he died in obscurity in the year 1200. But when Francis of Assisi came on the scene and met with considerable success, he seemed to be the leader of that new era of the Spirit predicted by Joachim. Although the year 1260 came without the new age being introduced, the program of Joachim was revived, new dates were set up, and the golden age was still expected. The group that tried to follow Francis's ideals of poverty fell into disfavor with the church, and in their persecuted condition they turned for spiritual strength to the prophecies of Joachim. These people, called the Spiritual Franciscans, were found primarily in Italy and southern France.[5] Perhaps the most prominent of them, Peter John Olivi (1248-1298), a teacher and theologian, wrote books that were held to be as important as the Scriptures. Consequently, in most of the arguments between the Spirituals and the papacy, the writings of Olivi are reexamined. His most important work, *A Commentary on the Apocalypse,* was based on Joachim's works and portrays the carnal church as ripening for judgment and awaiting the victory of the spiritual order. Olivi could not, of course, accept the 1,260th year as the beginning of the third age since his commentary appeared in 1297. Hence, he decided upon the seventh year after the death of Christ because this is the date that he assigned for the elevation of Peter to the primacy of the church. Thus these days would end in the year 1300. Olivi echoed Joachim in the identification of the Roman Church with Antichrist and in the description of the Age of the Spirit.

Johann Heinrich Alsted

It became obvious that Joachim and his followers had missed the date for the new age, but others still tried to take up the effort. During the era of the Reformation, a most unusual individual became interested in this cause. Johann Heinrich Alsted, who believed that the Second Coming would occur in 1694, was in most aspects of his life a typical product of the Reformed tradition.[6] A German Calvinist trained in Reformed theology and humanistic studies at Herborn, Alsted remained at his alma mater as a professor. A steady stream of writing flowed from his pen, causing his name to be known far beyond his native Rhineland. As this fame grew, young men from every country of Europe where the Reformed faith had gained a foothold came to hear his lectures.

When dissension broke out between the Reformed and the Arminians, and the Synod of Dort was called (1618) for the purpose of settling the dispute, Alsted was selected as a representative to the meeting. He participated in the victory of the Reformed position at the Synod, and, on his return, was promoted to Professor of Theology and later was elected rector of the school.

In the meantime, however, the Thirty Years War had begun, and the large armies marching through the Rhineland disturbed the quiet course of Alsted's life. The troops brought plague and fire in their wake, and the fortunes of Herborn declined. When Alsted was invited by Prince Gabriel of Transylvania to come to a new school that the Prince was organizing (1624), the desire for an undisturbed place to do his work caused him to accept this appointment, and he remained there until his death.

Although in much of his outlook he was a typical product of the Reformed orthodoxy of his day, in his espousal of millennialist eschatology Alsted departed from the Calvinist legacy. The orthodox Calvinists had inherited from the sixteenth-century Reformers a deep distrust of millennialism. Calvin had dismissed such teaching as a childish fantasy without scriptural support. Calvin castigated millenarians as those being ignorant of divine things or as malignant perverts attempting to overthrow the grace of God. His concern was the appearance and revelation of the Lord for a general resurrection and Last Judgment, and he felt that millennialism was a poor substitute for this hope. Calvin was also against using biblical numerics in speculations about the end of the age. In commenting on Daniel 12, a favorite book for such predictions, the Genevan reformer stated: "In numerical calculations I am no conjurer, and those who expound this passage with too much subtlety, only trifle in their own speculations, and detract from the authority of prophecy."[7] With this attitude, it is not surprising that Calvin never wrote a commentary on the Book of Revelation.

31

Alsted disagreed with this aspect of Calvin's teaching and defended the premillennial outlook in a book entitled *Diatribe de mille annis Apocalypticis.* This work was later translated into English under the title *The Beloved City.*[8] According to Alsted, there were two reasons for writing this book. First, it would help to establish a method of Bible study that could be applied to any other portion of Holy Scripture; and second, it gave him an opportunity to explain his millennialist position. In the foreword to the book, he laid down three prerequisites to the successful study of biblical prophecy. These were the help of the Holy Spirit, a diligent comparison of Scripture with Scripture, and an experience of fulfilled Bible prophecy. As the Thirty Years War was devastating his land at this time, he felt that this indeed was the end of the age. He admonished: "Let us sail therefore in the name of God, and comfort the desolation of Germany with this pious meditation."[9] The war, which altered the course of his life, seems to have influenced Alsted in the adoption of his eschatological views.

The Beloved City is a careful exposition of Revelation 20. After dealing in an introductory way with the author, subject, and context, Alsted gives a summation of this passage. He proceeds in this fashion: God will put the dragon, Satan, into the bottomless pit for a thousand years. Since Satan is imprisoned, he cannot stir wicked men against the church of God; therefore, the church enjoys outward peace, the righteous are raised from the dead, and multitudes are converted. At the close of the thousand years this happy condition is ended by the war of Gog and Magog, during which the church is again persecuted. After this conflict comes the Last Judgment and the final destruction of evil. Alsted then presents a word study of the entire chapter to support millennialism, and this "philological" section is followed by a logical analysis of the text. He deals with certain objections that might arise in the minds of his readers. He begins by stating that most of the objections could be reduced to the question of whether the church can anticipate any millennial happiness on earth before the Last Judgment. To prove that there will be a great day of earthly blessing for the church, he cites a number of Old Testament passages such as Isaiah 2:1-4; 34:1-17; Joel 3:1-2, 9-13; and Psalm 22:27; 86:9; and 117:1. These passages, which speak of the defeat of the enemies of God, peace on earth, and the conversion of the nations, if taken literally, would all point to the future millennial reign of Christ. Among these proofs he includes Daniel 12:11-12, which he felt showed that the millennium would begin in 1694. This passage states:

> And from the time that the continual burnt offering is taken away, and the abomination that makes desolate is set up, there shall be a thousand two hundred and ninety days. Blessed is he who waits and comes to the thousand three hundred and thirty-five days.

Alsted comments that "from the time" is to be understood as referring to the destruction of Jerusalem by Titus and that a day in prophecy is to be understood as a year. Thus, to the date of the destruction of Jerusalem in A.D. 69 we add 1,290 years, which makes A.D. 1359 "at which we must begin the Epocha or account of 1335 days, or years; and so we shall be brought to the year of Christ 2694 in which the thousand years in the Revelation shall have end; and they being ended the war of Gog and Magog shall begin, to which also the last judgment shall put an end."[10] (When the millennium is subtracted from this figure, the 1694 date for the beginning of the golden age was produced.) He later deals with other objections including to the bodily nature of the first resurrection and the reign of the resurrected saints on earth, and concludes by showing the doctrines which may be drawn from this passage. Within a short time of its publication, the book had a great influence in many of the Reformed lands. During the Puritan Revolution, his work, coupled with that of Joseph Mede, had a profound influence on English eschatological views.

Leonard Sale-Harrison

Yet the year 1694 passed, and the kingdom of God still was not established on earth. One would think that these examples would be sufficient to discourage efforts at setting a date for the Second Advent, but this was not the case. During the years between World War I and World War II, there were a number of very successful preachers of Prophecy who worked among the newly emerging fundamentalist churches. One of the most important of these was Leonard Sale-Harrison (c. 1875-1956), an interdenominational Bible teacher and speaker from Australia who held prophetic conferences in many churches in North America and published several books on prophetic subjects. One of his first works, *The Remarkable Jew*, appeared in 1928 and went through twelve editions selling over two hundred thousand copies.[11] His other best-selling books include *The Resurrection of the Old Roman Empire* (1928), which went into thirteen editions in twenty years, and *The Coming Great Northern Confederacy; or Russia's Future* (1928), which won such approval that sixteen editions were published. As these volumes were reissued, they were revised and changed in an effort to keep abreast with current affairs.

Of all his works, it is especially in *The Resurrection of the Old Roman Empire* that Sale-Harrison moves farthest toward dating the Second Coming. An edition published in 1939 represents his most complete teaching on the subject. Sale-Harrison was a firm believer in the pretribulation rapture and hence felt that exact dates ought not to be set. Yet, contrary to this belief, his matching of Scriptures with events in the life and times of Benito Mussolini seemed to pinpoint the time of the end of the age in the late 1930s or early 1940s. Using as his base for interpretation the image of Daniel, chapter 2, he believed that he lived in the closing days represented by the feet of clay and iron. The clay represented certain extremely democratic elements, such as the socialists, whereas the iron depicted "that strong body of men who will stand and support law and order."[12] The latter group, identified with the Fascists at times, will call for a superman or strong ruler (Antichrist) to bring order out of chaos. Mussolini, although not the final Antichrist perhaps, certainly would prepare the way for him.

With this as his underlying principle of interpretation, Sale-Harrison proceeded to explain how the Italian dictator, in conformity with biblical prophecy, was reviving the Roman Empire. Mussolini's territorial conquests, he believed, were an effort to make the Mediterranean into a Roman lake. In an attempt to copy Julius Caesar, the Duce was even trying to establish a state cult with himself at the center. As the dictator put it: "I am the State. I, because of God, I am called. I, because I am the superman incarnate . . . I am a law-giver as well as war lord." Sale-Harrison comments on this grandiose claim, "The man of sin will not claim much more."[13] Like Caesar, Mussolini took control of all the major offices of state and restored the ancient buildings of the city of Rome. He even planned to raise a huge statue in his own honor, a fulfillment of Revelation 13:14-15. Sale-Harrison cites the involvement of Italy in Austria, the Balkans, the Middle East, and Spain as examples of Italian efforts at controlling the old Roman lands. The attempted conquest of Ethiopia seemed to challenge Sale-

Harrison's interpretation, as this land was not part of the Roman Empire. He assured his readers, however, "Mussolini . . . must disgorge that for which he spent so much to acquire. The future Caesar Government will not have that land under its jurisdiction. The prophetic Word of God will again be proved accurate."[14] After a lengthy consideration of the pact between the pope and the Fascist state, he discusses Mussolini's favorable attitude toward Protestantism. The Italian dictator encouraged Bible societies in their distribution of Scripture, prohibited the sale of indecent literature, regulated the liquor trade, and discouraged swearing and drunkenness. Even this attempt at fairness in religion seemed to be a fulfillment of Revelation 17, which indicated that the real power during the end time would be political Rome rather than ecclesiastical Rome.

Among many other examples cited to prove that the coming of the Lord was near were the restoration of Rome, the use of Roman characters for writing in Turkey, the Bank of America becoming an international organization (it had formerly been the Bank of Italy, U.S.A.), the use of the Fascist emblem on ten-cent coins in the United States, draining of the marshes near Rome, and the rearmament of Italy. Other signs of approaching trouble seemed to synchronize with the restoration of ancient Rome. These included the growth of a company that would give everyone a number (The British Monomarks, Ltd.) thus fulfilling Revelation 13:16-18, the spread of fascism even to America, the advance of science through such developments as television and robots, the popularity of spiritism in the teaching of such men as Sir Arthur Conan Doyle, and growing anti-Semitism. Admitting that date-setting is a tricky business, Sale-Harrison stated that many great Bible students felt that the end would come in 1940 or 1941 and "even Gratton Guinness has no dates beyond 1934."[15]

Like many pretribulation premillennialists, Sale-Harrison was rather inconsistent.[16] If there are no signs required before the coming of the Lord to rapture His church, then why is so much time spent in reading current events into the Bible? Also, although he hesitated to set a precise year, yet by identifying Mussolini with the prophecies of Antichrist, Sale-Harrison, in essence, set the date within his own generation. Many premillennialists of the dispensationalist variety fall into the same date-setting trap. Prophetic preaching thus becomes a method by which one can relate the Bible to current events. This certainly can make for a literal interpretation of the Scriptures and the Bible becomes as relevant as tomorrow's newspaper, and perhaps just as erroneous.

The Biblical View and Date-setting

Thus, prophetic teaching that is too detailed and leads to date-setting can harm the very cause of prophecy. In each of the instances mentioned above, the dates passed and the age continued. Also, it should be noticed that if those scholars of repute were mistaken, less responsible teachers have fallen into even greater error. When Jesus was addressing His followers in the Olivet discourse (Matt. 24 and 25), He warned them to watch for His coming. He exhorted Christians to prayerfulness and service. In fact, though the Lord's words left open the time of His coming, they contained strong hints of delay. There would be persecutions, wars, and rumors of wars; the gospel was to be preached among all nations; and Jerusalem was to be trodden down by the Gentiles until their time was fulfilled. When He taught the parable of the talents He pictured a master who went into a far country and did not return for "a long time" (Matt. 25:19). So, rather than encouraging His disciples to expect His immediate return, Christ prepared them for a long wait. The apostles also had to deal with those who attempted to set dates as well as with those who doubted the truth of the Second Coming. Peter in his Second Epistle shows that this question was being hotly debated in his day (3:3-11). The Lord's promise to return is repeated in this passage, and the apostle's readers are reminded that there is no slackness on His part. God's time is not man's time, for with Him one day is as a thousand years and a thousand years as a day. He works out His own purpose without hurry or delay. Part of the Lord's purpose is to bring many more to repentance, and so there was still plenty of time for witnessing and preaching.

A close study of John 21 reveals the same outlook on the part of the Beloved Apostle. The Second Advent had been discussed by the disciples, and some believed that the words Christ spoke to Peter meant that John would not die. John did not try to set dates for the Lord's return, but rather was content to explain that Jesus said: "If it is my will that he remain until I come, what is that to you?" (John 21:23).

Paul seemed to support delay with respect to the Lord's coming in II Thessalonians 2. At the end of his life, when he was writing to the Philippians, he was still looking for the return of Christ (4:5). The same attitude of patient waiting for the Lord's appearance is stated in James 5:7: "Be patient, therefore, brethren, until the coming of the Lord."

Our Lord and the writers of the New Testament knew best when they exhorted Christians to look for His return but to be aware that the time could not be foretold. Perhaps nothing has discouraged evangelical Christians more from engaging in social action than the social ethic which encourages an excessive emphasis upon the date of Christ's return. If Christ will surely return this year or next, it is easy for many to believe that attempts to alleviate social ills are useless. Perhaps this has caused many Christians to ignore purposive social change that could improve the lot of their fellowmen. Consequently, many believers have ignored the clear teaching of Scripture concerning love for one's neighbor and for those who have physical as well as spiritual needs (Matt. 25). C. S. Lewis warned that a belief in the Second Coming of Christ must never preclude

> sober work for the future within the limits of ordinary morality and prudence. . . . For what comes is judgment: happy are those whom it finds laboring in their vocations, whether they were merely going out to feed the pigs or laying good plans to deliver humanity a hundred years hence from some great evil. The curtain has indeed now fallen. Those pigs will never in fact be fed, the great campaign against white slavery or governmental tyranny will never in fact proceed to victory. No matter; you were at your post when the inspection came.[17]

Although the examples of history and the statements of Scripture warn the believer against date-setting and a dogmatic interpretation of current events in regard to eschatology, the Christian is constantly exhorted to vigilance. The Word of the Lord still commands: "And what I say to you I say to all: Watch" (Mark 13:37).

37

Notes

1. For more information on Montanism, see G. Salmon, "Montanism" in *Dictionary of Christian Biography*, W. Smith and H. Wace, ed., III, 935-945; John De Soyres, *Montanism and the Primitive Church* (Cambridge, 1878); and Philip Schaff, *History of the Christian Church*, reprint (Grand Rapids: Kregel, 1962), II, 415-434.

2. Timothy David Barnes, *Tertullian, a Historical and Literary Study* (Oxford: Clarendon, 1971).

3. Quoted by Schaff, *History*, p. 425.

4. Marjorie Reeves, *The Influence of Prophecy in the Later Middle Ages* (Oxford: Clarendon, 1969).

5. David Saville Muzzey, *The Spiritual Franciscans* (New York: Columbia Univ. Press, 1907); and Emile Gebhart, *Mystics and Heretics in Italy at the End of the Middle Ages* (London: Allen & Unwin, 1922).

6. Robert G. Clouse, "Johann Heinrich Alsted and English Millennialism," in *Harvard Theological Review*, LXII (1969), 180-207.

7. John Calvin, *Calvini Opera*, W. Baum, E. Cunitz, E. Reuss, ed. (Brunswick, 1889), XLI, 302 f. and *Institutes of the Christian Religion*, J. T. McNeil, ed., F. L. Battles, trans. (Philadelphia: Westminster, 1960), III, 25, 996. For a full treatment of Calvin's eschatology the student may refer to Heinrich Quistorp, *Calvin's Doctrine of the Last Things*, N. Knight, trans. (Richmond, VA: John Knox, 1955).

8. Johann Heinrich Alsted, *The Beloved City*, William Burton, trans. (London, 1643).

9. Ibid., p. 1.

10. Ibid., p. 50.

11. This work was even published in revised form in 1954, in Wheaton, Illinois, under the title *God and Israel*.

12. Leonard Sale-Harrison, *The Resurrection of the Old Roman Empire* (London: the author, 1939), p. 100.

13. Ibid., p. 61.

14. Ibid., p. 91.

15. Ibid., p. 124. Henry Gratton Guinness (1835-1910) was an English inter-denominational evangelist who rivaled Charles Spurgeon in popularity. He wrote nine major works on prophecy, including *The Approaching End of the Age* (1879) and *History Unveiling Prophecy* (1905), which became classic expressions of the premillennialist viewpoint.

16. A "pretribulation premillennialist" is a person who follows the scheme of prophetic interpretation which believes there will be a secret "rapture" or removal of the church from the world prior to the "Great Tribulation" (i.e., the period of time immediately prior to the millennium).

17. C. S. Lewis, "The Christian Hope," *Eternity*, V (March 1954), p. 50. For an attempt to correct the evangelical·attitude of isolation from society, see Robert G. Clouse, Robert D. Linder, and Richard V. Pierard, *The Cross and the Flag* (Carol Stream, IL: Creation House, 1972).

3

Nineteenth-Century Roots

Ian S. Rennie

During the centuries, Christians believe, God has been leading the church in the understanding of the faith. In certain eras, particular truths have occupied special prominence. The pattern usually has been that at the beginning of such an era the biblical data has been interpreted in various ways, but gradually, often over many decades, a large measure of essential agreement has been reached. Therefore, biblical Christians, although believing that serious thought continually must be given to all areas of doctrine, are nonetheless united in believing that the Holy Spirit has guided the church into an understanding of the basic guidelines on such matters as the Trinity, the two natures of Jesus Christ, sin, grace, the atonement, and justification by faith. But eschatology—the study of last things—and its correlate, prophecy, are not included in this list.

Diversity in Prophetic Interpretation

The preceding statement on the lack of agreement on prophecy (and we shall use this word to include the area of eschatology as well) deserves some qualification. All Christians who take the Bible seriously as authoritative in all matters of faith and life do agree on the reality of predictive prophecy and on the fact that Jesus Christ shall personally return, that there shall be resurrection and judgment, hell and heaven. And this unanimity is not to be underemphasized, particularly when we realize that these subjects embody the great elements of prophetic concern. Perhaps this is also a salutary reminder that we should concentrate—and this is nowhere more true than in prophecy—on the majors. When we come, however, to the secondary matters of prophecy, such as the millennium, the tribulation, and the interpretation of the notoriously difficult apocalyptic symbolism of the books of Daniel and Revelation, then there is little agreement. And it is to this aspect of the subject that this chapter is addressing itself.

Perhaps another question that should be raised before dealing with the historical material is whether or not God intends to give us agreement on all secondary matters. Though many might argue in the affirmative, undoubtedly there are some who would contend that prophecy is one of those subjects on which God has seen fit—perhaps to stretch our faith, love, and hope—not to reveal Himself with any great measure of comprehensiveness or clarity.

At the same time God has created us with a desire to understand and systematize. As a result, we must hope that the divergent millennial views, so like the partial attempts of Apollinarians, Nestorians, and Eutychians to deal with the nature of our Lord in a bygone age, will find themselves resolved in a prophetic Chalcedon.

Perhaps the saddest thing about any system of absolutist assertions in the area of prophecy, such as those presented in Hal Lindsey's book, *The Late Great Planet Earth,* is that the proponents do not see the limited and partial nature of their own interpretations. In studying the roots of contemporary dispensationalism, we shall be looking at but one example of this tendency to absolutize the relative and partial knowledge given us. And even there we believe that God can use these efforts to point the way to a synthesis that is more faithful to the Word of God.

Amillennialism and Postmillennialism

Where did Lindsey's prophetic views come from historically? This is the subject to which we must now address ourselves. He is what is called a premillennialist, believing that Jesus Christ will return to earth and establish His reign of one thousand years, according to Revelation 20. It has often been pointed out, and with ample justification, that there were premillennialists—such as Irenaeus, that most-biblical of all the Church Fathers—in the early days of the

42

Christian era. It must also be stressed, however, that at this time the church did not give itself to serious theological endeavor in the area of prophecy. As a result, the views are inchoate, obscure, and unsystematic—vastly different from the premillennialism of *The Late Great Planet Earth.*

In the early fifth century A.D. Augustine, to whom so much of our doctrinal understanding is indebted, gave attention to the millennium amid the myriad other doctrines with which he dealt. He was an amillennialist, believing that the millennial period was not totally in the future, but that, since Jesus Christ already had bound Satan, the millennium was just another way of describing the blessings of the age of grace, the gospel, and the church. For over one thousand years, on past the Reformation of the sixteenth century, amillennialism was the basic prophetic view of Christians, although in the church age some interpreted the millennium as a specific period of time whereas others regarded it as a symbolic and an inexact number.

During the seventeenth century, the Puritans of Old and New England, so self-consciously the heirs of the Reformation, began a slight modification of their amillennial heritage. They believed, in common with all Christians of the time, that many of the prophecies concerning Israel in the Old Testament had a nonliteral, or symbolic, fulfillment in the church of the New Testament age. As they read the Old Testament prophecies, they saw pictures of the church enjoying great success, which was confirmed by the events of the Reformation. As a result, they believed the Holy Spirit would bring a worldwide revival before Jesus Christ returned, and that they were standing on the threshold of it. This was the foundation of postmillennialism, for this period of gospel blessing, whether a literal thousand years or not, was regarded as that of which the millennium was speaking. This view was dominant among English-speaking Protestants for over two hundred years, well into the nineteenth century. The dynamism and optimism engendered by this view fostered what are usually regarded by Christians as the most important developments of the last two centuries: the Evangelical Awakening, the modern missionary movement, and the building of a worldwide church. In the later part of the nineteenth century, postmillennialism became secularized through the influence of liberal theology and the idea of progress, but it is a calumny against some of the finest Christians who ever lived to take postmillennialism at its worst, as does Lindsey, and describe its adherents as believers in the inherent goodness of man.

43

Surely no progress can be made in the study of prophecy, or any other subject for that matter, until we agree to treat with integrity the approaches of those who hold differing points of view.

Early Premillennialism

Premillennialism appeared at various times throughout the Middle Ages. Its view of widespread declension in the church and chaos in society before the return of Jesus Christ, with a millennial period of earthly vindication of the righteous and oppressed, had a special appeal in days of disaster. At times it even shared a revolutionary character. This stream erupted once again in the Peasant Wars that accompanied the Continental Reformation, and for generations responsible premillennialism had to seek to dissociate itself from the violence of Münster, when it was brave enough to raise its head at all. The upheavals associated with the Thirty Years War in Europe (1618-1648) led at least one outstanding continental Protestant thinker, Johann Heinrich Alsted, to adopt premillennialism, and his work found a positive response among a number of the contemporary Puritans, faced with a government intransigently opposed to their view of personal, church, and national revival. The premillennial enthusiasm of some of the extreme left-wingers of the Puritan movement once again made serious Christians hesitant about this approach, and thus matters were to lie until the watershed of the French Revolution and the Napoleonic wars in the generation between 1789 and 1815.

Modern Premillennialism

The cataclysmic events around the turn of the nineteenth century led some Christians to expect the speedy premillennial return of Jesus Christ, and this was reinforced by the historicist interpretation of the Book of Revelation, which was held by virtually all Protestants. This approach assumed that in chapters 6 to 18 of Revelation we have a symbolic presentation of the history of the church and the nations and rulers associated with it. The prophetic days, whether 1260, 1335, or 2300, were understood as years, and the papacy was seen to be the Antichrist. It took a few years for thinkers to begin to work the matter out, but with events occurring just across the

Channel, British Christians, most of them members of the national church, were impelled to the task. The 1,260 years, which would culminate in the judgment of the Antichrist, were assumed to be taking place in Napoleon's handling of the papacy, and working back from there it was found, with delightful consistency, that this period of time would take one to a date that might be assumed as the emergence of the papacy. Assuming the end of the twenty-four hundred years would usher in the Second Advent of Jesus Christ, and dating its commencement from some time in the life of Daniel, it was believed, with the notorious historicist penchant for date-setting, that the return of Jesus Christ would certainly take place during the nineteenth century, quite likely during the 1840s or 1860s. Some became even more specific than that. Events were so ominous, and the historicist scheme so lucid, that there was no doubt in the minds of these early nineteenth-century premillennialists.

G. S. Faber kicked off the discussion with his *Dissertations* in 1806, which, however, were only a very general and unformed introduction to the subject. In 1813, William Cuninghame, a Scottish laird and lay-theologian, who was to be involved in the prophetic debates for a number of years, issued his *Dissertations on the Seals and Trumpets*. In 1815, another layman, J. Hatley Frere, one of the most important figures in the premillennial renaissance, published his *Combined View of the Prophecies of Daniel, Esdras, and St. John.* Then in 1816, Lewis Way, a wealthy Anglican clergyman who was in the process of reconstituting the London Society for Promoting Christianity among the Jews (L.S.P.C.J.), published his *Letters*, which announced the important fusion of Jewish missions and premillennial hope, with stress on the return of the Jews to Palestine and their national conversion just before the return of Jesus Christ. The Puritan postmillennialists and their descendants looked eagerly for the conversion of the Jews according to Romans 11, but this new stress on the Jews carried with it another and more literalistic interpretation of some of the Old Testament prophecies referring to Israel. When the prophets spoke predictively of Israel they meant Israel and not the church. Thus one of the most important planks of premillennialism was nailed down.

Perhaps an aside is necessary here about the word "literal." Hal Lindsey speaks disdainfully of the postmillennialists, and by implication, of the amillennialists, for rejecting the literal sense of much of

45

the Scripture. This gives the impression that they were akin to extreme theological liberals, denying the obvious sense of Scripture, and thus refusing to bow before the authority of the Word of God. One must strongly protest against this kind of innuendo, for it is altogether untrue and unfair. These Christians interpreted many of the Old Testament prophecies concerning Israel in a nonliteral way because this is the way they believed the New Testament interpreted these passages, applying them to the church, e.g., Joel 2 and Acts 2; Jeremiah 31 and Hebrews 8 and 10; Amos 9 and Acts 15. It was a matter of exegesis, not unbelief.

Premillennialism Confirmed

In the immediate post-Napoleonic era, events took place that appeared to confirm the premillennial view for a number of British Christians. As historicist premillennialists—and all premillennialists were such between 1815 and 1830—they saw a number of signs that indicated the nearness of the Second Coming. And it appeared as if these signs were being fulfilled before their very eyes. One sign was the conversion of Jews, and the aggressive ministry after 1815 of the L.S.P.C.J. with its trickle of Jewish converts convinced many that the turning of the Jews as a whole to Christ was about to take place. Then, according to historicist premillennialism, the return of Jesus Christ could not be far distant. Admittedly, the success of Jewish evangelism was being interpreted with almost postmillennial optimism; but the important thing for this study is not the basis in fact, but the mood of anticipation that was born.

Another sign of the nearness of the Second Advent was the preaching of the gospel throughout the world, and the partial decline, at least, of opposing forces. The modern missionary movement provided the former, although the premillennialists were not as imaginatively exuberant about its achievements as other Evangelicals. Events in Ireland also suggested that God was calling many out of the Roman Catholic Church. During the 1820s, many Irish Roman Catholic children began to attend schools provided and directed by Protestants, where the Bible was taught. Moreover, there were indications in several areas that adults were leaving Roman Catholicism. It looked also as if the Ottoman Empire, viewed as the bastion of Islam, might be losing its grip. Particularly if this were to

46

take place in Palestine it would be an added sign, for it would provide an opening for the return of the Jews.

In addition, there were signs of apostasy in much of the church. The premillennial view did not look for a widespread revival before the return of Jesus Christ, not even a revival to be followed by a brief time of apostasy, judgment, and tribulation. It was believed that the church already was sliding into apostasy, and thus the end was near. At first sight, to one who has read anything of early nineteenth-century evangelical history, this may appear a strange point of view. For on the surface, as far as Britain was concerned, it appeared that evangelical Christianity was progressing remarkably, and the prospects were favorable indeed. But this was not the whole story. Robert Haldane, the Scottish evangelist, because of his social position as well as his zeal, had strong bonds with the Anglican Evangelicals. In 1816, once the Napoleonic Wars were completed, his evangelistic passion made him one of the first British Christians to reach the Continent. He believed the Roman Catholic Church was apostate, but what he saw of Swiss, French, and to some extent German, Protestantism convinced him that Rationalism already had them on an equally broad road to destruction. He, together with Henry Drummond, the wealthy London banker (not the late nineteenth-century author of *The Greatest Thing in the World*), founded the Continental Society in London in 1819; and although its primary goal for Haldane was always the evangelization of Europe, to others the emphasis appeared to be on the examination of contemporary Protestant decline as a sign of the end of the age.

Evidence of apostasy was highlighted by another development as well. This was the growing concern among some Christians for the rediscovery of New Testament patterns of church life. Neither the Reformers nor the leaders of the Evangelical Awakening had been indifferent to the apostolic concept of the church, but for the former, New Testament doctrine had been of primary concern, and for the latter, New Testament evangelism and power. At this period, however, a number of Christians began to search for the New Testament experience of the church—for life in the Body. This phenomenon is well-described by some historians as the Restorationist Movement. In Britain it found its expression primarily in Plymouth Brethrenism and the Catholic Apostolic Church, both essentially breakaways from the Church of England. In America the net must be cast wider, to include the Campbellites, or Churches of Christ/

Christian Church, Mormons, and Seventh Day Adventists. We are, however, getting ahead of ourselves.

In the 1820s, although the search was in progress, crystallization into groups had not yet taken place. Interestingly enough, Robert Haldane, as early as 1804, through his writings on the mutual ministries of all believers in the apostolic church, had considerable influence on this development. As usual, Haldane was primarily an evangelist, and did not carry these views very far; but those who came under his influence, such as Alexander Campbell in America, and some of the Anglican Evangelicals in Britain, took them much further. And, of course, if you were looking for an apostolic replica, even the most alive church—and there were many—suffered by comparison. In fact, in some of these circles, British and American evangelical Protestantism was soon being described as apostate as well. If apostasy in the church was a sign of the Second Coming then there was apparently much of it around. The return of Jesus Christ had to be near at hand, and thus premillennialism was strengthened.

Added to apostasy in the church was a sense of upheaval and chaos in society as a whole. The fabric of British life was being strained in the post-Napoleonic world by the evidence of class tension in the Peterloo massacre and the demand for Parliamentary reform, by the movement for Catholic emancipation (Catholic Emancipation Act, 1829), and by the never-ending eruptions of the insoluble Irish problem. And, across the Channel, events were leading to the Revolution of 1830. These forces and events persuaded many that the Lord was at the door.

One further encouragement to premillennialism may be mentioned as well. This was the expectation by some that there would be a special ministry of the Holy Spirit in at least part of the church just prior to the Lord's return—a "latter rain"—and that this would be accompanied by charismatic activity. This may appear contradictory to what has been said about apostasy and more in line with post-millennialism, but all the historian can do at times is record what is apparently contradictory without fully being able to explain how such ideas could cohabit in the same mind. And when news of the expression of the charismatic gifts reached London from Scotland in the early summer of 1830, prophetic anticipation reached a new high in certain circles.

48

The Growth of Premillennialism in Britain

With all these forces at work, a clearly defined premillennial movement arose in Britain during the 1820s. Anglican evangelicalism was
ripe for new leadership and new ideas at this period, and the premillennialists provided it for a considerable part of the constituency.
The older generation of leaders, such as the Reverend Charles
Simeon of Cambridge and William Wilberforce, the former member
of Parliament and abolisher of the slave trade, were getting on in
years. Young men of the same caliber did not seem to be taking their
places, and a vacuum resulted. Evangelical Anglican Calvinism,
always moderate, was becoming more and more so, and there were
those who longed for a return to the old paths. Then there was the
concern for a more biblical doctrine of the church than the viable
but spiritually unrespectable Pietist view of the church within the
church—the Evangelicals making do with the anomalies of a traditional state church as long as they had freedom to preach the gospel.
There was also a realistic concern among some Evangelicals that the
stories of missionary success that they continually heard were not
altogether borne out by the facts. And there were those who feared
that some of the Evangelicals in Parliament had been taking too
liberal a line on such matters as Catholic emancipation. They wanted
a reassertion of the traditional ultraconservative position of the
virtual inviolability of the British Protestant Constitution. To these
issues and needs, the premillennialists appeared to provide the answer.
Not that they consciously devised a program to meet these situations,
but their emphases gave them a ready hearing in certain sections of
the Evangelical party which were concerned about such matters.

Edward Irving

The premillennial movement gained one of its most important
converts in the person of Edward Irving. A minister in London of a
Church of Scotland congregation for expatriates from north of the
Border, he had the entrée into evangelical Anglican circles which
leading Evangelicals from other state churches were accorded, and
which no English Dissenter could hope to gain. He had also been
assistant in Glasgow to the great Thomas Chalmers, which was an
introduction in itself. But, in addition, Irving was a genius; and for
the first few years at least, the attractive more than the erratic side
of his brilliance was in evidence. After his arrival in London in 1822,

49

his eloquence soon made him the center of much attention. Then in 1825, Hatley Frere led him into the premillennial fold. Never one to do anything by halves, Irving poured his torrential abilities into the new movement. Prophecy became the heart and soul of his ministry.

In the next year, at his beautiful home in Albury, Surrey, Henry Drummond began annual conferences for the study of prophecy with a wide section of respected Evangelicals in attendance, at least in the beginning. These were genuine study conferences limited to invited guests, and through them the premillennial faith was more clearly stated and its ramifications more fully explored. Some of the more traditional Anglican Evangelicals became unhappy about the stress on the apostasy of the church—by implication, at least, including even the Church of England—and even more so by the violent spirit and intemperate language of particularly the Scottish and Irish participants. But the Albury Conferences were to continue until 1830, doing yeoman service for the cause of premillennialism, until in the latter year the situation was radically altered by the appearance of the gift of tongues and the accusation by the London presbytery of the Church of Scotland that Irving, with his usual unguarded language, in attempting to stress the real humanity of the Incarnation, had actually become guilty of teaching the sinfulness of Christ's human nature.

John Nelson Darby

As Irving began to pass from the center of the premillennial stage —to die in 1834 and be remembered only as the instigator of the abortive Catholic Apostolic Church—a new champion was emerging in Ireland. John Nelson Darby was an evangelical clergyman of what in those days was still the United Church of England and Ireland. He was deeply distressed at the lethargy of Irish Anglicanism and the seeming blindness and even heresy of some of its leaders. The somber note of premillennialism accorded well with his experience and he entered the ranks. His searching mind and ardent spirit soon latched on to new ideas that were to transform premillennialism, associate it forever with his name, and produce the type of premillennialism known as "dispensationalism," which is presented in *The Late Great Planet Earth.*

Darby's new ideas naturally did not come to systematic coherence immediately, but the distinctiveness of his thinking was soon evident. Darby's first shift from the normal premillennial position came with his acceptance in the late 1820s of the literal-day position in regard to the prophetic time periods. This interpretation had been suggested by Samuel R. Maitland, someone who was well outside the evangelical camp, in his volume written in 1826 entitled *An Enquiry into the Grounds on which the Prophetic Period of Daniel and St. John has been Supposed to Consist of 1260 Years.* Although Maitland may have been wishing to improve Anglican relations with Roman Catholicism by abolishing the historicist hallmark of prophetic days counted as years, which regularly identified the papacy with the Antichrist, this aspect was not of significance for Darby, who, in line with all his fellow Evangelicals, had an ample and varied arsenal of anti-Catholic polemic. What was of significance was that the 1,260 days became three and a half years which, joined with forty-two months, would become the seven-year period of the Tribulation.

This alteration of the meaning of prophetic days also involved a change in the interpretation of the Book of Revelation, from historicism to what has been called "futurism." Thus the events of Revelation are assumed to take place during the Tribulation, not during the course of church history. This was to be another salient characteristic of dispensational premillennialism.

The next development of immediate significance was the idea of the secret rapture, prior to the Tribulation, after which Christ would return with His saints for the period of millennial rule. The origin of this idea has been debated often. Some have asserted that they have seen glimpses of this viewpoint in the reports of the Albury Conferences, known as the *Dialogues on Prophecy,* whereas others have attributed it to Edward Irving and his most immediate circle. Only recently there has been another full-scale attempt to discover the origin of this idea. Dave MacPherson, an American, writing in a breezy journalistic style, published a book in 1973 called *The Unbelievable Pre-Trib Origin.* Quoting from certain long-forgotten productions of the Catholic Apostolic Church, he insists that the secret rapture was clearly enunciated first among those who received the charismatic gifts at Port Glasgow, Scotland, in the spring of 1830. Margaret Macdonald, just fifteen years of age, received the spirit of prophecy, and among her utterances was one that distinguished between the second phase of Christ's coming, which would be public, and the first, which would be secret and hidden, observed only by believers, and which would raise them to be with Christ. It is doubtful that Margaret Macdonald was the first person to broach such an idea, and it is also doubtful that her presentation was as clear as MacPherson suggests. But it is likely that it was grist for Darby's mill. He visited Port Glasgow for some three weeks to observe the phenomena, for, as has been mentioned, many of the premillennialists looked for some such outpouring of the Holy Spirit prior to the Second Advent. Darby finally, and undoubtedly reluctantly, became convinced that the gifts were a delusion, but as he left Scotland he carried with him impressions which, after some years of reflection, would play their part in the formation of the teaching of the secret pretribulation rapture.

Finally, we must note Darby's new understanding of the relation of Israel and the church. He not only saw the Old Testament prophecies concerning Israel fulfilled in a literal Israel, as did all premillennialists, but he drew a rigid separation between Israel and the church, which was quite new. Darby had come to the conclusion that all Christendom, in its organized expression, was apostate. But he drove the implications further than others. What then was the true church? It was a heavenly people unknown outside the New Testament Epistles. Israel, on the other hand, was God's earthly people; and to it all the prophecies belonged, interpreted literally, since extensive literalism not only accorded with premillennialism, but was in harmony with the earthly nature of its calling. The heavenliness of the church also relates well to the secret rapture, in fact demands it, and is of a piece with it, since that which is heavenly must be raptured out of the earthly tribulation. The seventy prophetic weeks of Daniel were then introduced, with sixty-nine prior to the day of Pentecost, none during the church age and the seventieth being the Tribulation. The subsequent millennium was to have a decidedly Jewish cast. The church, therefore, was a parenthesis between the eras of God's dealing with Israel. This view of the relation of Israel and the church may have helped Darby to clarify and unify his thinking, but it also introduced an altogether new outlook that has made dispensational premillennialism the distinctive movement it is.

It took Darby a few years to work out with his colleagues all the implications of these positions—and he did have an able band of associates, many of whom, to use the English archaism, were of good family, a number being Oxford or Trinity College, Dublin men. In Ireland there were those represented by J. G. Bellett and Lord Congleton, who, during the 1820s, had begun to sever their ties with the organized churches, and whose small gatherings for the breaking of bread and mutual ministry set the pattern for the Plymouth Brethren assemblies and in certain cases antedated Darby's involvement. At Oxford there had been a group of high Calvinistic young evangelical Anglicans in the late 1820s who were earnestly seeking for a viable expression of the Body of Christ. Two of these men had met Darby in Ireland, where they had been tutors in the home of his brother-in-law, who would subsequently become Lord Chief Justice Pennefather. One, J. C. Philpot, found Darby an important link in the chain of his conversion; the other, Francis Newman, brother of the future cardinal, John Henry Newman, was profoundly influenced by the Irish clergyman. Although their own searches within a few years would remove them as far as possible from the incipient Brethren movement (the one becoming the doyen of the most extreme section of the hyper-Calvinistic Strict and Particular Baptists and the other a Unitarian), they did introduce Darby to Oxford, where he found fertile soil in such men as G. V. Wigram, and above all, Benjamin Wills Newton.

Darby's prophetic views, with which we are particularly concerned, came to their developed form through interaction with these friends. Of crucial importance were the annual Powerscourt Conferences, which first met near Dublin in 1831, the year after the closure of the Albury Conferences. The setting at the estate was similar to Albury, the pattern of discussion was similar, but now the hostess was a young widow, the wealthy and attractive Theodosia, Lady Powerscourt, who had once been present at the Albury sessions. The continuity of the two conferences was highlighted further by the presence of Edward Irving. Although he rapidly was coming under a shadow in England, his views were still, in early October, 1831, of sufficient interest to those whose intense search was leading them out of the established church that he was still welcomed as a resource person. But there was a difference. The Reverend Robert Daly, Anglican rector of Powerscourt, was the chairman for several years—which indicates something of the ecclesiastical ambiguity of the situation, as he was to proceed to become a well-known evangelical bishop. The real creative force behind the conference, however, was J. N. Darby, with whom the young widow was deeply in love.

In the Conference of 1831, there appeared to be a general acceptance of the literal-day theory, which implied the rejection of historicism and the acceptance of futurism. The secret rapture, in a still somewhat undeveloped form, was also given a considerable measure of acceptance, and in a few months was being taught at the new Brethren assembly in Plymouth. The view of the church as a parenthesis was put forward by Darby and some of his associates at the 1833 Powerscourt Conference. Although the details were not all developed, and it would be a decade or so before Darby stressed it as essential, the foundation had been well laid.

Darby's prophetic views did not enjoy widespread favor at once. The association with Edward Irving had to be lived down. Darby and his associates were also, as we have mentioned, in many cases fastidiously aristocratic or upper class; and although they committed themselves to serving Christ with exemplary self-denial, they did not readily communicate across the class barrier with the mass of British Christians. Outside of the Brethren, it was only among some of their former Evangelical Anglican confreres that dispensational premillennialism spread at all. A change, however, was soon to take place.

The Spread of Darby's Eschatology

In the years following 1843, events took place that opened up new scope for Darby's teachings. The first was the debacle of historicist premillennialism. As noted earlier, the historicists, with their date-setting, looked for the Second Coming in either the 1840s or 1860s. The date of 1843 (subsequently changed to October 22, 1844) was more common in America, under the aegis of William Miller, than in Britain. When the shock of nonfulfillment came, all forms of premillennialism suffered a blow from which it took a generation to recover. In Britain, the events in America were seen by many premillennialists more as a warning than a disaster, and as a result they maintained their historicist premillenarian framework. In the years of chastening they worked hard on their calculations, and as the 1860s dawned they were once again bold enough to be asserting that they knew, if not the day or the hour of the Second Coming, at least the decade and perhaps even the year. Hatley Frere, who by this time had been involved in the prophetic movement for half a century, insisted that the Jews would be back in Palestine with a rebuilt temple in 1865, that Roman Catholicism would be destroyed by 1864, and that

Louis Napoleon was the Antichrist, all of which were signs pointing to a virtually immediate return. Needless to say, the old man and his colleagues became a bit of a laughingstock, and the exodus to Darbyite premillennialism increased.

Then there was the revival of 1859. Proportionately no group in Britain benefited more from this vast spiritual movement than the Plymouth Brethren. As a recent spiritually alive movement, it was natural that many vibrant new Christians should see in its fellowship what they wanted. But more than this was the fact that this revival was predominantly lay led, and hardly anywhere were laymen better prepared for ministry than in the unclerical Brethren. As a result, in Britain, Brethren lay evangelists were at the heart of the revival. And through their ministries, hosts of working people entered the Brethren movement. And as the ecclesiastically more fluid days of revival passed, many of the lay evangelists, even though not Brethren, found a greater measure of acceptance among the Brethren than in their own circles. As a result, Brethren ideas, and particularly Darby's views on prophecy, began to reach a wider circle.

Another factor in the growth of dispensational premillennialism was the rise of the many-faceted movement known as "theological liberalism." The revival of 1859 did not have much of an intellectual orientation, and as a result it did little or nothing to meet or provide an alternative to the views that were already beginning to appear in the thoughtful sections of the English-speaking world. These premillennialists, however, were stalwart opponents of liberalism. There are undoubtedly various reasons for this, but one certainly would be their literal approach to biblical interpretation. Liberalism in one way and another rejected the literal and factual truth of many of the basic Christian doctrines. While many Christians were reeling under this massive and brilliant attack, the dispensational premillennialists, fortified by their eschatological literalism, maintained unbrokenly the historicity of biblical revelation. Many Christians who were looking for a way out turned to the leaders of this movement as a bulwark, and naturally accepted the whole package that went with it, premillennialism and all. Premillennialism also commended itself by its apparent realism in the face of liberalism. It pictured an increasingly apostate church prior to the Second Advent, and this was exactly what liberalism seemed to be bringing about. Postmillennialism in many places was also losing its biblical rootage as its sanguine outlook was overwhelmed by secular ideas of progress and evolutionary optimism. This left an eschatological vacuum into which premillennialism, as the only seemingly viable alternative, naturally flowed, since many evangelical postmillennialists, in the sections of the world particularly feeling the effects of liberalism, believed it was necessary to abandon a viewpoint that was assuming such ostensibly non-Christian overtones.

Added to these factors was the leadership of dispensational premillennialism. Darby was a man of overwhelming devotion, whose charismatic personality galvanized disciples throughout his long life. As the movement spread, particularly in America, it drew in some of the ablest Protestant evangelicals of the day. Although these men were not intellectuals, they were capable and activistic, and their lives gave every indication of the genuine piety and evangelistic concern that characterized the revival out of which they came. Because of Darby's strong doctrinal views, they were also men who gave way no more to the vapidities that were developing in American revivalism than they did to the vagaries of liberalism. Many of the premillennial leaders were among the most respected clergymen in American Protestantism.

The Faith Missions, which developed in the wake of the 1859 revival, were also centers of the advance of dispensational premillennialism. The China Inland Mission was the prototype, and Hudson Taylor had the closest of associations with the Brethren. The spiritual dedication and heroism of the early faith missionaries, as is always the case, was overwhelmingly attractive, and as Christians sought to follow the pattern, premillennialism was included.

There were other significant elements in the growth of dispensational premillennialism, particularly in America. One was the Bible school movement. These virtually unique American institutions began to grow up in the 1880s and 1890s to provide training for the many lay volunteers who wished to engage in home and overseas missionary work. Moody's Institute in Chicago, although not the first of such schools, became the prototype; and since Moody had imbibed a fair dose of dispensationalism in a rather typical unstructured form, and his colleague and successor R. A. Torrey in a more systematic way, it was natural that the burgeoning Bible school movement, with a few exceptions, should follow this line of thought. And as the Bible schools unintentionally became training centers for evangelical ministers as many of the theological seminaries opted for divergent views,

Darby's prophetic teaching became more widely accepted than ever. Another element of growth was the massive pietistic immigration from Europe in the latter part of the nineteenth century, which was to do so much to alter the face of American evangelicalism. These groups, in need of theological training for their leaders, turned naturally to the Bible schools; and as a result, dispensational premillennialism gained entrance and achieved almost instant and total success in a group whose importance, not only in Middle America but also in American evangelicalism, it would be difficult to overrate.

In Britain, Darby's premillennialism found a home among most of the Plymouth Brethren, some of the evangelical Anglicans, and a great many in the interdenominational evangelical world that grew out of the 1859 revival and gained added impetus from D. L. Moody's singularly successful ministry in Britain. In many ways these groups were the constituents of the fundamentalist movement in Britain. Although it is sometimes argued that there was no modernist-fundamentalist controversy in Britain, there certainly was a fundamentalist movement, which had conscious ties with the same movement in other parts of the world. While divisions took place in Britain during the 1920s, violent controversy was largely avoided, due at least in part to British politeness, the elastic nature of the fabric of state-church Anglicanism which was comprehensive enough to let even fundamentalist Evangelicals feel at home, and the relative lack of evangelical strength. Although the renaissance of Reformed theology in Britain among the descendants of the fundamentalists since World War II has caused some to deny a prevalent British dispensationalism in the first half of this century, all one has to do is look at the reports of the interdenominational youth organizations, which were so singularly effective in Britain, to realize that Darby had left an indelible mark that lasted at least until the beginning of World War II.

Darby's Influence in America

In America, Darby's impact was far greater. The Plymouth Brethren never have exerted the influence in American evangelical life that they have in Britain, but they have been more uniform in their dispensational premillennialism, and their ideas have been more widely accepted. We must keep in mind that when Darby arrived in America in 1862, on the first of his numerous visits, the Exclusive Brethren, of which he was the unofficial leader, were not as exclusive as they have become in the subsequent century. As a result, many ministers and Christians from other denominations came to hear, and were impressed with, this man who seemed so able an expositor of Scripture. It was particularly among eastern and northern Presbyterians and Baptists that Darby had his greatest extra-Brethren influence. These men were theologically oriented, Calvinistically committed, and aware and afraid of the emergence of theological liberalism, as was Darby. He spoke to their situation, and his prophetic teaching seemed an essential ingredient.

Associated with them were the representatives of the new interdenominational evangelicalism that was developing in America, as in Britain, in the wake of 1859 and Moody. And here Darbyism was warmly received. Prophetic periodicals were begun, such as *Waymarks in the Wilderness* and the respected *Prophetic Times.* Summer Bible conferences—the most notable at Niagara-on-the-Lake, Ontario, with the eminent St. Louis Presbyterian, James H. Brookes, as the leading light—were organized. And popular prophetic conferences were held in New York in 1878, Chicago in 1886, and Baltimore in 1892. These conferences were not as stridently dispensational since they were in large measure directed against theological liberalism. In this effort as broad a platform as possible was desirable. The key leaders, however, were committed to this eschatology, saw it as a strategic weapon against the enemy, and did all they could to commend it, without rocking the boat. For a short while in the early 1890s it looked as if this approach might be successful, but events were to prove otherwise.

Dispensational Premillennialism in the Early Twentieth Century

The strident period of dispensationalism began with the new century. The nondispensational leaders of premillennialism in America found they could not honestly participate in a movement whose dominant theology contained implications to which they could not subscribe. Their secession brought an end to the Niagara Bible Conference and might have wrecked the movement; but instead it made the movement more homogeneous and ready to move forward when the right opportunity arose. This opportunity came with the revival of 1904-08, which was the last in the chain of the movements of spiritual renewal that began with Wesley. Although it has been best known in the Western world as the Welsh revival, its greatest effectiveness was in the Third World. It did, however, spread to some extent throughout Europe and America and gave fresh dynamic to the anti-liberal and dispensational causes. In 1908, a presentation edition of W. E. Blackstone's *Jesus Is Coming,* a dispensational work first published a generation before, was sent to several hundred thousand ministers and Christian workers. Then in 1909, profiting from the same impetus, the Scofield Reference Bible was published, with notes that embodied with remarkable clarity and succinctness, amid a great deal of other material, the essence of the dispensational scheme. New and revived Christians were interested in Bible study, and here was a unique tool. Its orthodoxy was unambiguous in a day of battle, and its eschatology, more than ever, appeared to provide a valid interpretation of the current situation. Soon the badge of North American evangelicalism was the Scofield Bible. It was revised in 1917, with the result that its distinctive teachings were even more cogent and forceful than ever, and just at the time that the British mandate of Palestine provided an apparent fulfillment of premillennial hope in the promised return of Jews to their native land.

Throughout the modernist-fundamentalist controversies of the 1920s and 1930s, dispensationalism was a most frequent ingredient on the conservative side, undoubtedly contributing to the spirit of defensiveness and pessimism that characterized evangelical Christianity in that era.

In the post-World War II period, with the renewal of evangelical thought and life, eschatology has received a less disproportionate emphasis, the various millennial options have been more consistently canvassed, there has been greater humility in regard to detail, and perhaps above all, there has been a new awareness of the oneness of the people of God in all ages. In this light Hal Lindsey's book seems an unfortunate throwback to the past era; but in spite of this, one trusts that God will use his work as a small contribution to the final resolution of a fuller understanding of biblical prophecy.

4

Prophecy in the Old Testament

Carl Edwin Armerding

Recently I was asked by a student, "When are we going to study prophecy in our Old Testament course?" I knew what he meant, although we had just finished a class in Amos, and in fact the question arose as a result of conversations with a friend who was running a "Bible" class in which certain popular books about the Bible (not the Bible) formed the basis for study. His question pointed up the problem of definition that contemporary Christians constantly face. Because of the constant emphasis in certain evangelical circles during the past half century on what I call "futurology" (i.e., the study of what is going to happen in the coming generation), it is difficult for most of us to see that biblical prophecy has a much broader scope than simply the prediction of future events. In fact, the study of a prophet like Amos offers relatively little of interest to biblical futurologists; hence the conclusion of my student that we had not yet studied prophecy.

Who were the prophets in the Old Testament, and what were their primary concerns? If the future was not their major point of focus, what was? This question can be answered only when we turn to the prophets themselves, and, looking at their preaching, ask to whom it was directed, what formed the subject matter, and what place the future had in their message.

There are, in the Old Testament, three Hebrew words that describe the prophet. The *ro'eh* or "seer" (I Sam. 9:9) is described as a man who could see God's plan or discern His will, and as such was consulted as a kind of oracle in early Israel. In Samuel's case he also offered sacrifices, but whether this was part of his role as seer is not clear. A second term, *hozeh,* is roughly parallel to seer *(ro'eh)* both in meaning and function. Gad is described in the same passage (II Sam. 24:11) as David's *hozeh,* or seer, and as *nabi',* or prophet, showing that the terms, at that period, were roughly synonymous. This introduces the third term, *nabi',* usually translated "prophet," from a root that is still the subject of debate. The commonly accepted etymology of *nabi'* relates the word to the prophet's call by God,[1] but by biblical times the linguistic history of the word is of secondary importance. Even if *nabi'* does describe the origin of the prophetic utterance, as opposed to *ro'eh* and *hozeh,* which define its function, all three clearly refer to the type of activity we find illustrated in the lives and ministry of the biblical prophets, and it is to them we must turn now.

From Abraham to Elijah

Although Abraham is once called a prophet by a foreign king (Gen. 20:7), apparently corroborated by Psalm 105:5, and Moses could relate a promise of the Lord saying, "I will raise up for you a prophet like me from among you" (Deut. 18:18), it is not until the time of Samuel that prophecy begins in earnest. It is difficult to determine just what Samuel's prophetic role included, as he was also a prominent judge and probably a priest as well. One thing is clear: when Samuel, Saul, and others prophesied (lit: "acted as a *nabi'* "), it was in response to the coming upon them of the Spirit of God (I Sam. 19:20). That this sometimes produced acts of ecstasy (v. 24) has been the subject of much debate, but that it provided the stimulus for the prophetic utterance, and thus endowed it with the quality of divine revelation, is not in question. The continuing role of the prophet as channel for the Word of Yahweh is the first hallmark of prophetic activity.[2]

Nathan and then Gad appear as court prophets in the reign of David, and their function seems an advisory one within the court itself. Gad, as noted above, is called "David's seer" (II Sam. 24:11), and it appears from events recorded in I Kings 1 that Nathan also had an official role. In the case of Gad, the text states explicitly that he communicated the word of the Lord (Yahweh) to the king, a function that seems consistent with the nature and role of the prophets throughout Israel's history.

Various other prophets are noted as having some kind of official or unofficial advisory duty in relation to Israel's monarchs. Their exact relationship to the court is not always clear, nor is it necessarily always the same. Ahijah appears on the highway as a lone communicator of the Word of Yahweh to the first Jeroboam (I Kings 11:29-39), whereas Elijah, Micaiah the son of Imlah, and Elisha all function within the court but quite independently of it. The solitary and majestic figure of Elijah has fascinated students of the Bible, by his sudden appearance before Ahab (I Kings 17:1) with the solemn testimony, "As the Lord, the God of Israel, lives, before whom I stand, there shall be neither dew nor rain these years, except by my word." How and why he was admitted to the presence of the king is never explained, but it is obvious from the succeeding chapters that the king knew of the prophetic role and extended to the prophet immunity from the kind of prosecution that would normally be applied to such a figure. Ahab could call Elijah a "troubler of Israel" (I Kings 18:17), but it was only Jezebel the Phoenician who became so bold as to threaten the life of God's prophet.

In the planning of the battle with the Syrians that brought Ahab's life to an end (I Kings 22 and II Chron. 18), we find about four hundred official court prophets functioning in the Samaritan court, again with the task of advising the king on such matters as the expedience of joining battle or refraining from it. Although these prophets claim to have the word of Yahweh, and one of them, Zedekiah, specifically prophesies in Yahweh's name, it is clear that the true prophet of Yahweh is Micaiah, the son of Imlah. Micaiah, though apparently also attached in some way to the court, maintains that it is loyalty to the Lord alone that marks the true prophet of God. His advice, though admitted by Ahab to be generally unfavorable, passes the test for a true prophet of Yahweh as set out in Deuteronomy 13:1-3 and 18:17-22. His word "came to pass," which the true word of the Lord always does.

Elisha, like Elijah before him, advised kings on military matters (II Kings 6:9) and otherwise functioned as a political counselor to the ruling monarch (cf. II Kings 13:14). On an assignment passed to him with the mantle of Elijah, he anointed kings for both Syria and Israel (II Kings 8:7-15 and 9:2-6). He seems to have been constantly associated with a group of guild prophets called in the Bible the "sons of the prophets," though it is never quite certain if these young men are prophets in the full biblical sense.[3]

Classical Prophecy

The great era of prophecy comes with the rise of Amos and Hosea in the eighth century B.C. Although some scholars date Joel and/or Jonah earlier,[4] Amos and Hosea are thought by many to have been the first of those writing prophets whose ministry so powerfully influenced the next two hundred years. Contrary to certain theories popular a generation ago, neither prophet looked on himself as an innovator, nor did either consider prophecy to be a new ethical movement challenging the theology of an earlier time (cf. especially Amos 2:11 f. and 3:7). What Amos did in the social sphere, Hosea did in the religious sphere. Each prophet challenged the accepted norms by proclaiming them to be in violation of the law given by Moses, and of the covenant-election that had created the nation. The history of Israel, particularly God's redemptive activity in the Exodus, provides the touchstone for evaluating all subsequent life. The early period, when Israel's love for God was pure and untarnished, is the ideal, both for past and future. For Amos, this relationship has been polluted by a lapse in basic social justice, a lapse made all the worse by a vain show of religious piety. For Hosea, probably a younger contemporary, Israel has prostituted her relationship with Yahweh by going after other lovers. This is illustrated graphically by God's commandment that the prophet himself provide the object lesson. He was to take a "wife of harlotry and have children of harlotry" that God's persistent love for His whoring nation might be shown. Savage denunciations are heaped upon the priests, and at the same time some of the most tender love passages in all literature are reflected in God's appeals to His wandering people (e.g., Hos. 11:1-4, 8-9).

Both Amos and Hosea foresee a day when Israel will be cast off by God, and each likewise seems committed to an ultimate restoration.[5] For Amos, the day of God's restoration is preceded by, or is part of, a "day of Yahweh" (5:18-20) in which judgment and wrath are poured out upon the enemies of God. This concept, prominent both in Joel and Zephaniah, already was known to the people in Amos's day, though plainly they thought of it as a day of Israel's triumph rather than a day of judgment. Amos does not say that restoration will be a feature of this "day," but the closing chapter of his prophecy seems to imply that it is, since it visualizes a society in which an Israel, restored from exile, is peacefully settled in her land.

About half a century after Amos and Hosea, two prophets arose with a message of judgment for Judah. Isaiah of Jerusalem, one of the greatest of the writing prophets, directed his message of God's glory and ultimate triumph against all of the nations round about Judah, and finally and graphically against the covenant nation itself. False religion comes in for its usual castigation, and God is seen standing as judge and jury in a court case against Judah. The verdict, in light of the holiness of God as understood by the prophet through his own call, is "guilty!" Along with the message of doom comes the promise of a savior (9:6 f.) from the line of David and the root of Jesse (11:1-10), who will usher in a Messianic age of peace and security.[6] The concept that a remnant of Israel will return to the land from Assyria and later (in chapters 40–55) from Babylon, is a preface to promises both in Isaiah and Micah of an age when Zion will become the world's capital, the wealth of all nations flowing into it (Isa. 65 and Mic. 4). But neither Micah nor Isaiah could be characterized as futurologists. Both prophets use the future as an encouragement and consolation for those who will heed the message of judgment, though it is conceded that the nation as a whole will not listen.

Isaiah 40–55, often called "the Book of Consolation,"[7] presents God in universal terms as one who controls even the great Persian king Cyrus and his movements. These chapters, which many feel to be the greatest prophetic utterances of all times, offer comfort and strength to a people facing human disaster. The figure of the Lord's Suffering Servant looms large in chapters 42–53, and Christians from the time of our Lord consistently have seen here a prophecy of the vicarious suffering and redemptive work of Christ. Although it was not until New Testament times that the servant figure was combined with the messianic king in one person, the servant idea became one of the more prominent elements of prophetic expectation.

In Habakkuk, who lived in the late seventh century B.C., we find a prophet who seems to have done no public preaching. His message is not given directly to Judah. Rather, it is a message of hope extended to the beleaguered prophet whose confidence in God's control of history had been shaken by inexplicable events. The prophecy is a dialogue between Habakkuk and God. "How long, O Lord, will I call for help, and Thou wilt not hear?" (1:2, NASB). When the answer comes,"I am raising up the Chaldeans" (v. 6)[8], it is clear that the answer creates more problems yet. "Why art Thou silent when the wicked swallowed up those more righteous than they?" (v. 13). The silence of the heavens is broken only to remind the prophet that God will bring all things into judgment in His own time, that history is going somewhere, and that in the "midst of the years," before God brings all to consummation, "the just shall live by faith." Here is a prophetic message that is neither ethical preaching nor futuristic speculation. Rather, it is a genuine dialogue grounded in real life and asserting, despite the appearances, that God is the controlling force— a fact that faith can confidently appropriate.

Prophecy of Exile

Jeremiah and Ezekiel stand as Israel's two great interpreters of the Exile. Jeremiah, whose recorded ministry began in the days of Josiah, became known as "the prophet of doom." He, above all others, was the consistent pessimist. A constant advisor to kings, governors, and other high officials, Jeremiah's call was for acquiescence in the impending destruction by Nebuchadnezzar and his Babylonian forces. Naturally, this did not increase the prophet's popularity, but his proclamations were vindicated when the march of events made his view of history a reality. Ezekiel, writing from exile on the River Chebar, likewise explored the purpose of the Exile and, together with Jeremiah, proclaimed that God was to be glorified even in this horrible disaster. The glory of God, breaking forth from its geographical confinements, is the special stamp of Ezekiel's visions, together with his call to the shepherds of Israel to return to their true calling. Finally, Ezekiel envisions a new Jerusalem, with a new and different temple in its midst, a message that must have caused considerable discussion among the unfortunates in Babylon.

In the days of the Babylonian captivity, no figure stands so tall as Daniel. Here we come upon a new and different strain in the prophetic line. The Book of Daniel is replete with dreams and their interpretations, apocalyptic visions of the end time, and fascinating accounts of the author's life in the court of Babylonian kings. Long a favorite of futurologists, Daniel also had a message for his own day.[9] Both the prophecy and Daniel's own life stand as a testimony to the fact that God raises up whom He chooses to sit upon thrones and that His will is ultimately the determining factor in all future history. In the meantime, all people can take refuge in the power and goodness of God, an assurance that has meant much to oppressed believers in every age from Maccabean times until the present.

Post-Exilic Prophecy

There are three prophets who are prominent following the return from Babylon: Haggai, Zechariah, and Malachi. The first two, in the year 521 B.C., called the disheartened band of returned exiles to consider divine priorities and get on with rebuilding the house of God. Haggai's scathing sarcasm points up the futility of attempting to measure success in worldly or materialistic terms, whereas Zechariah offers hope to the little band. The day of small things (the restored community in Judea) will exceed in glory even the days of Solomon, and the mountain will become a plain before Zerubbabel. The Spirit of the Lord rather than any earthly power will accomplish this, together with a messianic figure or figures somehow related to Zerubbabel, the prince, and Joshua, the high priest.

Zechariah's last six chapters differ in style and content from the earlier eight. Much of the material, enigmatic in its own time, was later to confirm for the apostles of Jesus the authenticity of their Lord's first advent, and other passages speak of a restored Jerusalem into which the wealth of nations shall flow. A consistent favorite of futuristic Bible scholars, these visions provide much of the basis for discussions of Israel's place in the current prophetic timetable.[10]

Malachi, the last of the canonical prophets, rebukes irreverent priests and a disrespectful people. A call for fidelity in covenant relationships (including marriage) and generosity in giving to God is accompanied by a warning that the Lord is coming suddenly to His temple. In the intervening dark days, the faithful ones who fear the Lord will not be forgotten, and on "that day," God will spare them as a father spares his own son who serves him.

Summary

In summary, the message of the prophets is one of judgment and hope: judgment for those who ignore social justice and who corrupt religious activity, but hope for the little remnant which is faithful to the standards of the Lord's covenant. The future, like the past, is an integral part of their message, because only a God who controls the future and is guiding it to His own consummation can effectively warn of judgment or realistically offer hope. Inasmuch as the context for each of the prophecies is a national one, either Israel or Judah, the historical development and theological meaning of these two nations is central to biblical prophecy. Institutions like the monarchy, the priesthood, and the temple, with its forms of worship, all have a part in the story, both present and future.

It is here that interpreters of prophecy part company. That there is a God who controls history and who used ancient Israel to bring about His own purposes is universally agreed upon by Christians. That the prophets looked for a day of Israel's restoration is plain, though numerous contemporary writers seem oblivious to the fact that many of the prophecies were fulfilled in the restoration under Zerubbabel, Ezra, and Nehemiah. But there is another dimension to Israel's restoration, and that is found in the exalted language that points to a day when universal peace and justice will mark the earth. According to the prophets, Israel is an essential component of that time of peace and glory, and most Christians would agree that this is so. The problem arises when Christians define Israel. Is this a literal restoration of a national or cultural Israel (e.g., the state of Israel), or is this Israel after New Testament times to be equated with a spiritual body somehow identified with the Christian church?

It should be noted that this question, which often looms so large in discussion and debate, is not the crucial issue. The real thrust of prophecy, both for the original audiences and for the church today, is the confident assurance that there is both judgment and glory ahead. God is a God of power and love, and one who keeps covenant with His elect. History is going somewhere, whether it be to the millennial blessing of the pre- or postmillennarian or to the ultimate consummation in heavenly glory of the amillennialist. Ultimately, time will show us which hermeneutical scheme is correct, but in the meantime we can all find comfort, encouragement, and warning for the present in the message of the prophets.

Amos still speaks to those (whatever their persuasion) who assiduously maintain the forms of religion while ignoring the concerns of the poor and oppressed. Hosea still stands as the prophet of unrequited love. His God still waits to receive His unfaithful wife, and the appeal remains as poignant as when it was acted out in the prophet's own time. Isaiah still points forward to a time when

68

universal blessing and peace will mark the earth, when the lion will lie down with the lamb, and a little child shall lead them. The Suffering Servant, now seen in glory with His suffering behind Him, is still for Christians the basic figure of the loving vicarious sacrifice of Christ. Jeremiah, the weeping prophet, still calls us to see that God's purposes are bigger than any nationalistic or other humanly devised schemes, whereas his younger contemporary, Ezekiel, still graphically points to the glory of the Lord who is enthroned above the cherubim.

We could go on, but space does not permit, to speak of Elijah, Micah, and Nahum; of Daniel, Joel, Obadiah, and Jonah; and of Haggai, Zechariah, and Malachi. These all died looking forward to the day of consummation. That they did not understand all the details of its fulfillment is indicated in I Peter 1:10 ff. If we cannot agree on the details of that portion of their vision that is still unfulfilled, this fact should not trouble us. The message was for their time and our time, and it is a message directed to changing our life-style right now. Speculation about the future can sometimes blunt the thrust of the message; but, properly understood, the element of future prediction should form a powerful part of the prophetic proclamation. For the believer, there is a future; but for the scoffer the future element is all the more foreboding. The biblical context is hardly a setting for idle speculation; the issues are too important and immediate.

Guidelines for Interpreting Prophecy

In closing, a few guidelines for interpreting Old Testament prophecy seem in order. A passage of prophecy, like any other passage of the Old Testament, must be seen in its own historical and cultural context. Before extracting the meaning of the passage for today, we must carefully attempt to understand what it meant to the original hearers in the life-setting of the prophet and his people. The message may simply be the way in which God interacted with people and events in a distant land at a remote time in the past. There are, however, some special rules for prophetic Scriptures, which apply only seldom to other sections of the Bible.

First, look for different kinds of language such as figures of speech. Prophetic Scripture, like other biblical poetry, is rich in figurative language that should not be subjected to an unnatural degree of literalism. For example, when Ashdod and Egypt are

69

called to witness the demise of Israel (Amos 3:9), this is presumably a literary device to emphasize the horror of Israel's impending destruction and not a literal call to the Philistines and Egyptians to come and sit on the hillside outside Samaria.

Secondly, be aware of the nature of symbolic actions, events, persons, or things. Ezekiel's strange behavior in lying on his side or cutting and burning his hair (Ezek. 4 and 5), like Hosea's marriage and Isaiah's three-year experiment with nakedness (chap. 20), are symbols that depend for their interpretation on our understanding of the event in its time. The event in its own time, however, may have no specially striking significance; this resides only at the symbolic level.

Thirdly, in prophetic passages we should be cautious about the extent and nature of any predictive elements that may be present. Although it is usually true that there are didactic, or teaching, elements in the prophecy, it is not always true that there are predictions. And where there are predictive elements, the fulfillment may occur shortly after the prophet's utterance, or it may be something for the distant future. In some cases, the predictive element may be reasonably specific, as in the reference to Cyrus (Isa. 45:1), whereas in others it may be expressed in the most general of terms, as for example the variety of associations connected with the coming "day of the Lord." Sometimes there seem to be two or more fulfillments, as with the child to be born in the time of Ahaz and Isaiah (Isa. 7:14). The child was to be a sign to Ahaz, but at least from the New Testament perspective, and even in view of the Old Testament expectation, the child seems to demand some additional reference. Rather than look for two or more separate fulfillments, it is probably best to deduce a single meaning from the passage, a meaning that may be expressed in more than one fulfilling event. Thus, the situation when Christ came as a sign to His people is in many ways parallel to the situation that occasioned the original prophecy. In each case the child born is an indication of the direct intervention of God in history and represents a sign to the people.

Together with the question of multiple fulfillment, a student of prophecy should expect an indirect fulfillment by a correspondence of historical events. In Matthew's Gospel (2:15), the statement from Hosea 11:1 "Out of Egypt I have called my son" is treated as a prophecy of the sojourn of the infant Jesus in that country. In its original context, however, the statement is nothing of the kind. But when we see that Matthew is pointing to equivalent, analogous, or corresponding elements in the life of Christ and in the history of Israel, we can understand the principle behind his use of the passage.[11] That this principle does not give license for finding any and all kinds of symbolic, figurative, or nonliteral meanings should be evident. The significance intended by the author should initially control our investigation, to which may be added a possible expansion in the light of parallels between the New Testament and the Old. Thus, for the New Testament Christian there is a freedom to move away from both a sort of mechanical one-to-one view that reads predictive prophecy as merely a series of newspaper reports written before the event, and also too rigid a system of interpretation that limits the imagination and freedom to recognize divinely intended correspondences and equivalencies.[12]

Prophecy and the prophetic movement is one of the richest aspects of the Old Testament. Indeed, the characteristic emphases of that movement are to be found pervading much of the earlier Scriptures. That it has often suffered at the hands of its friends, especially with respect to its predictive elements, only makes it the more necessary to maintain a proper understanding of its function and dynamic. For the prophets, though continually persecuted and killed, were those who "announced beforehand the coming of the Righteous One" (Acts 7:52). It was Jesus Christ the Righteous to whom all prophetic history pointed. His coming, both as historically completed and as hopefully expected, forms the dual focus to which all prophetic themes move with increasing clarity. That the prophetic message was direct and challenging to its own time only increases the challenge to ourselves. They all died in faith, looking forward to the promise. We live now between the times. We have experienced the fulfillment in Christ, but still we look forward to the end. The final consummation will be ultimately and definitively the era of prophetic fulfillment, when they, with us, shall be made perfect (Heb. 11:40).

71

Notes

1. Cf. R. K. Harrison, *Introduction to the Old Testament* (Grand Rapids, Eerdmans, 1969), p. 711 and W. F. Albright, *From the Stone Age to Christianity*, 2d. ed. (New York: Doubleday, 1957), pp. 303 ff. Albright favors the concept "one who is called [by God], one who has a vocation [from God]."

2. Cf. Jeremiah 18:18 for a capsule statement of spheres of responsibility in Israel. The word *(dabar)* could come in various forms (direct speech, vision, dream, historical event), but it had its own power and ability (cf. Isa. 55:11). For an introduction to the subject, see J. G. S. S. Thomson, *The Old Testament View of Revelation* (Grand Rapids: Eerdmans, 1960), pp. 57-80.

3. H. L. Ellison, *The Prophets of Israel* (Grand Rapids: Eerdmans; and Exeter: Paternoster, 1969), p. 364, distinguishes between the professional or guild prophet and the true prophet of Israel.

4. Harrison, *Introduction to O.T.*, pp. 876-79 (Joel) and 914-18 (Jonah).

5. Various commentators consider the restoration passages, especially of Amos, to be from a later hand. Cf. various commentaries, and Harrison, *Introduction to O. T.*, pp. 868 ff. (Hosea) and 890-94 (Amos).

6. Attacks on the unity of Isaiah have concentrated on chapters 40–66, though the forward-looking material of chapters 1–35 is also considered exilic by many. However, the messianic projection seems so basic to the prophet's message that we may, for the moment, safely ignore such drastic conclusions.

7. Many scholars, including some conservatives, attribute this entire section to a sixth-century prophet in Babylonian exile. The traditional view has been ably defended in recent years by E. J. Young, *The Book of Isaiah*, 3 vols. (Grand Rapids: Eerdmans, 1965–72); O. T. Allis, *The Unity of Isaiah* (Philadelphia: Presbyterian and Reformed, 1950); and others.

8. A reference to the resurgent Babylonian forces, soon to topple the great Assyrian Empire and then establish themselves as the new "world" conqueror.

9. Partly because of the predictive elements, Daniel has stood in the forefront of critical attack. A survey of the extensive literature may be found in Harrison, *Introduction to O. T.*, pp. 1105-1127. Even if the final recension of Daniel comes from Maccabean times (a claim by no means settled), the prophecy is a powerful message to its contemporaries as well as to future generations.

10. See, e. g., D. Baron, *Visions and Prophecies of Zechariah* (Grand Rapids: Kregel, 1918, reprinted 1972) and M. F. Unger, *Zechariah* (Grand Rapids: Zondervan, 1963). A traditionally conservative amillennial view is seen in T. H. Laetsch, *The Minor Prophets* (St. Louis: Concordia, 1956), who relates all prophecies to Christ and His church.

11. See C. H. Dodd, *According to the Scriptures* (London: James Nisbet, 1952), for a standard treatment of the New Testament use of the Old. Cf. also chapters in *Hermeneutics* (Grand Rapids: Baker, 1967), by B. L. Ramm et al., and chapter 6, *"When the Time Had Fully Come,"* of this volume.

12. For a fuller treatment of the subject, see chapter 7, "Interpretation of Prophecy," by W. S. LaSor in *Hermeneutics,* by B. L. Ramm et al., (Grand Rapids: Baker, 1967), and chapter 13 in A. B. Mickelsen, *Interpreting the Bible* (Grand Rapids: Eerdmans, 1963).

5

Messianic Prophecies in the Old Testament

Walter C. Kaiser, Jr.

There are some 456 Old Testament passages that refer to the Messiah or messianic times attested in 558 separate quotations from the Rabbinic writings.[1] Whereas it freely may be conceded that some of these references are questionable due to the subjective methodology and "spiritualizing" tendencies in Rabbinic interpretation, nevertheless, the statistics alone remain as eloquent testimony to both the plethora of available Old Testament texts and the strong Jewish consciousness that the hope of salvation and the glory of God's people was indeed connected with the prospect of a coming ideal king who would rule the world.

The Nature of Messianic Prophecies

Before actually considering a selection of these passages, inquiry first must be made into the nature and character of these messianic passages. By what term or terms are we to refer to this doctrine? Is the doctrine a result of scattered predictions that later made sense when Christ appeared, or is there an eternal plan that knowingly was unfolded before the eyes of Israel and all the world? How many nations and how much material did the doctrine of Messiah embrace as it grew during Old Testament days? These questions must be addressed before we turn to the contents themselves.

Messiah or Servant?

What was this coming Redeemer-King most frequently called? Almost universally, He is today referred to as the Messiah. This is somewhat strange, since if one were to judge simply on the frequency of the terms used, we would have selected the biblical term "Servant of the Lord." This term is the most prominent, appearing in Isaiah 40–66 thirty-one times in connection with the coming Redeemer-King. Furthermore, these passages were cited more often by the New Testament writers than any others, except for those promises that were given to Abraham and David. The designation of "Servant," however, apparently was connected too often solely with the aspect of suffering and the death of the coming person; thus, the more regal term won out.

To be sure, "Messiah" does appear some thirty-nine times in the Old Testament, but the term was used to designate the "anointed" high priest four times (Lev. 4:3, 5, 16; 6:22), the patriarchs twice (Ps. 105:15; I Chron. 16:22), and Cyrus once (Isa. 45:1). In the majority of the passages, which appear in the books of Samuel and Psalms, it has reference to one of the "anointed" Israelite kings: Saul, David, or Solomon. This leaves only nine passages to refer exclusively to a coming ideal person, but all nine are hotly contested. But surely Psalm 2:2 and Daniel 9:25-26 clearly depict a Messiah who was yet to come. Perhaps I Samuel 2:10 and 2:35 could be added to this list.[2]

Regardless of the decision made on the term itself, the fact is clear: numerous texts refer to a coming king who will redeem men from their sin and who will possess an everlasting kingdom to which the nations of the earth must one day yield either willingly or unwillingly.

Prediction or Promise?

Although it may not seem to make much difference whether we think of the Old Testament words about Messiah's person and work as predictions or a promise, there is a vast difference for the biblical authors. A prediction is a foretelling, or a prognostication. It concentrates the hearer's or reader's attention only on two things: the word spoken before the event and the fulfilling event itself. Certainly, this is proper and legitimate, for it does magnify the greatness of God's Word and the accuracy of His accomplishing that ancient Word. It fails, however, to capture precisely that aspect that thrilled the Old Testament writers and saints.

Promise, on the other hand, embraces, as Willis J. Beecher remarked,

> . . . the means employed for that purpose. The promise and the means and the result are all in mind at once. . . . If the promise involved a series of results, we might connect any one of the results with the foretelling clause as a fulfilled prediction. . . . But if we pre-eminently confined our thought to these items in the fulfilled promise, we should be led to an inadequate and very likely a false idea of the promise and its fulfillment. To understand the predictive element aright we must see it in the light of the other elements. Every fulfilled promise is a fulfilled prediction; but it is exceedingly important to look at it as a promise and not as mere prediction.[3]

Since so much, if not all, of Old Testament prophecy falls into the class of a series of predictions with many of them having a series of results, the necessity for regarding these prophecies as promises rather than merely as predictions becomes obvious.

Separate or Cumulative?

Of even greater importance is the matter of the interrelation of these prophecies. Even granting that some may be in a series, are the series interrelated? Or are we dealing with disconnected and heterogeneous predictions randomly announced in the Word of God?

The marvel of prophecy is neither in an alleged separation of the prophetic word from history and geography nor in an unproven assumption that prediction is the main feature in prophecy. Rather, the amazing thing about Old Testament predictions concerning Messiah and His work is that they all make up one continuous plan of God. There is unity here—not diverse and scattered predictions. Each prediction is added to the continuous promise of God that was announced first to pre-patriarchal peoples, then enlarged and continuously supplemented from the patriarchs down to the postexilic era of Haggai, Zechariah, and Malachi. But it remained God's single, cumulative promise.

Precisely the reverse emphasis was the weakness of some of the great apologetic works on prophecy in the past. Indeed, they did show correctly how literally hundreds of predictions have come true in Messiah, but they either exhausted the reader and themselves in trying to show that the scattered Old Testament texts indeed did predict these seemingly unrelated facts and they were therefore entitled to use that text; or they often just assumed that the connection between the Old Testament Word and the accomplished events was understood by all, so that any whimsical impressions left by the selection of the precise Old Testament words was not worth considering in light of such vastly greater gains made in the interest of apologetics. But all along, the unity and cumulative force of the prophecies went begging for lack of interpreters and careful readers. The very repetition of previous prophecies in the later ones should have pointed to the fact that God's revelation was building on what had been announced previously.

Temporal or Eternal?

The duration of this continuous series of announcements in the single, ancient, but renewing promise of God must also be part of our concern when we speak of the character and nature of Messianic prophecy. Too often, reference is made to the fulfillment of separate prophecies as if they were the final enactment of all that God had intended. What should have been said instead was that there was a climacteric fulfillment in the first advent of Christ, i.e., an important change had been reached in the ongoing development of the promise. This was no final fulfillment, however, nor is any other event God's final fulfillment, for the promise is an everlasting promise enduring to all of eternity.

The time range of the messianic prophecies is staggering. It begins in Eden with a word about a "seed" that would remedy the Fall and continues on into a description of the everlasting kingdom of God where Christ reigns as sovereign Lord over the nations in the new heavens and the new earth. The sweep is breathtaking, but it also has a unitized character. Wherever the word of promise is met in the Old Testament, it also participates in that "eternal covenant" (e.g., Heb. 13:20) that made the Word so dependable and certain (Gal. 3:15-18; Rom. 11:29; Heb. 6:13, 17-18).

Cosmopolitan or National?

All of this brings up a delicate point in Jewish and Christian interpretation. If the promise made with Abraham on through to David and those who followed is eternal (Gen. 17:7, 13, 19; II Sam.

78

23:5; Ps. 89:29; Isa. 55:3), then what must be done with the persistent inclusions about Israel's national career and her geographical holdings?

Some Jewish and rationalistic scholars conclude that since Israel's geographical and political career is included so obviously in the center of the promise, that is all that the promise means. It was a prophetic hope expressing the demographic and political aspirations of the nation Israel, consequently all other applications to the church or especially to Jesus Christ are false and inapplicable. This conclusion fails to take the Old Testament itself seriously, much less the historical realities. On the other hand, an overwhelming number of Christian interpreters err in the same manner, only to the opposite side of the promise. They deny that the promise has anything left in it for national Israel, unless it be just incidental, now that the Christian era has arrived.

Willis J. Beecher of the old Princeton faculty said it best when he commented:

> ... If the Christian interpreter persists in excluding the ethnical Israel from his conception of the fulfilment, or in regarding Israel's part in the matter as merely preparatory and not eternal, then he comes into conflict with the plain witness of both Testaments [and we might now add "with history as well"]. . . . Rightly interpreted, the biblical statements include in the fulfilment both Israel the race, with whom the covenant is eternal, and also the personal Christ and his mission, with the whole spiritual Israel of the redeemed in all ages. The New Testament teaches this as Christian doctrine, for leading men to repentance and for edification, and the Old Testament teaches it as messianic doctrine, for leading men to repentance and for edification. . . . The exclusive Jewish interpretation and the exclusive Christian interpretation are equally wrong. Each is correct in what it affirms, and incorrect in what it denies.[4]

The promise, then, was national and cosmopolitan. Israel will yet receive what God's eternal covenant had unconditionally promised: a land, nationhood, king, worship, and riches. But so will the nations of the earth be blessed in Abraham's seed. Indeed, all the ends of the earth shall turn to the Lord (Ps. 22:27-28) and princes shall come from Egypt and Ethiopia and sing unto God (Ps. 68:31-32). So agreed Isaiah (49:12,22; 60:3,5,11; 61:6; 62:2; 66:19) and all the prophets. Was not the Jerusalem council convened to answer this very question? And did they not appeal successfully, to the satisfaction of the Jews present, to Amos 9:11-12? And if any doubt remains concerning the Jew, has not Paul spoken definitively in Romans 11?

We therefore conclude that the messianic doctrine is located in God's single, unified plan, called His promise, which is eternal in its fulfillment, with climacteric plateaus reached in its historical accomplishments. Finally, it is cumulative in its build-up, but national and truly cosmopolitan in its outreach to all nations, tribes, and peoples in all historical times.

The Unfolding Doctrine of Messiah

E. Jenni summarized the situation best when he observed that:

> The O.T. Messiah . . . has no real counterpart in the ancient Near Eastern milieu. Its source must, therefore, be sought within the O.T. faith. To be sure, many of the concepts which are a part of the picture of the Messiah are also to be found in the intellectual world of the Babylonians, the Egyptians, and other cultures of the Near East. But in these cases, they lack the specifically Israelite projection toward the final goal of history.[5]

It is to that Testament, then, that we turn to receive the word of promise, and some of its results in history up to the first advent.

The Roots of the Promise

At least two passages constitute the tap root of the promise in the pre-patriarchal era. The first was given to Adam and Eve in Genesis 3:15, and the other was given to Shem in Genesis 9:26-27.

In the former passage, the earliest beginnings of the Messiah can be ever so faintly observed. But make no mistake about it, the presence of a promise, which began a long series of amplifications that at once formed a doctrine of salvation, a direction for the universal history of mankind, and a cryptic statement about the outcome of the whole process, is as certain as words can be.

A divinely imposed hostility ("I will cause") between personalities (*enmity* is a word always used between individuals, never involving the lower creation) is announced in Genesis 3:15. The contest will at first be between Satan and Eve; then between Satan's "seed" and Eve's "seed." The collective or corporate nature of the word *seed* is most important for understanding any messianic doctrine, for it is the first of many to come. It involves the total group meant (either

80

all the physical or spiritual descendents) and then comes to its fullest realization in its representative head who epitomizes the whole group. Thus, the seed of Satan is, no doubt, all his spiritual descendants who are to live subsequently on the earth and who will one day be singularly represented and epitomized in the Antichrist who is to come according to later revelation. But the seed of Eve includes all her future spiritual descendants who will also be effectively represented in the One, Himself the "Seed," too, viz., Jesus Christ. (This is also Paul's insight into Moses' meaning, cf. Galatians 3:16, 29.)

The real surprise, however, is not the divinely implanted hostility between Satan and Satan's "seed"; it is that Eve's "seed," (a male descendant of Eve's seed) would be victoriously matched in a battle with Satan. He would mortally crush Satan, a victory which, Paul later added, would be shared by all the seed of Eve (Rom. 16:20).[6] How this victory would be actualized and what the wounding of this Man's heel meant had to await later unfolding revelation.

In the meantime, the circle of possible origins for this deliverer for man's desperate need is given in Genesis 9:26-27. With tantalizing brevity, the promise is simply, "Blessed be the Lord, the God of Shem, . . . he shall dwell in . . . the tents of Shem (KJV)." To be sure, the subject of "he shall dwell" is extremely difficult to ascertain. Charles Briggs strenuously argued that it was the same as the subject of the preceding clause ("God enlarge Japheth") and therefore this dwelling was an open prediction that God would one day come and "tabernacle" among the Semitic peoples.[7] This suggestion must not be dismissed as quickly as it has been customarily treated. Even if the subject is, as most argue, Japheth, then the text still identifies Shem as the fountain-head of all divine blessing. Non-Semitic peoples, like Japheth, will need to find their spiritual provision from the "Shemites."

The Promise to Abraham

In Abraham's day, the doctrine of Messiah took a giant step forward. God met with one of Shem's descendants and narrowed the circle from which the divine blessing should emanate even further.

The word to Abraham, Isaac, and Jacob centered on a promised *heir* (Gen. 12:3,7; 13:14-16; 15:4-5,13,18; 16:10; 17:2,7,9,19; 21:12; 22:17; 26:24; 27:28-29; 28:14). The promise of a "seed" brought to the patriarch's mind, no doubt, the ancient word given to

81

Adam and Eve about a "seed," indeed a coming "he" who would crush Satan's head. Thus, a "seed" is developing that at once includes all believers, but which also simultaneously has its ultimate sights set on a single heir *par excellence:* the One who would represent the many. When Abraham was asked to sacrifice Isaac on Mount Moriah (Gen. 22), the full meaning of what it meant to have the promise of God's *heir* came home to the patriarch with full force. God alone was capable of maintaining His promise, and, as if to underscore the point, God took an oath to confirm this word. He also was able to provide a substitute for bound Isaac. Is is any wonder, then, that Jesus insisted on the fact that "Abraham rejoiced to see my day, he saw it and was glad"?

Meanwhile, a series of fresh births of sons (like Isaac and Jacob), who stood in a direct line with this coming person, testified to the reality of the promise, and they themselves each revealed part of the accomplishment in their own historical times.

Along with promising an heir, the Lord included an *inheritance* of the land of Canaan as a gift to the patriarchs and their descendants forever (Gen. 12:1,7; 13:15,17; 15:7,18; 17:8; 24:7; 26:2-3; 28:13; 49:8-12). Thereby, the doctrine of Messiah was tied indirectly with an earthly philosophy of history. His kingdom would not only be spiritually located in the hearts of His men, but it would be located in our planet and in our history as well. He would, appropriately, complete history as He had begun it, with His people Israel in their land. Present-day Christians must not jettison this provison in the messianic doctrine for supposed theological or hermeneutical reasons when all along it is actually the result of "our Western dualism, docetism, and spiritualism."[8]

A third and climactic provision found in that same Abrahamic promise was the gift of a *heritage* that in the patriarch's seed "the nations of the earth shall be blessed" (Gen. 12:3; 18:18; 22:18; 26:4; 28:14). So excellent was this provision that it is uniformly called the "gospel" (e.g., Gal. 3:8). All nations, peoples, and tribes would be blessed (not "bless themselves"),[9] i.e., hear about: God's *heir*/Messiah, God's plan and philosophy of history wherein the nation Israel became God's timepiece, and a gospel rich enough to save all who would believe.

Thus God chose Abram from the line of Shem and made his seed the center of the promise for the future redemption of the entire world. As if to anticipate the royal predictions of Jacob (Gen. 49:

8-10) and Balaam (Num. 24:17), which ultimately rested in David's house (II Sam. 7), God promised to make Abram and Sarah ancestors of kings (Gen. 17:6,16; cf. 35:11).

Jacob, in his blessing, prophetically had given to his fourth son, Judah, the scepter of kingship that was to be his "until he comes to whom it belongs" (cf. "Shiloh" and Ezek. 21:27). That one was none other than Messiah, just as the angel announced in Luke 1:32-33. Similarly, Balaam saw royalty as a "star" and a "scepter" coming out of Israel. Messiah now was known to be not only from the "seed" of Eve, Shem, and Abraham; but more specifically, He was to be a reigning son from Judah's tribe.

The Everlasting Priesthood

Before Scripture spells out in detail all that this coming ruler would be like, it adds two other offices to His kingship: priest and prophet. Both of these promises also appear to be generic and corporate in nature—that is, they predict a series of men holding these offices while also envisioning a culminating personage as a climacteric fulfillment.

Even though all Israel had been characterized as a "kingdom of priests" before the Lord (Exod. 19:5-6) and had declined the offer because of God's awesome holiness, in Numbers 25:12-13, Phinehas's righteous act led God to promise that henceforth he and his "seed" after him would receive a covenant of an "everlasting priesthood." This prophecy was expanded on the eve of the demise of Eli's house. On that occasion, God said that He would raise up a "faithful priest" and "build him a permanent house and he would walk before his anointed [Messiah] forever" (I Sam. 2:35). Delitzsch summarized this aspect precisely when he said:

> The promise (I Sam. 2:35) is primarily realized all the better in the Zadokite high priest who stood at the side of the better kings from the house of David. But its ultimate fulfilment is found in the Christ of God, in whom according to Zech. 6:13 the ideal king and priest do not stand side by side but are united.[10]

The only correction needed to Delitzsch's statement is that already five hundred years earlier, David had contemplated in Psalm

110:4,6 this union of a "priest" "after the order of Melchizedek" and a victorious "Lord" who would judge the nations. No doubt, when David received this revelation in Psalm 110, he was having his "quiet time" in Genesis 14; and while contemplating the sweet victory that God had given to his man of promise, Abraham,[11] over the four foreign kings, his mind was filled with the prospect of a future victory when the Lord would one day also say to David's Lord, "Sit at my right hand."

The Prophet Like Moses

Likewise, Deuteronomy 18:15,18 pointed to "a prophet" who would come from among the Jews and be like Moses. Although it is technically true that the expression, "I will raise up to you a prophet," is not collective or generic but denotes only one prophet and no more, all the same the word is used here also in a distributive sense. It appears in a context that speaks of priests, Levites, and false prophets as classes. Nor is there any Pentateuchal passage authorizing later prophecy if this is not it. Indeed, all previous messianic prophecy has been generic, as is the prophecy that follows in the next period. Consequently, while focusing on that one prophet who was to come, the context leads us to expect a succession of prophets. This is exactly how Peter viewed our passage in Acts 3:21,24 as did Stephen in Acts 7:37. The line of true prophets was consummated in Jesus Christ.

Others distinguished between the great prophet and the Messiah (John 1:19-21; 4:19,25; 6:14; 7:40-42) whereas the unity of the two perhaps dawned on others (Matt. 21:9-11).

Already in Deuteronomy 33:5, Moses had been called "king" and in Exodus 34:3-8 he was Israel's first priest; indeed the judge of Aaron's office (Lev. 10:16-20) and the one who passed the high priesthood on to Eleazar (Num. 20:23-29). Thus Scripture provided for the ultimate unification of the Messiah's offices in Moses' functions; there was to be a resemblance to Moses' ministry as priest and king.[12]

Let there be no mistake, however. God's Servant will triumph (Isa. 52:13), for even though many will be shocked at His crucifixion (Isa. 52:14), this is nothing compared to the way kings will be stunned when He returns a second time (Isa. 52:15). So while He "made himself an offering for sin" so that His "seed" might live (Isa.

53:10), nevertheless, the Servant knew from eternity that the plan of the Lord would succeed (Isa. 53:10).

The Sure Mercies of David

The future redemption of the race was to come through the seed of the woman, the race of Shem, the promise to Abraham, the ruling scepter and star in Judah, the kingdom of priests in Israel, the priesthood of Phinehas, and the prophet like Moses.

But the best of all was now to be disclosed by Nathan the prophet in II Samuel 7 (cf. I Chron. 17). The same promise that had been extended a millennium earlier to Abraham and had continued through his seed in the meantime, is now given another gigantic push forward with the news that God would establish David's dynasty ("house"), kingdom, and throne forever. Furthermore, the duration was not only eternal, but the realm of the kingdom was universal. In flabbergasted tones, David thanks God in a prayer that divulges the fact that David understood this promise to be a "charter for all humanity" (II Sam. 7:19).[13] This accords with the eloquent heights of Davidic and Solomonic messianic Psalms such as 2, 45, 72, and 110. Yes, "all kings will fall down before him: all nations shall serve him" (Ps. 72:10).

The prophetic literature sharpens the specifics of this Davidic dynasty ("house"), authority ("throne"), and rule or realm ("kingdom"). This future king will be born in David's city of Bethlehem (Mic. 5:2), enjoy a miraculous birth ("sign" of Isa. 7:14), be called "God," the "Everlasting Father" (Isa. 9:6), and have the "Spirit of the Lord" resting upon Him (Isa. 11:2). He is to be the "one" good "shepherd" that will rule over Israel (Ezek. 34:23-24) as "king" in accordance with the "everlasting covenant" made previously with Abraham and David, but now in its enlarged form called a "new covenant" (Jer. 31:31ff.) or "covenant of peace" (Ezek. 37:24-28). All this is but a partial list of those "sure mercies" given to David (Isa. 55:3).

The Servant of the Lord

Intrinsically bound up with these themes of royalty and victory was the theme of the suffering Messiah. The principle of ransom or deliverance on the basis of an appointed substitute had already been taught by Moses as an "everlasting statute" in the Passover lamb

(Exod. 12:14) and in the two goats of the day of atonement (Lev. 16:34). The perpetuity of this principle finds its concrete embodiment in the person of Isaiah's Servant of the Lord.

The term *servant* is again a generic or collective term, which according to Isaiah's own teaching, often meant "Israel," precisely what the "seed" of the earlier promises signified (Isa. 41:8-10; 42:18-19; 43:9-10; 44:1-3,21; 45:4; 48:20; 49:3; Jer. 30:10; 46:27-28; Ezek. 28:25; and the plural word, *servants,* all coming after Isa. 53, *viz.* 54:17; 56:6; 63:17; 65:8-9,13-15; and 66:14). Notice, however, this is not merely ethnic Israel; it is Israel as possessor of the promise given to Abraham and David, national Israel and spiritual Israel.[14]

But then this servant also is to be distinguished from national Israel in that He is an individual who has a mission to Israel (Isa. 42:1-7; 49:1-9; 50:4-10; 52:13–53:12; Jer. 33:21; Ezek. 34:23-24; 37:24-25; Hag. 2:23; Zech. 3:8). The term is technical, but clear. Can anyone doubt that this "servant" is the same as the kingly Messiah when they share attributes (e.g., "my Spirit is on him" Isa. 42:1, cf. Isa. 11:2) and the same mission (e.g., "a light to the Gentiles" Isa. 42:6; 49:6, cf. Isa. 9:2).

The Son of Man

Although there are additional pictures of the Messiah such as a "top stone" or "cornerstone" (Isa. 28:16, Zech. 3:9; 4:7; and Ps. 118:22), we conclude with Daniel's "Son of Man." This also is Messiah, but Messiah as reigning and ruling king. He will come one day "in the clouds of heaven" and there shall finally be given to Him "dominion, and glory, and a kingdom, that all people, nations, and tongues, should serve him; his dominion is an everlasting dominion which shall not pass away, and his kingdom shall not be destroyed" (Dan. 7:13-14). Whereas modern scholarship is loath to bring together the figures of the "Servant of Yahweh" and the "Son of Man," neither Jesus nor some of His earlier predecessors at Qumran were at all hesitant to do so.[15] An obedient, serving, suffering "Son of Man" was not a contradiction in terms or mission, for He was one person with one mission and a single plan: God's Messiah as announced in His everlasting promise.

86

Notes

1. Alfred Edersheim, *The Life and Times of Jesus the Messiah,* vol. 2 (Grand Rapids: Eerdmans, 1953), Appendix 9, pp. 710-41. The distribution of the 456 Old Testament passages is as follows: Pentateuch—75, Prophets—243, Writings—138.

2. The other four references of the nine are: Ps. 20:6; 28:8; 84:9; and Hab. 3:13.

3. Willis J. Beecher, *The Prophets and the Promise* (Grand Rapids: Baker, 1963 [reprint of 1905]), p. 361.

4. Ibid., p. 383.

5. E. Jenni, "Messiah," *Interpreter's Dictionary of the Bible,* vol. 3 (Nashville: Abingdon, 1962), p. 361.

6. R. A. Martin. "The Earliest Messianic Interpretation of Genesis 3:15," *Journal of Biblical Literature,* 84 (1965), pp. 425-27.

7. Charles A. Briggs, *Messianic Prophecy* (New York: Scribner, 1889), pp. 82-83, note 1.

8. Henrikus Berkhof, *Christ, The Meaning of History* (Richmond: John Knox, 1966), p. 153.

9. The view held by A. Kuenen, *The Prophets and Prophecy in Israel: An Historical and Critical Inquiry,* translated by Adam Milroy (London: Longman, 1877), pp. 378-80, 456, 496 is well critiqued by Stanley Leathes, *Old Testament Prophecy* (London: Hodder and Stoughton, 1880), 33-61. Also see the excellent article by O. T. Allis, "The Blessing of Abraham," *Princeton Theological Review,* 24 (1927), pp. 263-98. The meaning of the Hebrew *Hithpael* is often a simple passive (e.g., Prov. 31:30; Lam. 2:12; 4:1; Mic. 6:16; Ezek. 19:12). Surprisingly, even the cautious and conservative Franz Delitzsch, *Messianic Prophecies,* translated by S. I. Curtiss (Edinburgh: T. & T. Clark, 1880), p. 31, takes the reflexive view because the passive meaning for the *Hithpael* is "Late"! Then he tries to slide the two views together and says, "Since the nations will deserve the blessing of Abraham they will on that account be blessed. . . . Spiritual blessings . . . fall to those who long for them" (!!).

10. Delitzsch, *Messianic Prophecies,* p. 45.

11. Beecher, *Prophets and Promise,* pp. 346-48.

12. H. L. Ellison, *The Centrality of the Messianic Idea for the Old Testament* (London: Tyndale, 1953). On page 16 he comments, " . . . It is the more remarkable that there seems to be no trace at all of Moses' prophecy of a 'prophet like unto me' being interpreted Messianically in rabbinic literature. In the New Testament it is used almost casually, as though its Messianic meaning would be accepted without cavil. . . ." Either it was suppressed, or "the rabbis never thought through the relationship of the Messiah to the Law."

13. For development of this translation, see Walter C. Kaiser, Jr., "The Blessings of David: A Charter for Humanity," in *The Law and the Prophets: O. T. Allis Festschrift,* edited by J. Skilton (Philadelphia: Presbyterian and Reformed, 1973).

14. See Willis J. Beecher's excellent discussion, *Prophets and Promise*, pp. 263-88.

15. F. F. Bruce, *The New Testament Development of Old Testament Themes* (Grand Rapids: Eerdmans, 1968), pp. 88-99.

6

When the Time Had Fully Come

Donald A. Hagner

It is in the Epistle to the Galatians—precisely where his argument depends so heavily on the Old Testament—that the apostle Paul sets forth the goal of the Old Testament anticipation as the appearance of Jesus Christ in history: "When the time had fully come, God sent forth his Son" (4:4). Ears attuned to the message of the Old Testament cannot miss the significance of a phrase such as "the fullness of time" or Paul's startling reference to his contemporaries as those "upon whom the end of the ages has come" (I Cor. 10:11).

Fulfillment of the Old Testament in the New Testament

If there is any theme that pervades the New Testament, it is the theme of fulfillment. That which had long been prophesied, which had been hoped for and anticipated through the turmoil of Israel's frustrating history, has now dawned upon mankind in the events recorded in the New Testament. The excitement is present from the beginning of the gospel age when Jesus announces, "The time is fulfilled, and the kingdom of God is at hand" (Mark 1:15); it is present at Pentecost when Peter declares, "This is what was spoken by the prophet Joel" (Acts 2:16). The wonder of the things that have transpired is apparent when they are later described as not only what the prophets prophesied but what they "searched and inquired about" and as "things into which angels long to look" (I Peter 1:10 ff.).

89

Indeed, these words lend an aura of mystery to the fulfillment that has come through the present goodness of God.

This insistent note of fulfillment throughout the New Testament has led some scholars, initially C. H. Dodd, to refer to New Testament eschatology as "realized eschatology." To the extent that such a designation reflects New Testament teaching it is suitable. The fact is, however, that despite the emphasis upon fulfillment in the New Testament, not all eschatology *is* realized. There remains more to come, specifically the complex of events associated with the return of Jesus Christ. In actuality we have, to use a distinction popularized by G. E. Ladd, fulfillment without consummation. Allowing for eschatology that is yet future, the thrust of the New Testament teaching may be designated appropriately as *"inaugurated eschatology."*

In the New Testament, eschatology already is present; the end has seen its beginning. The goal now being realized is none other than that looked forward to in the Old Testament. Accordingly, a large amount of space in the New Testament is given to Old Testament allusion and quotation as the events of the New Testament period are demonstrated to be the fulfillment of the Old Testament hope.

Although there is no reason to dispute that the post-resurrection church read the Old Testament with a new understanding and was active in constructing an apologetic from the Old Testament materials, there is also no need to dispute that the impetus for this new apprehension of the meaning of the Old Testament came from Jesus Himself. Luke repeats himself several times at the end of his Gospel in asserting that "beginning with Moses and all the prophets, he [Jesus] interpreted to them in all the scriptures the things concerning himself" (Luke 24:25 ff., 32, 44 ff.). Just as there was a slowness in comprehending the import of Jesus' words and deeds in His ministry, so now more than ever was there a slowness in understanding the illuminating events of that ministry. It is natural to suppose that in His post-resurrection ministry Jesus should be concerned with the matter of Old Testament interpretation, and we have every reason to believe that when the early church buttressed its kerygma with Old Testament evidence, it was dependent upon the initial instruction of Jesus. Thus, when he writes the following, Paul is ultimately relying upon Jesus' understanding of the Old Testament: "For I delivered to you as of first importance what I also received, that Christ died for our sins in accordance with the scriptures, that he was buried, that he was raised on the third day in accordance with the scriptures" (I Cor. 15:3 f.).

Sensus Plenior in the New Testament

The manner in which the Old Testament is used in the New Testament is often fascinating, if occasionally troublesome, to the Bible student. Some of the Old Testament material used is straightforwardly predictive. That is, it speaks of things that from the author's perspective are future. One would expect no difficulty with the New Testament fulfillment of predictive prophecy, yet there are instances where, in keeping with the fundamental principles of grammatical-historical interpretation, the fulfillment of the prophecy must be to the prophet's contemporaries if it is to be regarded as meaningful to them. Thus Isaiah 7:14 speaks of the birth of a child who is to serve as a sign to King Ahaz. Matthew, however, finding a deeper or fuller meaning in the verse, aided by the Greek translation's *parthenos*, or "virgin," as well as the name "Immanuel," argues that the birth of Jesus is the fulfillment of what the prophet had spoken (Matt. 1:23).

This phenomenon occurs frequently in the New Testament, and however one chooses to describe it, one is faced with the perception of a deeper, more significant meaning or a fuller sense contained within and alongside the primary or contemporary meaning. This fuller sense, or *sensus plenior* as scholars have come to call it, is described well by R. E. Brown as the divinely intended meaning, not clearly intended by the human author, but made evident by subsequent revelation. It is this fuller sense that the New Testament writers are alive to as they produce their writings under the inspiration of the Holy Spirit.

Fulfillment in Typological Correspondences

In addition to the fulfillment of predictive Old Testament passages, however, there is a different kind of fulfillment spoken of in the New Testament, involving a notion of fulfillment that is, unfortunately for us, more genial to the Jewish mind than to ours. This is fulfillment not of prediction but of a divinely intended pattern that is seen to occur in the history of salvation. The correspondences found in these repeated patterns are sometimes called "types," and the study of the phenomenon, "typology." Although much abused

91

in the past, there is no reason to deny the real presence of typological correspondence in the Old and New Testament. This, too, involves a fuller sense than was apparent to or intended by the original author and thus is seen only in the recurrence of the pattern in the light of subsequent revelational events.

This is illustrated by another of Matthew's fulfillment quotations. After the narrative of the flight of the Holy Family to Egypt and their return at Herod's death, Matthew adds: "This was to fulfil what the Lord had spoken by the prophet, 'Out of Egypt have I called my son'" (2:15). The passage quoted is from Hosea 11:1, where the words are nothing more than a historical reminiscence of the Exodus of Israel from Egypt. Matthew rightly sees a correspondence in the coming out of Egypt of God's son, Israel, and the Son of God, Jesus. The former event serves as a type of the latter.

But how can Matthew speak of fulfillment? Does this mean that we are to suppose that Matthew construed the Hosea passage as predictive prophecy? It is certain that Matthew would have allowed that these words of Hosea refer to the historical event of the Exodus. At the same time, however, within the historical allusion Matthew can detect a predictive aspect in the correspondence contained in the two instances of God's son being called out of Egypt. The key to understanding how mere correspondence can be understood as prediction and fulfillment is found in the Jewish conviction concerning the absolute sovereignty of God in ordering the events of history. Thus correspondences and patterns that can be detected in the history of salvation (or the history of God's dealing with man) are not accidental. They are divinely intended, the earlier ones (types) foreshadowing and thus pointing to the later ones (antitypes) that thereby are seen to fulfill their counterparts.

It is apparent immediately that for this kind of detection of parallels, the biblical writings provide an almost too-promising hunting-ground. The biblical writers themselves delight in this activity. Matthew sees a correspondence between the wailing of Rachel for the exiled captives that is mentioned by Jeremiah (31:15) and that of the Bethlehemites at Herod's slaughter of their male infants (Matt. 2:17 f.). The geographical proximity of the traditional site of Rachel's tomb to the town of Bethlehem probably strengthened the correspondence of the lamentation in Matthew's mind. Perhaps an even less substantial correspondence is seen a few verses later in Matthew when he refers to the dwelling of Jesus in Nazareth as ful-

filling the prophetic utterance: " 'He shall be called a Nazarene' "
(2:23). Matthew appears to be playing on the word *branch* in Isaiah
11:1, which in the Hebrew (*nezer*) has the same initial three con-
sonants as the name Nazareth. In effect, then, Matthew is saying this:
The sovereignty of God over history is such that the prophecy of
a branch from the root of Jesse (which finds its fulfillment in the
messianic personage of Jesus) is echoed in the very name of the city
where the intended descendant came to reside.

There is thus a "fuller sense" to much of the Old Testament as it
was read by Matthew and other New Testament writers. Correspondences that we would have regarded as merely interesting or even
fascinating are seized upon as possessing divinely intended significance. Far from being fortuitous, such correspondences suggest the
underlying teleological interconnection of these materials and therein
the outworking of God's plan in history. The question now arises:
Do all correspondences that one may detect in the Scriptures possess
divinely intended significance? Can we, starting with the premise of
the overarching sovereignty of God, find type and antitype in every
comparison of similarities that may present itself to our minds?
Indeed, how far can we go with the "fuller sense" of Scripture? Can
it encompass allegorical (as over against typological) understanding
of the Old Testament?

Controls on Typological Correspondences

Clearly there must be some controls on the way in which and the
extent to which the interconnection between Old Testament anticipation and New Testament fulfillment is conceived. Even in the case
of predictive prophecy, some caution is called for in defining a fuller
sense. Although the fuller significance of the prophecy may not have
been present to the original author's mind, it must at least be in line
with, and not alien to, the original prediction. In the case of typology, somewhat more freedom is allowable; but here, too, caution
must be exercised.

Properly speaking, the designations *type* and *antitype* should be
reserved for correspondences or patterns located within historical
events. Typology thus focuses on the parallels that can be detected
between a historical sequence in the past and a historical sequence
present to the writers of the New Testament. It grows out of the
process of salvation in history. The earlier acts of God are seen in

93

retrospect as the foreshadowings of His later acts. In the sovereignty of God, the complex of events recorded in the New Testament is seen typologically as the fulfillment of the earlier pattern.

Typology finds its proper controls in being limited to analogy or correspondence within patterns of actual historical occurrences. The correspondences themselves should be of intrinsic importance to the narrative rather than merely incidental accompaniments. A clear example of valid typology is found in the correspondences in the redemption experienced by Israel in the events of the Passover and Exodus from Egypt and that redemption procured by the sacrifice of Jesus Christ making possible a new exodus from the bondage to sin. The analogies that can be detected here are substantial, central rather than peripheral, and rooted in the saving activity of God in history.

Of course, many analogies and correspondences between Old and New can be detected that are not historically rooted or not central to their respective narratives. These often may be interesting and instructive in themselves, but without New Testament warranty they should not be understood as divinely intended "typology." When such illustrative correspondences are seen, they should be regarded as "accidental" rather than specifically and intentionally designed by the will of God. The analogies that are brought forward here usually exhibit an *ex post facto* inventiveness that rightly disqualifies them. This is the case, for example, when the minutiae of the tabernacle furniture, having in themselves no intrinsic importance, are ascribed great typological significance with reference to New Testament truths. There is a legitimate use of the tabernacle in typological correspondences, but it involves the central ideas of the sacrificial ritual and the presence of God with man, rather than mere accompanying details. The historical patterns connected with the tabernacle are correctly understood as foreshadowings of the historical patterns narrated in the Gospels.

Misuse of Allegory

Allegorical interpretations of the Old Testament, insofar as they depart from historical patterns (which is what distinguishes allegory from typology), are to be regarded as essentially illegitimate appeals to *sensus plenior*. In allegory there are no controls. One produces from the Old Testament what one has predetermined to produce, and the product bears no necessary relationship to the source from which it is derived. Thus Philo, the Alexandrian contemporary of Jesus, can find in the narrative of the Pentateuch a grand allegory whose real interest is an exposition of Platonic Idealism. In this way, timeless or "spiritual" truths are extracted from documents that on the surface look time-conditioned and "earthly." Whereas one may admire Philo's adeptness in finding Platonism in the Mosaic writings, it must be admitted that both the method and the results are arbitrary.

The New Testament itself affords no allegorical use of the Old Testament in the strictest sense. There are, however, some passages in Paul's Epistles that are akin to allegory. Indeed, in Galatians 4:24, Paul uses the Greek verb *allēgorein*, "to speak allegorically," as he writes that Hagar the slave and Sarah the free woman "are two covenants," the old producing slavery and the new, freedom. Another passage where Paul comes close to what looks like allegory is in I Corinthians 10:4 where he writes of the Israelites in the wilderness that "they drank from the supernatural Rock which followed them, and the Rock was Christ."

These two passages are often set forth as classic examples of an allegorizing use of the Old Testament in the New Testament. Yet they also may be regarded as extensions of typology as it has been described above. That is, if these passages represent allegory, it must be noted that it is a rather severely controlled "allegory." First, it seems quite clear that Paul preserves the historicity of Sarah, Hagar, and the Rock. Thus, although he says the two women *are* two covenants, he does not mean that they were not real women in history. In the same way, when he says the Rock *was* Christ, he does not mean to deny that the Israelites drank from an actual rock. Nor is Paul arguing about the real meaning of the women and the rock. In the first instance, what Paul does is draw an analogy. The case of the two women is like the case of the two covenants, involving their children in slavery or freedom. This kind of correspondence is similar to what we have discussed above as typology. Moreover, Paul does not move away from the literal sense of the Old Testament passage, importing a meaning alien to the original; he discovers instead an essential continuity in the effects of the women and the covenants. Thus, although Paul suggests that he is speaking "allegorically," we may with some justification see in this material a moderate extension of the principles of typology.

This may be the case also in Paul's identification of the rock with Christ. He may be saying only that there is a typological correspondence between the rock, which repeatedly gave supernatural provision to the people of God, and Christ, who is the Archetype of supernatural provision in giving us the sweet water of salvation. Taking Christ as the culmination and thus as the pattern of all supernatural provision, one may easily suggest that where such provision is present, there is Christ. More probably, however, Paul begins with this analogy and extends it by implying that the pre-incarnate Christ was actually present with the people in the wilderness, and that where there was supernatural provision, it was He who was the source of it. Thus, the true Rock from which they drank was Christ. Essentially, then, what we have here is typological correspondence enhanced by the conviction of Paul (and the early church) that references to Yahweh in the Old Testament (translated *kyrios*, or *Lord*, in the Septuagint) can be understood, especially when found in a salvation context, as referring to the pre-incarnate Christ. Here we are confronted not with allegorizing, but with an example of a very specialized Christological interpretation of the Old Testament.

Therefore in the case of the two women and the Rock in the wilderness, as indeed in other instances of alleged allegorizing on Paul's part (e.g., I Cor. 5:6-8; 9:8-10), we do not find allegory in its stricter sense. If we choose to name it "allegory" at all, we must immediately add that it is a use of allegory carefully controlled against the abuse that has come to be associated with allegorical interpretation. Since these controls are in line with those referred to under typology, it seems more desirable to regard these passages as extensions of typology, and the I Corinthians 10:4 passage as reflecting a specialized Christological hermeneutic.

Controls Exercised by New Testament Writers

We may now summarize what we have presented about the *sensus plenior* of the Old Testament. That the New Testament writers are alive to a fuller sense of the Scriptures they possessed is evident not only in their understanding of some straightforwardly predictive passages, but particularly in their frequent use of typology. Discerning a teleological interconnection between the recorded words of the Scriptures and the events that had occurred in their own time, they interpreted the latter as the intended fulfillment of the former. The New Testament writers avoid allegory and by and large are restrained in their use of typology, sharing the following controls: (1) that there be a recognizable, linear continuity between the original meaning of the Old Testament and its New Testament counterpart; (2) that the correspondences be located in patterns of historical sequence, particularly involving no violation of the historical aspect of the Old Testament material; (3) that in its original context, the Old Testament material employed be of central and not merely peripheral importance.

It must be frankly admitted, however, that the New Testament writers do not always exercise these controls in their employment of typology. Yet what is remarkable is not the extent to which they depart from these controls but, given the climate of their time, the extent to which they abide by them. These men, after all, were completely caught up in the excitement of the fulfillment of God's promises to them in their day. It was of the risen Lord, who had so recently been in their midst, that they were able to say, "For all the promises of God find their Yes in him" (II Cor. 1:20). With this basic premise and their view of the inspiration of the Scriptures, one might have expected a much greater and freer—indeed, almost a limitless—use of typology and abundant allegorical exegesis as well.

Midrashic and Pesher Interpretations

There was no lack of rather fanciful handling of the Scriptures contemporary, or nearly so, with our New Testament authors to provide precedent and stimulus. We have already mentioned the highly allegorical exegesis produced by Philo. This type of allegorizing was not unknown even in Palestine. More common in Palestine, however, was the exegetical practice of the rabbis known as *midrash*, where the Scriptures were studied diligently to discover hidden meanings that were relevant to present circumstances. The midrashic technique involved an atomistic approach, wherein a single word or phrase, regardless of its meaning in its own context, could become the source of fresh meaning by the use of free association of ideas and wordplay. Therefore, even what seemed a most trivial item in the sacred text could become, through the ingenuity of the interpreter, the bearer of new significance and meaning.

Perhaps most interesting and important to the New Testament reader is the *pesher* interpretation as found in the writings of the Dead Sea community of Qumran. This monastic community believed that the eschaton—the end of the age and the consummation of

97

God's plan for Israel—was imminent. Accordingly, all Scripture spoke of the time period in which the community was called to exist. Any apparent meaning of the Scriptures that once may have made them relevant to their original historical context was superfluous. The *true* meaning of the Scriptures was the hidden meaning, hitherto inaccessible, but now made known at the end of the age through the interpretation revealed to the Teacher of Righteousness, the leader of the community. The interpretative technique applied to the Scriptures is atomistic like that of *midrash* discussed above. Everything in the text is forced into subservience to the controlling theme of fulfillment. But it is not a matter of an ancient text being relevant to the present, but rather the single true concern of that text from the beginning in every detail. *Pesher* interpretation, as found, for example, in the Qumran sect's commentary on Habakkuk, proceeds on the one-to-one basis of "this is that." Since the text is read entirely in the light of contemporary events, the reader is repeatedly shown that eschatology is imminent. He reads about his own time as spoken of by the prophet.

When one considers the widespread currency of allegorical, midrashic, and *pesher* interpretation in the first century, one only can think it remarkable that the New Testament writers were not more influenced by these types of interpretation than they were. We already have seen that there is no allegorical interpretation of the Old Testament in the New Testament, at least of the more unrestrained kind as found in Philo. When comparing the procedure of midrashic and *pesher* interpretation with the interpretation of the Old Testament in the New Testament writers, one is immediately impressed with an important difference. As a rule the New Testament writers avoid the atomistic approach that is so typical of these types of interpretation. That is, as demonstrated by C. H. Dodd, the Old Testament materials used come generally from more extended portions of the various books quoted. Thus, the quotation material is understood in its original context as a totality. The violation of the historical context and significance of the Old Testament writing that is so typical of the atomistic approach is thereby avoided. The text is not made totally subservient to the controlling presupposition of the interpreters. Instead, it speaks for itself, is seen to be in line with, and thus prophetic of, the fulfillment that has occurred.

Nevertheless, there is some common ground between midrashic and especially *pesher* interpretation on the one hand, and New Testament interpretation on the other. The New Testament writers, after all, believed more strongly than the men of Qumran that "this is that." And for them it was not a matter of eschatological fulfillment about to occur, but of eschatological fulfillment that *had* occurred. As these New Testament writers labored to proclaim the fulfillment and thus to show the interconnection between the Old Testament and the events they had witnessed, it is unthinkable that they could remain completely uninfluenced by current Jewish modes of argument. Consequently, it is that in the New Testament we occasionally encounter a use of the Old Testament that sounds strange to our ears, that appears somewhat contrived, and that is difficult to defend on carefully reasoned hermeneutical principles.

Conclusion

Generally, we are far too dispassionate in our reading of the New Testament. If we are truly to understand these writers, and more specifically their use of the Old Testament, we somehow must recapture the excitement that so dominated them. They knew that the end of the ages was upon them, that eschatology had begun in the ministry, death, and triumphant resurrection of their Lord. It was this that the Old Testament had in prospect from the beginning. It now had arrived and was the source of the joy and power of the early church. To be sure, there was the eager expectation of the consummation of eschatology in the return of this same Jesus. But that did not control their thinking. Instead they were controlled by the excitement of what had occurred in their midst, of which they themselves were witnesses: the present reality of the Kingdom. These men, as they read their Holy Scriptures, rightly understood them to be speaking of their day, whether by direct prediction or by *sensus plenior*. The history of salvation had reached its goal; the time had fully come.

7

Guidelines to the Interpretation of Daniel and Revelation

C. M. Kempton Hewitt

Peals of thunder, loud noises, flashes of lightning, and earthquakes. Howls of torment and wrath, angels wrestling with evil powers, and portents of blood and fire in heaven. Scarlet women on scarlet beasts. Death on a pale horse and stars named Wormwood. Charging rams and collapsing kingdoms. What does it all mean?

Of such stuff is the so-called apocalyptic literature made. All of these figures and symbols appear in the Bible and have been disputed and debated for generations, both before and after the first advent of Jesus. Can they be understood? Is this violent, confusing part of the Word still useful in our time? Or should it be set apart and considered a kind of second-class citizen to the rest of Scripture?

This brief introduction to apocalyptic literature will concentrate on the books of Daniel and Revelation. It will identify both the canonical (i.e., books belonging to the Bible, as agreed upon in the case of the Old Testament by both Jewish and Christian tradition, and in the case of the New Testament by Christian tradition) and noncanonical evidences of apocalyptic writings, as well as the idea of the apocalyptic. The problems one encounters in understanding apocalyptic writing will be discussed. Suggestions as to those general areas where we might profitably learn more from Daniel and Revelation will be made. Finally, guidelines for reading and studying these two books will be offered.

Any attempt to understand the apocalypses better must begin with humility and awe. In both Daniel and Revelation, the writers themselves admit to an overwhelming sense of inadequacy in the face of the awesome visions confronting them. We can readily identify with Daniel:

> And I, Daniel, was overcome and lay sick for some days; then I rose and went about the king's business; but I was appalled by the vision and did not understand it (Dan. 8:27).

John on Patmos was so shaken by his vision of Christ that he "fell at his feet as though dead" (Rev. 1:17).

It was not only the prophets themselves who experienced such wonder and awe. The early Christian scholar, Origen, one of the greatest intellects of all Christian history, posed the question:

> And who, on reading the revelations made to John, could fail to be amazed at the deep obscurity of the unspeakable mysteries contained therein, which are evident even to him who does not understand what is written?[1]

With this sense of humility and, at the same time, challenge, we open these books.

What Are the Apocalyptic Books of the Bible?

The book of Daniel in the Old Testament and The Revelation in the New Testament are clearly apocalyptic. Other apocalyptic passages, however, are found throughout Scripture. In the Old Testament, Ezekiel 1:9-10; 37:40-48, and chapters 38 and 39; Zechariah chapters 12–14; Isaiah chapters 24–27; and most of Joel contain symbolic visions and oracles that are apocalyptic in mood and style. In the New Testament, the so-called little apocalypse or book-within-a-book is found in Matthew 24, Mark 13, and Luke 21. This "little book," which is parallel in all three gospels, is sometimes referred to as the "synoptic apocalypse" or the "little apocalypse" because only small fragments of this parallel material are found in John's Gospel. Beyond this, apocalyptic material (varying amounts, according to one's definition) occurs throughout the New Testament.

Beyond canonical Scripture, however, the list of apocalyptic literature is extensive. Among the books of the so-called Pseudepigrapha, the most important are IV Ezra, the Similitudes of Enoch,

102

II Baruch, and the Testament of the Twelve Patriarchs. The New Testament Apocrypha contains the Apocalypses of Peter, Paul, Thomas, Stephen, John, the Virgin Mary, and others.

In addition, fresh information about apocalyptic literature has come to light through the discovery of the Dead Sea Scrolls. We now have evidence of twenty documents either written or preserved by the Qumran community. Although these books take many different forms—books of discipline, psalms, liturgies, and commentaries— much of this material is apocalyptic.

From this brief summary, it is clear that apocalyptic literature was, for both the Jewish and Christian communities, not simply an amusing, obscure footnote but an important and beloved part of faith. Although some would claim that this interest was present only in a fringe of the community, the fact remains that Jesus spoke in apocalyptic terms, as reported by all of the synoptic Gospels. This language and thought also are clearly present in the Epistles, especially II Thessalonians and II Peter.

What Makes a Book "Apocalyptic"?

Our English word *apocalypse* comes from a Greek word *apocalupsis,* meaning "unveiling."[2] The last book of the New Testament, for example, is sometimes referred to as "The Apocalypse," taken from the first words of the Greek text, "The revelation [apocalupsis] of Jesus Christ . . . " (Rev. 1:1).

Although the word *apocalypse* itself suggests clarity, there is no other body of Scripture that has occasioned greater disagreement. Within recent studies of the New Testament, the great debate of the late nineteenth and early twentieth centuries was focused on the question of apocalyptic elements in the Gospels. This debate, closely associated with the name of Albert Schweitzer, established the necessity of dealing with apocalyptic thought.

Many speak and write as though the characteristics of apocalyptic literature are clear and universally accepted. It may come as some surprise, then, to learn that there is no generally agreed-upon definition. There are, however, marks to which many scholars point: all apocalyptic literature focuses on conflict, a conflict always set in the framework of eschatology. By *eschatology* is meant that a second, distinct age, a creation by God, is looming over our present age, and will break in upon history at some point in time.

103

There are other marks of this kind of biblical literature. Almost without exception the revelation takes place through visions and dreams. These visions are replete with symbolism, often involving animals and numbers. History often is presented in symbolic images or allegories, so that a master code book might be needed to understand it. Angels and demons enter the struggle, often with violent and bloody consequences. Usually implicit in this struggle is a portent for the inauguration of a New Age, sometimes associated with a Messiah.[3]

Furthermore, apocalyptic writers lived during times of hardship, usually including persecution. This condition no doubt affected the writers. Some even say that without persecution, apocalyptic literature would never have been written.

Overarching the apocalyptic scene is a sense of mystery and urgency that has excited the imagination of Jews and Christians alike—especially in times of conflict and persecution—and challenged men of faith to search for a "hidden key" by which the biblical apocalypses might be understood.

The inescapable purpose of apocalyptic literature, however, is to reveal. Ironically, this fact is frequently neglected by interpreters of the apocalypses. For, above all, these books look at the inner meanings of what has taken place in the past, what is now happening, and what will happen in the future. It is from this sweeping telescoping of history and the future that the sense of urgency comes. That these revelations take place through visions is an important clue. It is as though the one who is experiencing the vision is handed a transforming lens that converts the confusion and turmoil of history into a clear, integrated verbal picture.

With a modern, experimental camera, the picture is taken, and the camera ejects a square, gray piece of paper. At first the image is amorphous and nebulous. As it is exposed to the light, however, a beautiful, sharp photographic image emerges. In many ways this illustrates what the apocalyptic writers attempted for their readers. The verbal picture they presented is an earthly reflection of heavenly thinking, a picture with a whole new, apparently unrelated, set of references. When read by those who "understand" (Rev. 13:18; Dan. 12:10), this verbal picture, with its metaphors and symbolism, is clear. To others it is an impenetrable mass of veiled figures.

The inability to find meaning in apocalyptic visions and dreams is experienced by those having no "understanding" (a favorite term in both Daniel and Revelation) for the concerns, convictions, and commitments they represent. This was the situation of the pagan neighbors in whose midst the writers and recipients of these apocalypses lived. This also applied to those Jews and Christians who had no time for the apocalyptic viewpoint. This hidden, or coded, nature of apocalyptic writings was purposeful to an extent, for it protected the writer and the community from further persecution.

Others do not "understand" because they live in another time and place. This is our problem as twentieth-century Western Christians. To illustrate this phenomenon, the story is reported of American naval pilots, who, when captured and pressured by their North Vietnamese captors to name other fliers still operating, responded with such names as Mickey Mouse, Donald Duck, and other Walt Disney figures. Their responses were reported in propaganda broadcasts to the world. The North Vietnamese remained unaware that the replies were fictional characters and, in effect, they relayed a coded message that the captured pilots were alive. Obviously, only a Westerner would recognize Mickey Mouse and Donald Duck as fictional. We shall see later how these features of apocalyptic literature are consistent throughout the Old and New Testaments.[4]

What Are the Problems of Interpreting the Apocalyptic Books?

We must now turn to two of the more difficult questions concerning the apocalypses of the Bible:

(1) To what extent are these also prophetic?

(2) Do these books really predict the future?

Daniel

The obvious temptation when trying to answer the first question is to compare Daniel with the prophets Jeremiah and Ezekiel, both of whom lived during the conquest and exile imposed upon Judah and its capital, Jerusalem, by the Babylonians. The differences between the books, however, appear to be vivid.

Daniel, as a part of the Old Testament canon, was not found among the prophets, but in the section called *Kethubim* or, literally, Writings, along with Psalms, Job, Proverbs, Ruth, Song of Solomon, Ecclesiastes, Lamentations, Esther, Ezra, Nehemiah, and I and II Chronicles. Only later was Daniel placed among the prophets, where it is found today in most Catholic and Protestant editions of the Bible.

Furthermore, Daniel refers to Jeremiah in a way that seems to place them in different strata. For example, Daniel quotes Jeremiah by name as if he were a person of great authority living in quite a different age and circumstance (Dan. 9:2). This is unparalleled elsewhere in the Old Testament prophets. Although Daniel does not specifically refer to Ezekiel by name, there is no doubt that Daniel was influenced by him. One example is Daniel 4:10-18, which concerns Nebuchadnezzar's dream of the great tree. The similarities between this and Ezekiel's oracle of 31:1-9 (against Egypt) are too close not to imply influence.[5] Other examples could be cited.

All of this, at first glance, might lead one to conclude that Daniel was not a prophet in the sense that Jeremiah and Ezekiel were. A deeper look, however, makes such a conclusion difficult. For example, Daniel is divided most conveniently into two parts. Chapters 1–6 contain a narrative account of the youth Daniel and his three Jewish friends in the Babylonian court, whereas chapters 7–12 present visionary material (with the exception of the marvelous prayer in 9:3-19), reflecting all of those characteristics outlined above that we term apocalyptic. We might suppose that chapters 1–6, which must be classed as "wisdom" or biographical material, do not belong in the prophets. But there is considerable biographical material in Jeremiah and, to a lesser extent, in Ezekiel. Furthermore, the visionary nature of Daniel 7–12 certainly is wholly consistent with the prophets (see Jeremiah 1:13 f. and chapter 24; Ezekiel 8–11; and Zechariah 1–5 and 7).

What is it, then, that raises the question of Daniel's place among the prophets? In addition to those factors already mentioned, it is important to be aware of the apparent absence of oracles (messages from God, spoken by God through the prophets to individuals and nations) for the people of Daniel's time. Even this must be carefully qualified, for Daniel does contain oracles—the reports of vision experiences to Darius the Mede (Dan. 11:1 ff.), for example. This, too, is consistent with the earlier great prophets. Still, there is something quite distinctive about Daniel, and this brings us to the second question concerning history and prediction.

It is precisely this concentration on prediction, as well as the total commitment to apocalyptic thought forms, which differentiates Daniel from Jeremiah and Ezekiel. Prophets such as Jeremiah and Ezekiel are concerned with prediction. Both, for example, envision a restored, perfected Israel. But there are two important differences when the predictions of these two books are compared with those in Daniel.

First, Jeremiah and Ezekiel are best thought of as a special kind of preacher, that is, prophets speaking the word of the Lord ("oracles") to the people of their time about all facets of life, not just the future. The source of the oracles is found in a deep religious experience of call and successive vision experiences. Jeremiah, for example, was deeply concerned for the religious abuses of his people, especially the corruption of many of his contemporary religious leaders. He also was outraged over rampant social injustice, a concern, incidentally, not present in Daniel. Ezekiel also addressed contemporary political, religious, and ethical concerns.

Second, when Jeremiah and Ezekiel speak of future hope, their vision is, on the whole, not eschatological. Rather, they see the future salvation of Israel as taking place within history, often in terms of a perfected past. In Jeremiah there is hope for a "new covenant" (Jer. 31:31 ff.), which is really a vastly improved Sinai covenant. He speaks the promise that one day "houses and fields shall again be bought in this land" (Jer. 32:15), that is, a return to the "good old days." In other places, Jeremiah makes it clear that the future will be better than the good old days. Ezekiel holds out the hope for a perfectly shaped land with the temple at the center (chapters 40–48). He speaks of a second conquest of the promised land, this time with no rebels allowed (20:38). In both Ezekiel and Jeremiah, good and evil men are mixed among the people of Israel. God's judgment is to weed out the good from the bad and establish with this remnant a renewed Israel.

In Daniel the picture is different. Here, God's judgment is a "them/us" matter. The forces of right (Israel and God) are arrayed against the forces of evil (Satan and his minions). There is no hope in history for improvement or perfection. Rather, there must be an end to history as we know it (the "eschatological" element of biblical thinking). This climactic end is God's judgment on the world. It ends the conflict between God's people and the forces of evil. God's conclusion to life as we know it is a triumphant, cataclysmic intervention that is violent and militaristic.

Jeremiah and Ezekiel are willing to struggle with the political realities of the time, and Daniel is not. For Daniel, there is total and final pessimism for the political possibilities of history; the only solution is to look beyond history to God's solution.

In summary, then, Daniel is prophetic literature, heavily indebted to the great prophetic tradition, but also a pioneer book that breaks new ground in its viewpoint, thought forms, and theology. There is much that is new in Daniel, and this new element includes more than the apocalyptic viewpoint. The six stories in chapters 1–6, for instance, have a familiar ring. After reflection, most readers are reminded of the Joseph stories in Genesis. Actually, the posture which the four (Daniel, Shadrach, Meshach, and Abednego) strike is similar to that of Joseph: victims of fate, unbending loyalty to the faith of the Hebrews, willingness to compromise to an extent by serving a pagan king, unparalleled success in a foreign court, ability to interpret dreams and visions, moral uprightness, testing by cruel frivolity of unsympathetic foreigners, and, above all, possessing special wisdom. The picture in both Genesis and Daniel is singularly attractive. Both Jewish Haggadah (Jewish interpretation of Scripture, narrative in style and designed to increase devotion) and Christian catechesis have drawn heavily upon these five personalities. Well they might, for this is what was intended, at least in Daniel's case. These stories are told to provide the example of individuals who are to be emulated, especially in a time of testing. (It may be that there are echoes of this in the two witnesses of Revelation 11.) At least in part, then, Daniel is essentially Wisdom Literature. This means that in addition to being the first apocalyptic book of the Bible, it is also the first prophetic book to use wisdom as a consistent motif.

Revelation

Remarkably, Revelation is the only book in the New Testament dedicated entirely to prophecy. This, upon reflection, is startling simply because the act of prophesying as well as the office of prophet is referred to frequently in the New Testament as a contemporary phenomenon (cf. Eph. 4:11; I Cor. 12:28; Acts 15:32), and yet the only clear example outside Revelation is the account in Acts 21:7-14 concerning the warning given to Paul by the prophet Agabus of Judea.

Although the Epistles are written by apostles (Rom. 1:1; I Cor. 1:1; II Cor. 1:1; Gal. 1:1; Eph. 1:1; Col. 1:1; I Peter 1:1; II Peter 1:1) and servants (Rom. 1:1; Phil. 1:1; Titus 1:1; II Peter 1:1; Jude 1) of Jesus Christ, there can be no doubt that Revelation is written by a prophet. Although John never refers directly to himself as a prophet (perhaps because he did not consider himself worthy to be counted in the same category with the two prophets described in Revelation 11), the book is clearly set within the brackets of prophecy.[6] The first and last sentences of Revelation make this clear: "Blessed is he who reads aloud the word of the prophecy . . . " (Rev. 1:3), and "I warn every one who hears the words of the prophecy of this book . . . " (Rev. 22:18). There can be little doubt that John, who was ordered to prophesy (Rev. 10:11), thought of his book as a prophetic message from Jesus Christ which was to be read throughout Asia in services of worship as the message of God through one of His prophets.

John, however, is not in such a minority as it may seem. Indeed, references to prophecy occur frequently in the New Testament. Apostles prophesy (Acts 27) and so do great numbers of worshiping Christians, as is implied in I Corinthians 14.

"The testimony of Jesus is the spirit of prophecy" (Rev. 19:10), says John, and it is made clear that Jesus' work of affirmation through His Spirit is the spirit of prophecy. Once this link with testimony is made, the door is open for other insights concerning the prophetic nature of Revelation. In Revelation, participation in the prophecy and testimony concerning Jesus Christ is not limited to a special class of officeholders called prophets. In many ways, Revelation is a call for hearers to enter into the experience of testimony and prophecy. Although we know very little about the prophesying that took place in the early church, it seems probable that it was not limited to prediction, nor was this always a professional function.[7] Thus, the call for hearers to take part in prophecy—as we have it in Revelation—is consistent with what is said concerning prophecy elsewhere in the New Testament.

But what is the nature of this prophetic activity? Here lies the importance of Revelation, for most of what we know about the form and function of prophecy in the primitive church comes from our study of the Apocalypse. The answer to this question is far more complicated than in the case of Daniel. A rich clue is to be found in the public nature of prophecy. From what is known, it is clear that prophecy took place in the context of Christian worship. The Apocalypse is not an exception, for it is a book rich in liturgical elements and was certainly meant by John to be read throughout Asia in services of worship. Equally important is the fact that the vision came to John on Patmos while he was worshiping (Rev. 1:10).

Certainly, prophecy was used by God in the churches for a purpose somehow distinct from proclamation and teaching, and yet in some ways similar to them.

What was this purpose? What set prophecy apart from other acts? Above all, prophecy grew out of the moving, ecstatic experience of being overcome by God's Spirit in such a way that words spoken while "in the Spirit" came not from reflection and study, but solely from God for the benefit of His people. From the reference in I Thessalonians 5:20 ("Do not despise prophesying"), we can conjecture that there were those who did not take kindly to having the orderly, planned course of public worship interrupted by these spontaneous outbursts. This is confirmed by the guidelines Paul felt necessary to lay down in I Corinthians 14. As for the purpose of prophecy, then, we can only say that these words spoken through the Spirit were for the guidance of believers, and that the intention was to clarify issues, whether generally acknowledged or unrecognized, confronting the congregation.

Viewed in this light, Revelation takes on a sense of urgency and relevance. John's concern that those hearing the report of his vision listen, understand, and alter their lives accordingly could not be clearer. Because his words are inspired, this prophecy has that same urgency and relevance for us today.

The Problem of Prediction

What is the central purpose of Daniel and Revelation? Is it to unveil? Since the apocalyptic writer takes one part of the prophet's function—to predict—and elevates it above all others, how does he predict? And what?

Alvin Toffler and others have brought a new word into our vocabulary—"futurism." This discipline begins from the observation that because change is now occurring so rapidly, we must develop facilities for anticipating the result of these changes so that individuals and institutions may gird themselves for change. If this is not done, the shock resulting from the rapidity of change may well overwhelm and incapacitate persons and even entire nations. An example of this is the current energy crisis, which possibly could change our entire way of life.

In many ways the purpose of the apocalyptic writers was much the same as that of the futurists of today. Just as many today are

110

skeptical of both the method and premise of futurism, we know that many in the age of apocalypticism were also skeptical. Thus, the New Testament book of II Peter defends Christian apocalypticism!

To carry the illustration further, the predictions of Daniel and Revelation are of much the same nature as that of Toffler's *Future Shock* (leaving aside, for a moment, the divine inspiration of Daniel and Revelation); the most detailed predictions are really illustrations of how change has affected men up to and including the present moment. Although the futurists cannot tell us in detail precisely how life will be in 1984, they can assure us that it will be different from what it is now, show us the broad shape of what that change may be like, and encourage us to develop skills to cope with it. Similarly, in both Daniel and Revelation we are left with a general impression, or a marked conviction. It is this: the present struggle in which we are engaged must be seen for what it is—the earthly dimension of a cosmic-wide struggle between God and the forces of evil. Our task is to keep the faith ("endure," says John in the Apocalypse), realize that what we do and say reflects this struggle, and wait for God's solution to the matter in His sweeping judgment.

What Can We Learn from Daniel and Revelation?

It is almost as important to focus on what we *cannot* learn from these two books as on what we can. The history of their interpretation has many tragic chapters. Persistently, there have been those who have tried to make Daniel and Revelation a detailed script for the near future. Space does not permit us to recount the stories of those who misled their followers by the easy identification of apocalyptic symbols and figures with historical counterparts of their time.

Not only the caveat of our Lord, " . . . of that day or that hour no one knows, not even the angels in heaven, nor the Son, but only the Father" (Mark 13:32), but also the command to conceal the revelation until the end (Dan. 12:4, 9) ought to prevent men from attempting to use the apocalyptic books as a kind of time-chart for guessing exactly when God will break in upon us. If nothing else, the repeated failure of well-intentioned Christians to name the day, season, year, or hour ought to make us immediately suspicious of those who by their own cleverness have claimed to break the final seal.

On the other hand, it is also unfortunate that Daniel and Revelation have been frequently neglected by Christians. The apparent

111

obscurity of both books has caused many simply to pretend that they do not exist. Even the great commentator John Calvin, who wrote on all the other books of the Bible, failed to write a commentary on the Book of Revelation!

Actually there is a great deal that is new in Daniel. The apocalyptic view of history becomes an alternative to the traditional view of history in the Old Testament. This view can give us a fresh understanding of events in the church and the world. The message of apocalyptic theology is that we need not be cynical when things do not get better (as they never seem to), because God is in control of history and will direct it to His own solution. Jews and Christians alike have found new hope through Daniel's message in those times when there seemed to be no hope for improvement.

Theologically, Daniel is a rich treasury of new ideas. Daniel is among the first in the Old Testament to state clearly a belief in a resurrection. Against the backdrop of the rest of the Old Testament, this is a revolutionary claim. The promise of resurrection fulfills the hope held out to those who embrace the faith (Dan. 12:2, 13). Further, the example of the four courageous Hebrew young men should strengthen our faith in difficult times.

We must remember, in all humility, that Daniel is not only a book for Christians (as members of the "new Israel"), but also, by historic claim, the book of the Jews. Who can doubt that the story of Shadrach, Meshach, and Abednego entering the "fiery furnace" for their faith (Dan. 3) was in the hearts and minds of those millions of Jews who were marched into the death camps of Hitler's Third Reich? And because of man's inhumanity to man, which will persist as long as human history continues, we shall never outlive our need for the Book of Daniel.

The Book of Revelation is necessary to complete the New Testament canon. Without it we would know very little about the form and function of prophecy in the primitive church. Although addressed to seven specific congregations that really did exist in Asia Minor, the message of the Apocalypse transcends the time in which it was written. Certainly, for example, we can see how the issues in our own lives and in the swirl of history taking place around us mirror the conflict in Revelation between the saints who keep the testimony of the Lamb who conquers and the earth-dwellers who sing the praises of the beast who blasphemes. Every Christian generation in every place is involved in the struggle portrayed in the Apocalypse, regardless of time or circumstance.

The imagery and symbolism of the Apocalypse have enriched not only the theology and thought of Christians throughout the centuries, but also have exercised vast influence over Western art and music. The search that many have conducted fruitlessly for the hidden key to unlock the details of the Apocalypse has left them blind to the sweeping drama of John's visions. Just as most readers rush by the grandeur and richness of the penitential prayer in Daniel 9:3-19, so they miss the wealth of liturgical references in Revelation with their implications.

For example, the center of activity in the Apocalypse is the heavenly throne. By means of piling up prepositions (*in, on, out of, from*), John visualizes the action of the Apocalypse rushing to, orbiting around, hovering in the midst of, and streaming out of the throne of God and the Lamb. The book's orderly sequence (series of sevens) begins in a blaze of verbal color, in the midst of which rules the "one seated on the throne." To begin the action of judgment, the Lamb—the Lord, Jesus Christ—approaches the throne of God and there accepts the symbol of His office as Lord of history—a scroll "sealed with seven seals." As the Lamb breaks each seal, the course of the conflict unfolds. The battle is in the Lamb's hands; through Him all the events of history, affecting all men in every place, head toward their final goal. When the details are woven together, we have a breathtaking pictorial tapestry, a verbal mural, of the central conviction of Christian apocalyptic. This conviction is that an all-powerful and transcendent God is directing the destiny of our whole universe toward His own purposes. Further, the Son carries out the mission of His Father on earth not in subjection to or in conflict with the Father, but in perfect obedience to Him.

How Should We Read and Study These Two Books?

To suggest that Daniel and Revelation are closed books to all but the most erudite of scholars would be wrong. Yet, more than anywhere else in the Bible, a friendly and trustworthy guide is needed in this territory.[8]

But how should one choose a guide? Fortunately, we have an abundance of commentaries on all levels, and especially for Revelation.[9] (This abundance, however, further complicates the problem of

113

choice.) A good place to begin is with the short introduction to Daniel and Revelation as found in a good Bible dictionary. Also helpful are introductory volumes to the Bible such as R. K. Harrison's *Old Testament Introduction* (Grand Rapids: Eerdmans, 1969) and E. F. Harrison's *Introduction to the New Testament* (Grand Rapids: Eerdmans, 1964) or similar volumes. After this, one may want to begin a more detailed study by working through the text with a one-volume commentary of the Bible.

From this study it soon will become clear where the issues and debates are. For example, commentators generally divide on the question of date, authorship, and the identity of the four kingdoms in Daniel 7. The lines of division were drawn very early. As early as the third century A.D., a pagan philosopher named Porphyry (*ca.* A.D. 232-303) set out to prove that Daniel was written during the critical period of the Maccabeans, or about 165 B.C. Jerome, an early Christian saint and scholar, objected violently to the spirit of Porphyry's exegesis but accepted, in the main, the results of his research. Since that time, scholars have disagreed, sometimes violently, over the question of the date and authorship of Daniel. If one wishes to study Daniel seriously this issue must be confronted, because a more precise understanding of the details in Daniel pivots to a large extent on whether one believes the book was written during the Babylonian Exile (i.e., in the sixth century B.C.) or during the turbulent days of the Maccabeans (i.e., in the second century B.C.).

The issues are even more complex in Revelation. One obvious example is how one is to understand the message to the seven churches of Asia when John addresses them in Revelation 1:4—3:22. Is one to believe that these messages were intended only for Christians in those places, for that time? Or do these churches represent successive eras in the church's history? Or are those messages relevant to some churches at certain times throughout the church's history? Or is it true perhaps that all of what John is commanded to speak to the "angel of the church" is relevant for all churches in all time? Those commentators who consume most of their writing space in juggling these rather tired questions should be avoided in favor of those who lead us to more fresh and constructive insights.

Look for balance in your guide. Because both Daniel and Revelation are such fertile ground, there is a rich history of interpretation. Those commentators who are aware of this history will better be able to help you avoid cul-de-sacs that others have followed in the past. Those unaware of this history are condemned to repeat it. Be wary of easy answers by those who claim to understand everything fully. It is certain that both Daniel and Revelation follow a type of blueprint that controls the development of each book. If we had this blueprint, it would be much easier to follow the action. We need to be aware, however, that no one has ever discovered this master plan and explained it in a way that is acceptable to all, or even to the majority of Christian scholars.

Perhaps the wisest advice regarding the interpretation of apocalyptic literature comes from Christianity's first great theologian, Irenaeus, Bishop of Lyons (*ca.* 130-200). In his influential treatise, *Against All Heresies,* he deals at length with Old Testament prophecy, especially that of Isaiah, Jeremiah, and Daniel. He explains Daniel and Revelation in some considerable detail (Book V), but cautions against trying to discover such matters as to whom the number of the mark of the Beast (666) refers. Rather, says Irenaeus,

> It is . . . more certain, and less hazardous, to *await the fulfillment of the prophecy,* than to be making surmises, and casting about for any names that may present themselves, inasmuch as many names can be found possessing the number mentioned; and the same question will, after all, remain unsolved. (Emphasis mine.)[10]

Here is wise counsel. Even before the New Testament existed as such, Irenaeus saw how unfruitful the search after the details of apocalyptic revelation really is. He believed strongly in prophecy nonetheless, as a means of proclaiming Christ and His kingdom. His example is worth following.

Above all, do not begin or end with what others say about Daniel and Revelation. Read these books as they were read and heard by the first readers and hearers. With an open and prayerful attitude, wait for God to speak and challenge you where you live. In the end, this is the best and most authentic use of these books.

Notes

1. G. W. Butterworth, *Origen On First Principles* (New York: Harper Torchbooks, 1966), p. 274.

2. In the Old Testament a Hebrew verb (*galah*) is used with approximately the same meaning. It is significant that of the twenty-three occurrences of this word in the Old Testament, eight of them are in Daniel, seven of them in chapter 2!

3. Some scholars would suggest that *pseudonymity* ought to be included in such a list. This element is undoubtedly present in some books, but it is by no means a consistent factor. The New Testament Book of Revelation, for example, is not written pseudonymously. Again, there is such great disagreement in the case of Daniel that no general claim can be made without dispute arising.

4. A selection of texts illustrating these features is offered in chapter 12 of C. K. Barrett's *The New Testament Background: Selected Documents* (London: SPCK, 1956; and New York: Harper, 1961).

5. The reference to Daniel in Ezekiel 14:14,20 cannot be to the canonical Book of Daniel.

6. The word *prophecy* is used five times, and the word *prophet* eight times in Revelation. The verb *to prophesy* is used only twice.

7. The references in I Timothy 1:18 and 4:14, for example, seem to suggest that prophecy within his own congregation played a major role in the calling of young Timothy as an evangelist.

8. At various times in the church's history Daniel and Revelation have been reserved for "mature audiences" only. Certainly this is not a safe or reasonable course to follow. The writer of Hebrews points out that there is a time to "leave the elementary doctrines of Christ and go on to maturity . . ." (Heb. 6:1). He goes on to list some of those "elementary doctrines." In this list are "the resurrection of the dead, and eternal judgment" (Heb. 6:2), both of which are spoken about at length in Daniel and Revelation!

9. A remarkably extensive bibliography on Revelation can be found in *I Saw a New Earth*, by Paul S. Minear (Washington: Corpus Bks., 1968). Dr. Minear's book is a superb study guide and would be an excellent place to begin one's study of the Apocalypse. Compare also the commentaries in the bibliography at the end of this book.

10. *The Ante-Nicene Fathers* (Grand Rapids: Eerdmans, reprinted 1973), vol. 1, xxx. 3, p. 559.

8

Evangelical Alternatives

James Robert Ross

If one should ask what the orthodox or evangelical doctrine of the last things is, an honest answer would have to recognize that there are more differences among Evangelicals on eschatology than on any other single aspect of our faith. Regrettably, these differences of opinion based on different interpretations of prophetic passages too often have led to bitter theological debates, even actual divisions, among sincere Christians. It is the purpose of this chapter to explore some of the more obvious and more basic differences in prophetic interpretation among Evangelicals.

Reasons for Our Differences

Why do significant differences of prophetic interpretation flourish among Christians who otherwise share a common faith? In the first place, biblical "prophecy" includes a variety and abundance of material. There is more eschatological material in the New Testament than many casual students suspect. Besides the Book of Revelation, which is devoted completely to eschatology, there are extended passages such as Matthew 24 and 25 and many references to last things found in every New Testament book. And when we try to comprehend and integrate the many Old Testament prophecies into our understanding of last things, the task becomes truly overwhelming.

117

Besides straightforward prose and poetry, the Bible includes much "apocalyptic" writing that uses a symbolic style very foreign to the modern interpreter (see chapter 7). This abundance and variety of biblical material in both content and style make it difficult to arrive at a single comprehensive system equally acceptable to all interpreters.

A second problem, not often recognized as such by conservative expositors, is simply that the Second Coming of Christ has been delayed more than nineteen centuries. As a former teacher of mine put it, "The main problem with the Second Coming is that it hasn't happened yet." The "delay of the Parousia," as it is often called by scholars, means that Christians have had to reassess in each generation the significance of the history of the world and of the church up to their own time as it relates to the teaching of the Bible on the consummation of the age. For example, most Christians have been concerned to discover in their own time and in the immediately preceding generations some fulfillment of the biblical prophecies. But as each generation passes, the task must start afresh. The result is a long line of interpretations, each sincerely attempting to relate the prophecies to its own age.

A third reason for our differences simply is that we often are tempted to do something with the biblical prophecies that is impossible to carry out. Man has a natural craving to know the future. He also seems to have a natural intellectual drive to develop comprehensive, logically airtight systems for every area of knowledge. Therefore, we often are tempted in the interpretation of biblical prophecies to find answers to the wrong questions about the future, questions with which biblical authors may not have been concerned. Furthermore, our desire for logical order frequently leads to rather artificial attempts to tie all the prophecies together into consistent, sometimes impressive, systems of interpretation. But if there are indeed many gaps in the biblical material—that is, if there are many aspects of the end time that are not fully revealed—then we are bound to come up with divergent systems when we try to construct them too comprehensively.

Finally, our differences on prophecy stem from the fact that our interpretation of the last things is related intimately to our overall theological bias. Eschatology is not a mere appendage to the Christian faith. Rather, it is at the very heart of our faith, and we cannot do justice to the Bible's picture of the uniqueness and finality of Jesus Christ without relating Him to the total picture of God's redemptive work, including the "last things." Contrary to the way we often think, Jesus Himself is the most important of the "last things." Or we might put it another way: the Bible, especially the New Testament, is an eschatological document throughout. We are coming to realize that eschatology determines our entire approach to the Bible and that we must begin with eschatological concerns before we can make sense of the Bible.

Before turning to a detailed study of evangelical alternatives, a few terms should be defined and a quick look directed to one chapter in the Bible that has been the pivot upon which the major differences turn.

The major schools of prophetic interpretation usually are classified according to their interpretation of Revelation 20 and its relationship to the Second Coming of Christ. This chapter tells of a time when Satan is bound for a thousand years so that he no longer deceives the nations. During this same "thousand years," those who live in the "first resurrection" rule with Christ. At the end of the thousand years, Satan is loosed from his prison in the abyss and deceptively persuades the nations to follow him into one last desperate rebellion against Christ. He is defeated and cast into the lake of fire. Thereupon follows a second resurrection and the final judgment of those raised to stand before the "great white throne."

The three schools of interpretation are known as premillennialism, amillennialism, and postmillennialism. The root of all three words comes from two Latin words, *mille* and *annum,* translated "a thousand years." The prefix in each case refers to the interpretation of the thousand years in relation to the Second Coming of Christ. *Pre*millennialism teaches that Christ will come again *before* the millennium, the thousand years. *A*millennialism and *post*millennialism both teach the Christ will return *after* the millennium. However, amillennialism does not believe the millennium means a period of political peace and prosperity under the rule of Christ. Rather, it refers only to the spiritual rule of Christ in His church during the period between His first appearance and His second coming. This simplified diagram shows the basic differences between the three schools of interpretation:

Premillennialism

| first appearance of Christ | church age | Second Coming of Christ | 1,000 year rule |

Postmillennialism

| first appearance of Christ | church age leads into 1,000 year rule | | Second Coming of Christ |

Amillennialism

| first appearance of Christ | church age = 1,000 year rule | Second Coming of Christ |

Premillennialism

The order in which we will examine these three approaches does not imply the relative merit of each view. Premillennialism, however, does seem to have some historical priority. Many of the church fathers from the second and third centuries held to something that would be called "premillennialism" today. *Chiliasm,* from the Greek word *chilia* meaning "thousand," is the older term applied to the view that the return of Christ to rule for a thousand years would result in a time of universal peace, prosperity, and righteousness.

In recent years, a particular form of premillennialism known as dispensationalism has become a prominent form of this view. Indeed, in many people's minds, premillennialism is synonymous with the dispensational form of the teaching. Daniel 9:24-27 is a most important key to the dispensational scheme of premillennialism. According to this passage, "seventy weeks" are decreed by God to complete His redemptive plans. That is, "seventy weeks" from the time of the commandment of the Persian king "to restore and build Jerusalem" are required to accomplish all that the prophets foretold of God's plans for Israel and His special use of them in saving the world. The "seventy weeks," however, do not mean weeks of days but weeks of *years.* Accordingly, God's prophetic plans for Israel will require 490 years (70 x 7).

Whether or not we can date precisely the beginning of these seventy weeks of years, it is obvious that much more time than that has already elapsed. But the dispensationalist believes that God's prophetic design for Israel was interrupted following the sixty-ninth

120

week, that is, at the crucifixion of Christ. As Daniel puts it, the "anointed one [Hebrew, *messiah*] shall be cut off." What happened next was the establishment of the church and the calling into it of people from all nations throughout the world. But this event was *not* predicted by the prophets. Neither does the church have anything to do with God's prophetic designs for Israel. In other words, God's "prophetic time clock" stopped running after the sixty-ninth week of Daniel. It will begin to run again only when God turns back to work with Israel and to accomplish through them what the prophets foretold. Consequently, there is one more "week," or seven more years, left to God's grand design for Israel.

But according to the dispensational scheme, God does not work at the same time through *both* Israel and the church. Therefore, the existence and ministry of the church of Christ upon this earth must be concluded before God's prophetic time clock begins to tick again and the seventieth week of Daniel can be fulfilled. The removal of the church from the earth to be with Christ in heaven during this final seven-year prophetic week is called the "Rapture." Passages in the New Testament, e.g., I Thessalonians 4:13-18, are taken to describe this removal of the church from the earth, when Christians— both the living and the dead—are caught up to meet the Lord in the air.

After the Rapture of the church from the earth, however, there is still a seven-year period to be fulfilled before Christ's personal and glorious return to the earth. This seven years is interpreted as the "great tribulation" (Matt. 24:21; Rev. 7:14).

The Tribulation may be characterized briefly as follows: (1) Israel again will be the focus of God's work on the earth. She will be restored to her own land and will rebuild the temple to resume the Levitical sacrifices prescribed by the Law. (2) International political power will be headed up in a Satanic ruler called the Antichrist, Beast, or Man of Sin (I John 4:3; Rev. 13; II Thess. 2:3). (3) Apostate Christendom, called the Harlot in Revelation 17, will ally herself with the Antichrist and will prosper through this spiritually adulterous union for a period of time. (4) Sin will increase among men and will reach a depth and intensity never before seen, except perhaps in the days of Noah. (5) The wrath of God will be poured out upon the earth in a series of cataclysmic judgments. (6) When the Beast turns against Israel, an international crisis will be generated, climaxing in the "battle of Armageddon."

The Tribulation, the seventieth week of Daniel, will last seven years. Just as the nations gather against Israel and threaten to annihilate her, Jesus, the Son of David, will appear with His saints to execute vengeance upon the Antichrist, his armies, and his allies. This appearance is described in Revelation 19. Thus, the Second Coming (Rev. 19) *precedes* the thousand-year rule (Rev. 20).

The premillennialists, both the dispensationalists and others, see the millennium as an important step in the fulfillment of biblical prophecy. Many Old Testament prophecies that describe a messianic kingdom of political justice, social harmony, material prosperity, and spiritual renewal are supposed to find their fulfillment in this period.[1]

Following the millennium there is a brief rebellion by Satan, and this is followed by the resurrection of those not caught up with Christ at the Rapture. These dead stand before the "great white throne judgment" and are judged according to all their works, which are recorded in the books of heaven. The wicked are cast into hell.

Then the new heavens, the new earth, and the new Jerusalem appear as the eternal home of all those saved from every age, including Old Testament saints, members of the church from all over the world, Jews who are faithful to God during the Tribulation, and even those born during the millennium whose hearts are genuinely obedient to Christ.

This summarizes the most basic points in the premillennial scheme of interpretation, at least from the dispensational perspective. There are, however, some aspects of this scheme that historic or traditional premillennialists do not accept. The latter, for example, reject the strong distinction between Israel and the church, which leads to the conclusion that God's work with Israel requires the church's removal from the scene *via* the Rapture. Instead, the Rapture of the church is at the Second Coming of Christ in glory *after* the Tribulation. Thus this view usually is called the "post-tribulation rapture," as opposed to the dispensationalists' "pretribulation rapture" view. In addition, there are numerous differences over details in the entire scheme. But it is not our purpose here to explore all of these variations. It is sufficient to point out that the premillennial view does *not* require belief in a secret Rapture of the church before the Tribulation some seven years before the actual Second Coming.

Amillennialism

The second major system of prophetic interpretation is *amillennialism*. The negative *a* is perhaps an unfortunate prefix. It implies that adherents of this view simply reject belief in the millennium. Of course, some theologians do reject belief in any sort of fulfillment of the prophecies, including the millennium. We are concerned, however, only with evangelical amillennialism, that is, an interpretation that accepts the authority of all of Scripture but that takes a less political or nonliteral view of many of the prophecies of the messianic reign. Amillennialism's most fundamental presupposition is that the kingdom of Christ is spiritual and inward and that the prophecies depicting it in more physical and political terms are to be interpreted figuratively or symbolically.

According to amillennialism, the reign of Christ began upon His ascension and with the outpouring of the Holy Spirit at Pentecost. Since that time, He has continued to exercise His royal power through the influence of the gospel and the work of His Spirit upon the minds and hearts of men. The thousand-year rule described by John in Revelation 20 is understood as a symbolic way of describing a very long rule of Christ. Some of the evidence for this interpretation is (1) the symbolic use of numbers throughout The Revelation, (2) the lack of any direct reference elsewhere in Scripture to a thousand-year reign, (3) the conviction that on this earth the presence and influence of the risen Christ should not be conceived in a physical or political manner. The first resurrection described in Revelation 20 is interpreted as the new birth. The binding of Satan does not mean that he is completely prevented from tempting anyone. Rather, by the power of the gospel and the spiritual lordship of Christ, Satan is hindered in his work and is to that extent "bound."

The amillennialist also claims that many of the Old Testament prophecies, which the premillennialist expects to be fulfilled in the millennium, already have been fulfilled, many of them before the birth of Christ. For example, the promise of the land of Canaan made to Abraham and his children was fulfilled in the conquest and occupation of Canaan under Joshua. Again, many of the prophetic predictions of a return to the land and a renewal of God's blessings upon the nation of Israel were fulfilled literally, according to the amillennialist, in the return of many of the Jews to their land in 538 B.C. following the Babylonian exile.

123

Therefore, the most critical difference between the amillennialist and the premillennialist is in the interpretation of the rule of Christ —whether or not an earthly, political manifestation of His rule is required by the prophecies. Although there are variations among individual amillennial interpreters, most of those who are evangelical look for a progression in evil toward the close of this present age. As men turn away from God and become unreceptive to the gospel, the world is prepared for the appearance of the Antichrist or the Man of Sin. Then will be fulfilled many of the prophecies of Revelation regarding a Satanic political power and its persecution of the saints. At the same time, the awesome judgments described in The Revelation will be poured out upon the earth. These judgments will be climaxed by the Second Coming of Christ, the resurrection of all the dead, and the final judgment. Then appears the heavenly city, the new and eternal spiritual creation, prepared by Christ for His Church. The lost are cast into the lake of fire.

Some amillennialists, however, reject a belief in the future fulfillment of many of the details of the Tribulation. It has been pointed out that The Revelation was written in a time when the church was actively persecuted by the Roman government, probably during the reign of Domitian, A.D. 81-96. Many of the allusions to the Beast and the Harlot in Revelation are strongly suggestive of the Roman government. This line of thought emphasizes that The Revelation was a kind of underground protest document written by a first-century Christian to condemn the Roman government and to encourage Christians who were suffering persecution to remain faithful to Christ as Lord, rather than to Domitian, who claimed to be *dominus et deus*, lord and god. Therefore, many of the visions of Revelation, especially preceding chapter 19, are intended not as predictions but as veiled descriptions of the actual conditions prevailing at the end of the first century.

Admittedly, the above line of interpretation is identified sometimes with a more critical and less conservative theological perspective. But it is certainly possible to hold to the authority of Scripture and also recognize a degree of validity in this understanding of the original historical intent of the book.

Postmillennialism

Probably the least understood of all the views on the future reign of Christ is that known as postmillennialism. And in terms of actual adherents, evangelical or otherwise, it is today a minority view. However, an evangelical defense of postmillennialism has recently been made by J. Marcellus Kik. According to Kik,

> The *postmil* looks for a fulfillment of the Old Testament prophecies of a glorious age of the church upon earth through the preaching of the gospel under the power of the Holy Spirit. He looks forward to all nations becoming Christian and living in peace one with another. He relates all prophecies to history and time. After the triumph of Christianity throughout the earth he looks for the second coming of the Lord.[2]

This, of course, is a statement by a theologically conservative postmillennialist. The postmillennial position, however, often has been identified with an early twentieth-century liberalism. There was a theologically liberal postmillennialism based on an optimistic view of human nature and a belief in the historical progress of culture and religion toward the social and spiritual perfection of man. Again, it must be emphasized that the concern of this chapter is with *evangelical* alternatives, such as that expressed by Kik. Kik does not believe in a future millennium on earth because of a supposed innate perfectibility of man based on a naive view of human nature and the impact of sin on man's social and political institutions.

The postmillennialist believes, like the amillennialist, that the rule of Christ is something that began with His ascension and continues by means of the ministry of the gospel and the transforming power of the Holy Spirit. Consequently, the postmillennialist takes more seriously, or at least more literally, the socio-political aspects of the biblical prophecies. In other words, he believes that the millennium is not simply a symbol either of the rule of the saints in heaven with Christ or of the spiritual rule of Christ in the hearts of Christians. Rather, he expects the rule of Christ, exercised by the Holy Spirit and mediated by the word of the gospel, ultimately to transform dramatically men's social, political, and international relations.

The evangelical postmillennialist believes that both the premillennialist and the amillennialist have underestimated the power of the gospel. Futhermore, he sees in certain passages of Scripture, such as the parables of the leaven and of the mustard seed (Matt. 13:31-33), biblical evidence that the kingdom is not ushered in suddenly and cataclysmically but slowly, quietly, and almost imperceptibly.

125

The postmillennialist believes that passages such as Matthew 24, which speaks of a time of extreme moral corruption and of a tribulation before the return of Christ, should be interpreted as fulfilled in the rejection of Christ by His own nation and the ensuing troubles that came upon the Jews, culminating in the destruction of Jerusalem in A.D. 70.

The postmillennialist looks forward to an actual "golden age" on earth, a time when men as a whole will love God with their whole heart and their neighbors as themselves. This "millennium" need not be precisely one thousand years in length, but to the postmillennialist, like the premillennialist, one of the sure promises of prophecy is that the earth will enjoy an extended period of peace and righteousness.

Therefore, the Second Coming of Christ *follows* this golden age. At that time, the resurrection and judgment will take place. Following these supernatural events, this present earthly, physical existence will be no more. In the resurrection, when Christ has delivered the kingdom up to the Father (I Cor. 15:24), all prophecies will have been fulfilled, and eternity will involve a completely spiritual life in perfect fellowship in the presence of God.

A Comparison of the Three Alternatives

The above summarization of the three most distinct schools of evangelical eschatological interpretation has not allowed a detailed exposition with substantiating arguments and counterarguments for any of the three views. (For more thorough explanations of each view the reader is referred to the bibliography at the end of the book.) Only in a couple of instances have differences that exist within each school been indicated. Of necessity, the particular views set forth above are somewhat generalized and simplified. Specific prophecies may be subject to different interpretations even among adherents of a major school of thought. The summarization is intended nonetheless to help the reader grasp the inner dynamic and the basic presuppositions of each view. To that end, the following comparison is offered by way of conclusion to the exposition of the three alternatives above.

Of the three views, premillennialists have the stronger interest in prophecy. A tally made of books published on prophecy will show that the majority are by premillennialists. This is not because there are more premillennialists around than a- or postmillennialists, but because the premillennialist seems to have a more enthusiastic approach to the topic. He probably will preach more often on the "signs of the times." He likely will be praying more often, "O Lord, come." Indeed, the premillennialist sometimes is inclined to excesses in his zeal to proclaim the Second Coming and to understand how and when the ancient prophecies are being fulfilled today.

Premillennialism usually shows more interest in the Old Testament prophets and in the nation of Israel than do the other schools. It is, indeed, a rather "Jewish" approach to prophecy, and I use the word without any pejorative connotations. The premillennialist usually believes that many of the Old Testament prophecies of the messianic kingdom await a future fulfillment. Furthermore, if some of the prophecies were fulfilled in a literal manner, for example, in Jesus' birth (Mic. 5:2), then we have every right to expect other prophecies to be literally fulfilled at the Second Coming. And it is not thought incredible that the kingdom of God will be politically, socially, and materially fulfilled in the millennium.

Postmillennialism and premillennialism have at least this much in common: From their study of the prophecies, they both expect a more complete fulfillment of them on this earth than we have yet witnessed in the establishment and history of the church. The postmillennialist, however, has difficulty with a resurrected, glorified Christ personally returning to this earth and exercising a righteous political rule from some particular place on earth, such as Jerusalem. This seems to him, first of all, to be an inconceivable mixing of the temporal and the eternal. Perhaps more important, the postmillennialist believes that the rule of Christ through the proclamation of the gospel and the genuine conversion of man has the potential to transform the political conditions of human existence in this world. According to the postmillennialist, both premillennialism and amillennialism are defeatist theologies. Both refuse to admit that Christ spiritually—that is, through the Holy Spirit—actually has the power to control the world that is rightfully His.

The amillennialist and the postmillennialist have this in common: Neither expects Christ to return to this earth. The Second Coming means only judgment, probably annihilation, for the old creation. The purpose of the return of Christ is not to take over this world but to take His church to be with Himself and to bring an end to all earthly, historical existence. The amillennialist is scandalized at what he considers to be a very carnal, physical conception of the kingdom of Christ. There is a very real sense in which the difference here between the amillennialist and the premillennialist is as much a difference in their view of the church as it is their view of the end time.

The amillennialist interprets the church as being itself very much an eschatological phenomenon—that is, the church is the fulfillment of many, if not most, of the prophecies of the messianic kingdom. Although these prophecies admittedly are cast in the political and social categories to which ancient Israel was accustomed, the amillennialist believes that the predominantly spiritual, nonpolitical nature of Christ's ministry points to a spiritual, nonliteral interpretation of the earthly, nationalistic prophecies. The amillennialist would see an earthly, political rule of Christ in the millennium not only as unnecessary, but as a sort of contradiction to the way Christ already has shown His kingdom to operate in the hearts of men as the gospel is preached to them and as they submit themselves to His lordship.

The amillennialist also differs from the postmillennialist insofar as he does not expect the gospel to slowly but surely permeate all of human life. Instead, he expects the power of Satan to continue in force among those who do not confess Christ, and he does not expect that this age will be consummated by a golden age of peace and righteousness. In this respect, the amillennialist can be almost as pessimistic about the course of this world as is the premillennialist. The amillennialist is not, however, usually as concerned with the imminent return of Christ and with the interpretation of signs that indicate its nearness.

Finally, a few words on my personal eschatology. I am personally committed to a form of historic premillennialism. However, I do not accept the extreme distinction between the church and Israel made by the dispensationalists. Neither do I find it profitable to speculate about the nearness of Christ's appearing. I feel that such attempts smack of pagan soothsaying, and, in any event, they aim at a knowledge more exact than that of Jesus Himself (Matt. 24:36).

I also feel that many premillennialists do not take sufficient account of the historical context of many prophecies, both the writings of the Old Testament prophets and the Book of Revelation. It is no honor to Scripture to read back into the text our own fanciful interpretations even if those interpretations are "literal."

128

The question for the faithful interpreter of Scripture is not whether he should interpret literally, but whether he should let the original inspired author say what he wishes to say under whatever form and style he chooses. On many occasions a "literal" interpretation does violence to prophecies, particularly those couched in poetic or apocalyptic terms.

On the other hand, I find that the amillennial interpretation is based on what I consider to be an unbiblical disjunction of the "spiritual" and the "physical." The many prophecies that promise political justice, physical health, and material prosperity are not necessarily "unspiritual." The ministry of Christ included the physical, and it is believable to me that the blessings that were experienced in a limited way at that time will become universal when He appears the second time.

The postmillennialist, I think, overlooks the fact that the proclamation of the gospel was not intended to produce the universal peace that the prophecies predict. The trend of prophecy is to expect a great apostasy before the appearing of Christ. I admit to the postmillennialist that this has often led to a spiritual defeatism, but I do not believe it is necessary. There is a tendency to quietism in the premillennial view. But also from the premillennial perspective, hope in the ultimate transformation of the social and political conditions of existence can be a productive dynamic in the Christian's concern for and involvement in the world for which Christ died and which some day He will completely liberate from the Satanic bondage to which it was subjected by man's Fall (Rom. 8:20).[3]

Notes

1. Some of these prophecies are Ps. 72; Isa. 2:1-4; 11; 65:17-25; Jer. 29:10-14; 33:10-16; Ezek. 11:14-21; 34:20-31; 37; Hos. 14:4-7; Joel 3:18-21; Amos 9:11-15; Zeph. 3:9-20; Zech. 14:9-21.

2. *An Eschatology of Victory* (Philadelphia: Presbyterian and Reformed, 1971), p. 4.

3. For the further development of this theme see chapter 15, "Living Between Two Ages."

9

The Kingdom of God

George Eldon Ladd

The Old Testament

One of the central prophetic themes of the Old Testament is the coming of the kingdom of God. Although the phrase itself does not appear, the idea is prevalent. The prophets constantly look forward to a day when "the Lord alone will be exalted" (Isa. 2:17). This means that all hostile powers that oppose the rule of God will be subdued; God's people will be gathered together in obedience to the divine rule; and nature itself will be delivered from the plague of evil to become the ideal setting for a redeemed people.

It is often thought that the prophecies of the Old Testament must be interpreted literally, and all one has to do is to piece together the diverse prophecies of the Old Testament to give a comprehensive program of the end of the age and the coming of God's kingdom. In fact, it is not the nature of prophecy to give such a complete program of the end. God spoke to the fathers through the prophets in "many and various ways" (Heb. 1:1). The words mean literally "in many parts and in many ways." Each prophetic word in the Old Testament is partial and fragmentary.

To illustrate: There are three very diverse messianic personages in the Old Testament that it is practically impossible to conflate into a consistent, harmonious unity. Isaiah foresees a Davidic king who "shall smite the earth with the rod of his mouth, and with the breath

131

of his lips he shall slay the wicked" (11:4). He is a son of David—a man arising from among the people, but one who will be supernaturally endowed by the Spirit of the Lord to establish the rule of God in all the earth.

On the other hand, Daniel sees "one like a son of man" come with the clouds of heaven to the throne of God to receive the kingdom of God and then to establish it on the earth (7:13-14). How can the Messiah be both an earthly Davidic king and at the same time a heavenly superhuman being?

Isaiah also sees a suffering servant — one who comes in humility and weakness to pour out His life in suffering and death to redeem His people (chap. 53). How could the Messiah be both a mighty, conquering king and a weak suffering servant? The Jews never knew how to put these three prophecies together. Christians see their fulfillment in the two advents of Jesus Christ. The point is that the Old Testament does not speak of two advents of one redeeming person; nor does it tell us that this Redeemer would be the pre-existent Son of God—the Word who became flesh and dwelt among us (John. 1:14). The important point is that the Old Testament cannot be finally understood apart from its fulfillment in the New Testament.

There are, however, several constant features in the prophetic expectation of the coming of the kingdom of God. It is always a dynamic hope. By this we mean that it is never a golden age produced by forces working within history—it is established by an act of God. As we have seen, there are three diverse messianic personages in the Old Testament. Often, however, there is no Messiah: it is God Himself who redeems His people. "Then the Lord your God will come, and all the holy ones with him" (Zech. 14:5). "Behold, your God will come with vengeance, with the recompense of God. He will come and save you" (Isa. 35:4).

The prophetic hope is always an earthly hope. Greek thought distinguished sharply between the body and the soul, and looked for an afterlife when the soul takes its heavenly flight from the earth. The prophets always conceive of the earth as the dwelling place of men. Salvation therefore is never the salvation of individual souls; it includes the redemption of the earth.

This redemption of creation is expressed in different ways. Sometimes it is described as life on this earth made perfect. Danger, evil, cruelty, and violence will be removed: "They shall not hurt or destroy in all my holy mountain" (Isa. 11:9). The earth will become remarkably fruitful: "The mountains shall drip sweet wine, and all the hills shall flow with it" (Amos 9:13). Isaiah, however, sees this transformation from the old order to the new world in such radical terms that he speaks of new heavens and a new earth (65:17; 66:22).

The new age is pictured sometimes as coming through a day of judgment that will involve a cosmic catastrophe. "I will utterly sweep away everything from the face of the earth," says the Lord. "In the fire of his jealous wrath, all the earth shall be consumed" (Zeph. 1:2,18). There is no Messiah in Zephaniah: judgment and establishment of the kingdom is the work of God Himself.

The kingdom of God is always a social rather than an individual hope. God will act to save His people. In the Old Testament, this hope is always given in terms of Israel. Although the nation as a whole is sinful and rebellious, God finally will save a repentant remnant (Amos 9:8; Isa. 4:2-4; Mic. 2:12). The fate of the Gentiles is pictured in different ways. Sometimes the Gentiles are to serve Israel (Amos 9:12; Mic. 5:9); sometimes they are to be converted (Zeph. 3:9; Isa. 2:2-4; 42:6-7).

The Old Testament is silent not only about the incarnation of the Son of God and His two advents, but also about the church age. Therefore, it is impossible to structure our eschatology on the basis of the Old Testament; we must see how the New Testament interprets the Old Testament—how God has spoken to us in His Son (Heb. 1:1 f.).

The Teaching of Jesus

The central theme of Jesus' teaching is the coming of the kingdom of God. The idiom occurs fourteen times in Mark, thirty-two times in Luke, but only four times in Matthew. In its place, Matthew substitutes "the kingdom of the heavens." These two phrases are quite interchangeable, as a comparison of Matthew 19:23 with Matthew 19:24 and Mark 10:23 will show. Furthermore, Matthew speaks of the "mysteries" of the kingdom of heaven (Matt. 13:11) whereas Mark speaks of the "mystery" of the kingdom of God (Mark 4:11).

By the kingdom of God, Jesus meant the new eschatological order to be established by a divine visitation similar to that which the prophets hoped for. A new terminology emerges in the Gospels

133

that became common in Jewish and rabbinic literature—that of the two ages: this age and the age to come. Although this terminology is not found in the Old Testament, it is an easy development of the prophetic theology of the kingdom of God. This age is the time of sinfulness, evil, and rebellion against God; the age to come will see the perfect establishment of God's rule in the world and the purging of all sin, evil, and rebellion. The New Testament interprets the evil of this age in terms of satanic and demonic power. Satan is the "god of this age" (II Cor. 4:4), who has been allowed in the sovereign wisdom of God to exercise great power in human affairs (Matt. 4:9). Satan is a spirit hostile to God and does all he can to frustrate the will of God. Allied with him are evil spirits—demons —capable of taking possession of the human personality. From one point of view, the theology of the entire New Testament can be understood in terms of a titanic conflict between God and Satan, the powers of light against the hosts of darkness. The ultimate enemies of God are not sinful men or pagan nations but evil spiritual powers. But since this conflict involves the destiny of men as individuals and of human history as a whole, the conflict is waged on the scene of human history. This is one of the fundamental presuppositions of the Bible—that there is a real invisible spiritual world of both good and evil that impinges upon and determines human existence and destiny. The theology of Satan and demons is a positive one: evil is not merely human ignorance, failure, or error; nor is it blind fate or irrational chance. Evil has its roots in personality, and it is greater than men and stronger than men. It is God's purpose finally to subdue and destroy these evil powers and deliver men from their enslavement.

This divine victory will be achieved only in the age to come, which will witness the kingdom of God. Or better, it is the coming of His kingdom that will inaugurate the age to come. The term "kingdom of God" is used of the divine visitation (Matt. 6:10, cf. Rev. 12:10), but in the Gospels, it is used more often of the new era to be inaugurated by the coming of God's reign. In this sense, the kingdom of God and the age to come are interchangeable terms. This is proven by the incident of the rich young ruler. When he asked Jesus how he might inherit eternal life, he was asking about life in the age to come —the life of the resurrection (Dan. 12:2). In His reply, Jesus speaks about entering the kingdom of God (Mark 10:23 ff.), about being saved (Mark 10:26), and about receiving eternal life in the age to

134

come (Mark 10:30). Thus Mark 9:47 speaks of entering the kingdom of God, whereas Matthew 18:9 speaks of entering life. Usually, this future age is spoken of simply as the kingdom of God into which the righteous will enter and from which the unrighteous will be excluded (Matt. 5:20; 7:21).

This age will end and the new age of God's kingdom will be inaugurated by the coming of the heavenly Son of Man. It is indisputable that the early church believed that Jesus taught that He Himself was destined to be the heavenly Son of Man prophesied in Daniel, who would inaugurate the kingdom of God. Matthew reports the disciples as asking what would be the sign of His *parousia* and the consummation of the age (Matt. 24:3). The discourse that follows speaks at length of the coming of the heavenly Son of Man with power and great glory to gather the elect into the kingdom of God (Matt. 24:30-31). The Son of Man will come in His glory to sit upon the throne of judgment to decide the destiny of men. The righteous will inherit the kingdom of God (Matt. 25:34), which again means to enter into eternal life (Matt. 25:46), whereas the wicked will suffer the judgment of eternal punishment. The parable of the weeds and wheat teaches that the Son of Man will send His angels to gather all causes of sin and all evildoers out of His kingdom; then the righteous will shine like the sun in the kingdom of God (Matt. 13:41-43). The future destiny of men will be decided by the Son of Man on the basis of their relationship to Jesus (Luke 12:8; the parallel verse in Matthew [10:32] does not refer to the Son of Man but only to Jesus in both His historical and eschatological mission).

The parable of the judgment of the nations implies that it will be the eschatological mission of the Son of Man to win the final victory over the demonic powers of evil, for the place of condemnation is called the eternal fire prepared for the devil and his angels (Matt. 25:41). The coming of the kingdom of God will witness the complete expurgation of evil from God's creation.

Life in the eschatological kingdom of God—life in the age to come—will be resurrection life. Although the Gospels do not say much about resurrection, Luke reports a saying that equates the attainment of the age to come with resurrection (Luke 20:34 f.). Resurrection life will mean a transformed existence very different from the life of this age. There will be no more death; therefore, the need for procreation will no longer exist.

135

The Gospels say very little about the conditions in the kingdom of God. That it will involve a transformation of the whole created order is reflected in Matthew 19:28. The "new world" (RSV) is literally the "regeneration" of the world. Although the word for "regeneration" belongs to the world of Hellenistic—Judaism and not to Aramaic idiom, it expresses the theology of resurrection and world renewal.

The primary interest of the Gospels in the age to come is its soteriological (saving) dimension—the restoration of fellowship with God. The pure in heart will see God (Matt 5:8) and enter into the joy of their Lord (Matt. 25:21,23). The harvest will take place and the grain be gathered into the barn (Matt. 13:30,39; Mark 4:29; cf. Matt. 3:12; Rev. 14:15). The sheep will be separated from the goats and brought safely into the fold (Matt. 25:32). The most common picture is that of a feast or table fellowship. Jesus again will drink wine with His disciples in the kingdom of God (Mark 14:25). They will eat and drink at Jesus' table in the kingdom (Luke 22:30). The consummation is likened to a wedding feast (Matt. 22:1-14; 25:1-12) and a banquet (Matt. 8:11; Luke 14:16-24). All of these metaphors picture the restoration of communion between God and men, which had been broken by sin.

The new element that provides the distinctive center of Jesus' teaching is that in His own person and mission, a real fulfillment of the Old Testament hope has taken place in history before the consummation of the age. "The time is fulfilled" (Mark 1:15). In an early sermon in Nazareth, Jesus cited the messianic prophecy of Isaiah 61:1-2 and added, "Today this scripture has been fulfilled in your hearing" (Luke 4:21). When John was in perplexity because Jesus was not fulfilling his proclamation of an eschatological kingdom, he sent emissaries to Jesus to ask whether He was indeed the coming one; Jesus replied by quoting the messianic promise of Isaiah 35:5-6, indicating that the prophecy was being fulfilled in His own mission. This note of prophetic fulfillment is sounded again in Luke 10:23-24 (cf. Matt. 13:16-17), where Jesus asserts that His contemporaries actually are witnessing what the Old Testament saints longed to see.

The present fulfillment of the Old Testament hope short of its consummation can be understood in light of the basic meaning of the kingdom of God as the divine reign or rule. In the mission of Jesus, God has entered into history in His kingly power to defeat the powers of evil and to bring to men a foretaste of the blessings of the

136

eschatological kingdom while they still live in the old age. This is explicitly affirmed in Matthew 12:28. One of the most characteristic works of Jesus was freeing men from demonic bondage. When accused of employing satanic power, Jesus replied that He cast out demons by the Spirit of God (Luke 11:20, "the finger of God"), and this was a sign that the kingdom of God had come upon them. Here is an unambiguous statement as to the presence of the kingdom of God, and it is entirely intelligible if the kingdom of God is His kingly power. God's power has come among men in the mission of Jesus to free them from satanic bondage. This is clearly affirmed in Matthew 12:29. Jesus has come from God into this age (the strong man's house) to deliver men from his power (plunder his goods), and this He can do because by the power of God's kingly rule in His own person He has defeated Satan (bound the strong man). Before the eschatological destruction of Satan, God in Jesus has inflicted on him a preliminary defeat.

The present defeat of Satan is also seen in the mission of Jesus' disciples, who also proclaimed the kingdom of God and cast out demons (Luke 10:9,17). Interpreting their experience, Jesus said in symbolic, mythological language that He saw Satan fallen from his position of power. Such a saying must be taken figuratively rather than literally; it means simply the defeat of satanic power.

When the Pharisees asked Jesus to give them a timetable for the approach of the eschatological kingdom, Jesus replied that the kingdom of God was already in their midst (Luke 17:20-21), but in an unexpected form. It was not accompanied by the signs and outward display the Pharisees expected and without which they would not be satisfied. They were blind to the in-breaking of God's rule, which was expected at the end of the age but was already occurring in the mission of Jesus.

The difficult saying in Matthew 11:12 can be understood in this context. The verse is best rendered, "the kingdom of heaven has been coming violently." John was the greatest of the age of the prophets; since John, something new has been at work in the world: the power of the kingdom of God in the mission of Jesus. The mighty working of the kingdom of God, however, requires a response—a mighty response—of men: "Men of violence" must "take it by force." Jesus frequently indicated that His mission demanded a powerful reaction from men (Mark 9:43,45,47; Luke 14:26; Matt. 13:44 ff.; Mark 10:21); they must be willing and ready to engage in any action,

137

however radical, to respond to the presence of the kingdom of God. Because the kingdom of God has come among men, they must receive it here and now, like little children with perfect receptivity, to enter into the eschatological consummation (Mark 10:15).

Because the kingly rule of God has broken into history in the mission of Jesus, it has brought to men the blessings of God's reign. It has inaugurated a new situation that also is called the kingdom of God. This is the meaning of Matthew 11:11, that the least in the kingdom of heaven is greater than John. Although he was the greatest of the prophets, he belonged to the old order; and the new age that Jesus' mission ushered in brings blessings so much greater that the least in the kingdom of heaven is greater than John—greater not by virtue of position or personal stature but by virtue of the blessings he enjoys.

This is the meaning of the sayings that speak about a present entrance into the kingdom (Matt. 21:31; 23:13; Luke 11:52; Mark 12:34). The kingdom as the new age of blessing means the presence of the eschatological salvation (Luke 19:9-10), restoration to the father's house (Luke 15:11 ff.; cf. esp. v. 24), the forgiveness of sins (Mark 2:7), the gift of righteousness (Luke 18:14), and eschatological joy in the presence of the bridegroom (Mark 2:19). The fellowship enjoyed in the new order is illustrated most vividly in the frequently repeated table fellowship of Jesus with His disciples. The metaphor of a feast was a common Jewish metaphor of the eschatological salvation. The fellowship of Jesus with His disciples and those who followed them was an anticipation of the joy and fellowship of the eschatological kingdom. Mark early sounds this note of table fellowship (Mark 2:15 ff.), and it was so typical of Jesus' ministry that His critics accused Him of being a glutton and a drunkard (Matt. 11:19). The religious significance of this meal is reflected in Jesus' words, "I came not to call the righteous, but sinners" (Mark 2:17). He was fulfilling His messianic mission when He gathered sinners into fellowship with Himself. In response to the protest of the scribes and Pharisees that He frequently engaged in such fellowship with people outside the pale of legalistic Judaism, Jesus gave the parables of the shepherd seeking his lost sheep, a woman searching for a lost coin, and a father freely forgiving and accepting a penitent son (Luke 15). The keynote is the joy in heaven over a sinner who repents (Luke 15:7, 10), as a father's delight over a son who comes home (Luke 15:24).

138

The coming of the kingdom in history before its eschatological consummation is illustrated by the parables of the kingdom (Mark 4; Matt. 13). The "mystery of the kingdom" (Mark 4:11) is precisely this: the disclosure of a new fact in redemptive history, namely, that the kingdom has come in history in an unforeseen and unexpected way. The background for this mystery or new revelation (see Rom. 16:25) is the Old Testament expectation, further developed in Judaism, that the coming of the kingdom would be an apocalyptic event, disrupting society in the eschatological judgment, an act of God bringing the old fallen order to its end and inaugurating the age to come. Jesus indeed shared these views; but the new revelation of the kingdom is that it has come in an unexpected way without disrupting society, demanding of men a response that was personally meaningful. The kingdom in Jesus' mission was not like a stone shattering the godless nations (Dan. 2); rather, it was like a sower scattering seed that required fruitful soil for effective growth. The present coming of the kingdom does not mean the judgment and separation of men; this will take place in the day of eschatological judgment. Until then, the wheat and the weeds grow together; the sons of the kingdom and the sons of the evil one will live together in the mixed society of this age. The presence of the kingdom in Jesus' mission is not a world-shaking event but a small, insignificant movement of a Jewish teacher and a handful of followers—as insignificant as a grain of mustard seed. Yet in the consummation, it will be like a great tree. At present, it is like a handful of leaven in a great bowl of dough; but one day, it will fill the bowl; it will have no competitors. These two parables are parables of contrast—the small unexpected form of the presence of the kingdom contrasted with its greatness in the day of consummation. *How* this greatness is to be achieved is not a part of the two parables. The parables of the tares and of the dragnet indicate that the kingdom will attain its final greatness by an eschatological act of God.

Insignificant as the presence of the kingdom is, it is yet of superlative value, and, like a treasure or a matchless pearl, should be acquired at any cost. Furthermore, the present action of the kingdom is working in an unexpected way in that it has set up a movement that is gathering into it both good and bad men (the dragnet). Publicans, sinners—even a traitor—were in the circle of Jesus' followers. The eschatological judgment not only will purify society as a whole (weeds), it also will purify the mixed fellowship of Jesus' followers.

139

In spite of this unexpected present coming of the kingdom in Jesus and His followers, the kingdom remains the supernatural act of God that uses the agency of men and yet transcends all human ability and activity (Mark 4:26-29); it will inevitably come to eschatological harvest.

The in-breaking of the eschatological kingdom in Jesus' person, words, and mission created a new fellowship. Jesus addressed His offer of the kingdom to Israel as a whole—the natural sons of the kingdom (Matt. 8:12) by right of covenant promises. The disciples were admonished to preach only to Israel—sons of the covenant (Matt. 10:5-6). Israel as a whole, however, rejected Jesus' message and is therefore destined to experience the judgment of God (Matt. 23:37-39). Jesus predicted the fall of Jerusalem in history (Luke 21:20-24; 23:27-31) and the destruction of the temple (Mark 13:2; cf. 14:58; 15:29). The historical fall of Jerusalem and the end of the Jewish nation are to be understood as a judgment of the kingdom of God in history.

Yet not all Israel rejected Him. Many responded to His repeated summons, "Follow me" (Mark 1:17). Jesus' disciples were not bound together by any formal teaching like the schools of the scribes, or any formal organization like the Qumran sectarians; they were bound together only by personal allegiance to Jesus—by the fellowship of the kingdom of God. From His disciples he chose twelve to participate in His mission (Mark 3:14). The number *twelve* is symbolic, reflecting the constitution of Israel in twelve tribes and indicating that Jesus' disciples formed the true Israel. It was not a closed fellowship but was open to all who would join the company of Jesus' followers in response to the challenge of the kingdom.

The New Testament does not identify the kingdom with the church. The kingdom is the rule of God, and the realm of His blessings; the church is the people of the kingdom who have received it, who will inherit it, and who witness to it.

The Gospels indicate that in some unexplained way, Jesus' death is essential to the coming of the kingdom. At the last supper with His disciples, Jesus gave them a cup that represented His "blood of the covenant, which is poured out for many" (Mark 14:24). These words take us back to the founding of the old covenant in Exodus 24:8 and to the promise in Jeremiah of a new covenant that God will make with His people in the kingdom of God, issuing in a perfected fellowship. Israel will be regenerated, their sins forgiven, and perfect knowledge of God effected (Jer. 31:31-34). The words of Jesus about the blood of the covenant implicitly claim that this promise of the new covenant in the kingdom of God is about to be fulfilled through His own death. This new covenant, however, is now established not in the eschatological kingdom but in history; it nevertheless looks forward to the coming of the eschatological kingdom (Mark 14:24; I Cor. 11:26). Jesus looked forward beyond death to the perfect fellowship of the consummated kingdom. The meal symbolized the messianic banquet in the kingdom of God, but it also symbolized Jesus' death. Thus His death and the coming of the kingdom are somehow inseparable. This same prophetic theme appears vividly in the Revelation of John. The lion of the tribe of Judah who alone is able to open the book of human destiny and bring history to the kingdom of God is the Lamb who has been slain (Rev. 5:5-6).

The necessity for Jesus' death is further affirmed in His present role as the Suffering Servant. He who is destined to be the eschatological Son of Man in the consummation of the kingdom is first of all the suffering Son of Man who "must suffer many things and be rejected by this generation" (Luke 17:25). The essential relationship between Jesus' death and the coming of the kingdom is illustrated by the fact that the sayings about His death refer to Him as the Son of Man (Mark 8:31; 9:31; 10:33 f.). The Son of Man by definition was an apocalyptic figure who would come with the clouds as the messianic figure in the eschatological consummation (Dan. 7:13 f.). Before He fulfills His eschatological role, however, the Son of Man must appear on earth in a mission of humility and suffering as the Servant of the Lord to "give his life as a ransom for many" (Mark 10:45). The eschatological consummation is linked with what God is doing in history in Jesus, especially in His death.

Conclusion

It is clear how the New Testament reinterprets the Old Testament prophecies. Jesus is destined to be the heavenly Son of Man of Daniel 7 to inaugurate the eternal rule of God. Before that day, He must appear as a man among men, as a meek and humble Son of Man, to fill the role of the Suffering Servant.

Furthermore, the Gospels reinterpret the people of God. In the Old Testament, it is the nation of Israel; Gentiles must become Jews to share the blessings of God's rule. In the Gospels, Jewish nationalism is rejected (Matt. 3:9). The people of God are Jesus' disciples. Also, Jesus foresees that this new people of God must include Gentiles (Matt. 8:11; 21:43).

Again, the enemies of God's rule are spiritual before they are political. The victory of God's kingdom in the future (Matt. 25:41) and in the present (Matt. 12:29; Luke 10:18) is a victory over spiritual powers.

A key concept about the kingdom of God, which the prophets were not permitted to see, was that the kingdom first must come on the spiritual level in the person of the incarnate Son of God before it would come with power and glory to fill all the earth. Jesus brought the kingdom with Him, and He will bring the kingdom in power and glory when He comes as the heavenly Son of Man. Even so, come, Lord Jesus!

10

The Return of Christ

Richard N. Longenecker

A dramatic shift of thought has taken place in the Western world during the past half century, resulting in a greater emphasis upon personal relevance and actualization in the present—with a corresponding disinterest in either past or future events. And Christian theology has in large measure been affected by this prevailing climate of opinion. The term *eschatology*, therefore, is often understood today more in terms of the "depth-dimension" of redemption than of any "length-dimension"—that is, it concerns the presence of eternity in human existence and the implications of this for all areas of contemporary life rather than a state of affairs in the future. Continuing the stance of many nineteenth-century interpreters, a sharp dichotomy often is effected between *prophetism* (frequently defined only as the ethical message of God that carries a moral demand for men of every age) and *apocalypticism* (the detailing of the course of future events), with the former accepted as religiously valid for today and the latter viewed as only one form of human speculation from a bygone period. Adopting such a perspective, many today think of the Christian doctrine of the return of Christ primarily in terms of "trans-history" and not "post-history"—that is, as signaling an encounter of God with men that lacks any specific horizontal direction.

Undoubtedly, such an emphasis is in many ways laudatory. It is to be preferred, in fact, to its converse—a preoccupation with future

Scripture quoted in this chapter is from the New International Version, the Revised Standard Version, and the author's own translations.

events that has no bearing on Christian living today. Yet, the compelling appeal of "eschatological actualization" must not be permitted to disintegrate the Christian's hope for the future or to dismiss as irrelevant the temporal return of Christ. It was just such an attitude that seems to have been entertained by some Christians at Corinth with regard to the resurrection of the body, for Paul had to defend not only the possibility and nature of a future resurrection (cf. I Cor. 15:35 ff.) but also the relevancy of this truth for his converts' faith and daily living (cf. I Cor. 15:12 ff.). And his comment to them in their confusion is pertinent as well for us in ours: "If only for this life we have hope in Christ, we are to be pitied more than all men" (I Cor. 15:19).

The basic themes of biblical Christianity have to do with (1) promise, (2) hope, and (3) fulfillment—that is, with God's promise, man's hope in response to the divine promise, and fulfillment that culminates in God's Messiah, Jesus of Nazareth. In that the Scriptures present God as working out His promise progressively in and through history, both by way of preparation for His Messiah and by way of extending the application of the redemption effected by His Messiah, the Christian cannot live his life in the present without also taking note of God's activity in the past and without awaiting God's final consummation in the future. On the other hand, in that God's promise concerns the redemption of men and all that pertains to men, the Christian cannot think of the past or await the future without seeking the relevance of all of this for life today. It is confidence in the God who has promised and who has progressively brought His promises to fulfillment that creates expectation, and it is this expectation that makes life presently significant and meaningful. Only as the historical or temporal and the existential or personal aspects of Christian faith meet in happy union is there a healthy, vital, and biblical faith. And both of these features are involved preeminently in the discussion and future reality of the return of Christ.

The Nature of the Christian's Hope

Its Two-Advent Structure

The eschatological message of the New Testament includes both realized and futuristic elements. Peter is recorded as beginning his sermon to the assembled crowd at Pentecost with the assertion

144

that what believers were experiencing in the outpouring of the Spirit was what the prophet Joel foretold when he proclaimed: "In the last days, God says, I will pour out my Spirit on all people" (Acts 2:16-21, quoting Joel 2:28-32). The realized element in this first sermon of the Christian church is highlighted by Peter's change of the prophet's wording from the somewhat ambiguous "afterwards" *(meta tauta)* to the more specific and eschatologically significant "in the last days" *(en tais eschatais hēmerais,* v. 17) and by his insertion of the phrase "and they will prophesy" *(kai prophēteusousin,* v.18) as evidence of the fact that the Spirit had indeed been "poured out." Yet, in his address to those gathered in the temple courtyard, while proclaiming "how God fulfilled what he had foretold through all the prophets" (Acts 3:18), Peter also speaks of future "times of refreshing" and a future coming of the Messiah, "who has been appointed for you—even Jesus, [who] must remain in heaven until the time comes for God to restore everything, as he promised long ago through his holy prophets" (Acts 3:20-21). And this tension between the "already" and "no longer," on the one hand, and the "still to come" and "not yet," on the other, continues throughout the whole of the New Testament. The writer to the Hebrews, for example, begins on the premise that he and his addressees are living "in the last days" *(ep' eschatou tōn hēmerōn)* when the progressive revelation of God has come to culmination in the Son (Heb. 1:1-3); yet he also speaks of awaiting "the world to come" *(tēn oikoumenēn tēn mellousan)* which Jesus, our incarnate and perfected Pioneer, will lead us into (Heb. 2:5 ff.). And in spelling out the nature of Jesus' sacrifice, he affirms that "he has appeared once for all at the [climax] of the ages *[epi sunteleia tōn aiōnōn]* to do away with sin by the sacrifice of himself" and "was sacrificed once to take away the sins of many people" (Heb. 9:26-28a); yet, he also proclaims in that same context that "he will appear a second time, not to bear sin, but to bring salvation to those who are waiting for him" (Heb. 9:28b). The letter of I Peter likewise declares that these are "the last times" *(ep' eschatou tōn chronōn,* 1:20; cf. II Peter 3:3; Jude 18; I John 2:18), yet looks forward to the coming of salvation in "the last [final period of] time" *(en kairō eschatō,* 1:5; cf. II Peter 3:4-10).

This two-advent structure of eschatological thought lies at the very heart of the Christian faith, distinguishing it from both a mere historicism and a mere futurism. This means, in the first place, that

145

the future for the Christian is not something completely unknown or entirely random, but that it is inextricably rooted in the redemptive events of the past and in the experience of being "in Christ" in the present—and completely determined by these realities. To employ the familiar imagery of World War II, it is V-Day that is awaited, which will complete what was inaugurated on D-Day. Or, to put it more biblically, the Christian looks forward to the marriage of Christ and His Bride, which will consummate the previous pledge of betrothal. In the second place, it means that Christians must not delude themselves into thinking either that all of God's promised blessings are theirs here and now or that all of them are only for "the sweet bye and bye." He who insists upon the fullness of heaven now will find himself either living in a "fool's paradise" or becoming terribly disillusioned. Yet he who awaits only the future lives his life much too meagerly now. With Paul, though we have experienced release from the condemnation of sin, we possess a consciousness of sonship, and are beneficiaries of the ministry of the Spirit (Rom. 8:1-17), "we wait eagerly for our adoption as sons" (Rom. 8:23) and are confident that "he who began a good work in us [you] will carry it on to completion until the day of Christ Jesus" (Phil. 1:6).

Its Personal Character

The eschatological message of the New Testament also is intensely personal in character. It is not a declaration about abstract principles to be followed, some state of Nirvana to be attained, or the interplay between the forces of nature that will result in some type of "good" for man. Rather, it stems from a personal and loving God whose avowed purpose in redemption is to bring man to his intended fullness "in Christ." It concerns man in his creatureliness, sinfulness, sonship, and glory. And it looks forward to the consummation of God's redemption in terms of personal reunion and loving fellowship. The imagery of the Bible for the relationship established by God with His people is that of the marriage relationship (cf. Isa. 54:5-8; Hos. 2:1-23; Eph. 5:31-32; Rev. 19:7-9), signaling the intensely personal character of our relationship with God both in this life and in the future. This means that when the Christian contemplates the future, he must not think primarily in terms of events and their relationships, or of provisions and their enjoyment, but his attention is to be fixed on Christ, and his joy is to be found in union with him, indeed, as expressed so beautifully in song:

146

The bride eyes not her garment,
   but her dear Bridegroom's face;
I will not gaze at glory,
   but on my King of grace.
Not at the crown he giveth,
   but on his piercèd hand.
The lamb is all the glory
   of Immanuel's land.

The Focus of the Christian's Hope

In the study of the futuristic message of the New Testament, a number of features seemingly clamor for attention. Among these are such themes as "the signs of the times," "the Second Coming of Christ," "the resurrection of believers," "the Tribulation," "the millennium," "the future of Israel," "the 144,000 redeemed," "the battle of Armageddon," "the marriage supper of the Lamb," "the binding of Satan," "the great white throne judgment," "the new Jerusalem"—with further subdivisions possible within many of these topics. The array of subjects has appeared to some almost endless, quite formidable, and somewhat esoteric. And a number of pious commentators have evidently seen it to be their task in life to increase the complexity with generous doses of fantasy and rationalistic speculation.

Two things, however, need to be said with regard to this profusion of eschatological themes. In the first place, such a list must not be taken as a series of unrelated matters, for each represents one aspect of a single complex of future events. And second, the focus of the New Testament's teaching regarding this complex of events is upon the return of Jesus Christ, which is referred to by the employment of such roughly synonymous expressions as Christ's "presence" or "coming" *(parousia)*, His "appearing" or "manifestation" *(epiphaneia)*, His "revelation" or "disclosure" *(apokalupsis)*, and "the day of the Lord" or "the day of our Lord Jesus Christ."

In what is probably the earliest extant prayer of the church—that prayer incorporated by Paul into his closing subscription to the Christians at Corinth—the focus of early Christian thought regarding the future is clearly identified in the Aramaic expression *Marana tha,* which in its context is clearly a prayer addressed to the exalted Jesus and means "O Lord, come!" (I Cor. 16:22). Likewise,

Paul's central concern in all of his eschatological treatments is Christ's return. In I Thessalonians 4:13-18, for example, the apostle encourages believers with regard to their deceased loved ones and their own purposes in life by spelling out the Christian's hope in terms of "the coming of the Lord," and in I Thessalonians 5:1-11 he continues the discussion, discouraging the setting of dates and urging preparedness, in terms of the equivalent expression "the day of the Lord." Even when he has to correct the understanding of his Thessalonian converts in II Thessalonians 2:1-12, and thereby finds himself entering into such esoteric matters as "the apostasy," "the man of lawlessness," "that which restrains," and "he who restrains," he captions his entire treatment as a discussion "concerning the coming of our Lord Jesus Christ and our being gathered to him" (v.1)— and he goes on to speak of his subject as "the day of the Lord" (v. 2), and "the manifestation of his coming" (v. 8). This same rough equivalency of eschatological expressions and this same futuristic focus are also to be found in the opening thanksgiving of I Corinthians 1:4-9. Here, Paul not only gives thanks for the grace of God that has enriched his converts' lives (vv. 4-6) but also calls them to an eager waiting for the coming "revelation of our Lord Jesus Christ" (v. 7). He then goes on to speak of "the day of our Lord Jesus Christ" (v. 8)—which event in context is surely the return of Christ that is certain to come because "God is faithful, who has called you into fellowship with his Son Jesus Christ our Lord" (v. 9).

Paul's discussion of the resurrection in I Corinthians 15 also focuses in its futuristic aspects upon Christ's return. It is "at his coming" that those who are Christ's will experience a resurrection like unto Christ's own resurrection (v. 23). And this focusing upon the return of Christ in consideration of the future continues throughout the Pauline writings. In Philippians, believers are exhorted to think and act not only in response to Christ's example of humble obedience (2:5-11) but also in light of the fact that "the Lord is at hand" (4:5), and in Titus 2:13 "the blessed hope" of which the gospel speaks is defined as "the glorious appearing of our great God and Savior, Jesus Christ" (understanding the Greek *kai* to be explicative).

The preaching and writings ascribed to Peter also evidence this same perspective. In his sermon of Acts 3, he is presented as appealing to the crowd in Solomon's colonnade: "Repent, then, and turn to God, so that your sins may be wiped out, that times of refreshing

148

may come from the Lord, and that he may send the Christ, who has been appointed for you—even Jesus. He must remain in heaven until the time comes for God to restore everything, as he promised long ago through his holy prophets" (vv. 19-21). And in II Peter 3, to those who derisively ask, "Where is this 'coming' he promised?" (v. 4), he retorts that those who deny the return of Christ have forgotten the power and long-suffering of God, for "the day of the Lord will come!" (v. 10). Similarly, the writings ascribed to John reflect this same emphasis with regard to the future. First John 2:28, for example, exhorts believers to continue in Christ "so that when he appears we may be confident and unashamed before him at his coming." And all of the Apocalypse of John is written between the pronouncement of 1:7:

> Behold, he is coming with the clouds,
> and every eye will see him,
> even those who pierced him;
> and all the peoples of the earth
> will mourn because of him;

the confirmation by the exalted Jesus in 22:20a:

> Yes, I am coming soon;

and the response of the believing community in 22:20b:

> Amen. Come, Lord Jesus!

It is the return of Christ, therefore, that is the focus of the futuristic message   the New Testament. Any attempt to shift this focus, whether in theory or in practice and for whatever reasons, can rightly be called "sectarian" because it alters the thrust of the biblical proclamation. Although each of the various themes of New Testament eschatology is significant within the larger mosaic of scriptural teaching, the main thrust of Christian proclamation can be so distorted as to make the message no longer Christian. It is not, after all, learned discourses on "the signs of the times" that form the apex of eschatological preaching, else Christianity becomes only another form of esoteric Gnosticism. Nor is the Christian's "blessed hope" a deliverance from the Tribulation (whether understood in "pre-," "mid-," or "post-trib" fashion), the arrival of the millennium, the redemption of the 144,000, the establishment of the New Jerusalem, or anything of the like—though some who proclaim a form of Christian theology evidently think so. Rather, the Christian focuses upon

149

the fully sufficient redemptive work of Christ in the past, the reign of Christ by His Spirit in the present, and the return of Christ to consummate God's redemptive purposes in the future. It is, therefore, the return of Christ that should be preeminent in the Christian's expectation and in his proclamation regarding the future.

The Basis of the Christian's Hope

The Christian's hope for the future differs from all human longings not only in its structure, character, and focus, but also with regard to the indelible stamp of certainty that it bears. This is because it is not a product of human speculation but springs from the promise and unfolding redemption of God. And in that progressive revelation of God's promise and that progressive unfolding of His redemptive activity, at least five factors can be enumerated as comprising the basis for the Christian's hope.

Rooted in the Covenant Promise of God

In the first place, the certainty of the Christian's hope for the future is rooted in the covenant promise of God. When God's covenant with Abraham and his descendants was established, it involved irrevocable implications not only for this life but also for the future. Thus Jesus, in Mark 12:26, could quote Exodus 3:6 in argumentation with the Sadducees on the subject of the resurrection, "I am the God of Abraham, and the God of Isaac, and the God of Jacob," and conclude from this that a living, personal relationship with God continues beyond death, for God "is not the God of the dead, but of the living." Likewise, the promised new covenant of Jeremiah 31:31-34 includes the declaration by God Himself: "I will be their God and they shall be my people" (v. 33 KJV)—a declaration which engenders the conviction that if God establishes contact with men and is willing to be called their God, then that relationship is of such a nature that even death cannot break it.

It is on the basis of this covenantal relationship of God with men, as expressed particularly in God's foreknowledge, predestination, call, and justification "in Christ" (cf. Rom. 8:29-30), that the apostle Paul can pose his almost defiant rhetorical questions: "What, then, shall we say in response to this? If God is for us, who can be against us? He who did not spare his own Son, but gave him up for us all—how will he not also, along with him, graciously give us all

150

things?" (Rom. 8:31-32). It is on this basis also that he can declare that believers are "more than conquerors" over all the spiritual powers and physical forces that may be found to oppose them (Rom. 8:33-37). And it is on this basis again that he can conclude his recitation of "holy defiance" with the affirmation: "I am convinced that neither death nor life, neither angels nor demons, neither the present nor the future, nor any powers, neither height nor depth, nor anything else in all creation, will be able to separate us from the love of God that is in Christ Jesus our Lord" (Rom. 8:38-39).

It is this same covenantal consciousness that impels Paul to back up his statements about eagerly awaiting "our Lord Jesus Christ to be revealed" and about being blameless "on the day of our Lord Jesus Christ" with the notation that "God, who has called you into fellowship with his Son Jesus Christ our Lord, is faithful " (I Cor. 1:7-9). And it is this consciousness that lies behind the assertions that Christian faith and knowledge rest upon "the hope of eternal life, which God, who does not lie, promised before the beginning of time" (Titus 1:2), and that undergirds the exhortation of the writer to the Hebrews to "hold unswervingly to the hope we profess, for he who promised is faithful" (Heb. 10:23).

Expressed in the Teaching of Jesus

Not only is the Christian's hope rooted in the covenant promises of God, but in the New Covenant it has been expressed in the teaching of Jesus. However difficult its details may be to interpret, the eschatological message of Jesus in the synoptic Gospels certainly highlights the expectation of Christ's Second Coming. Matthew's depiction of the Olivet discourse brings to the fore this feature in the question of the disciples: "When will this happen, and what will be the sign of your coming [parousia] and of the end of the age?" (Matt. 24:3). And in Luke's portrayal, Jesus' futuristic teaching in the region of Perea avowedly concerns "the day the Son of man is revealed" (17:23-37). John records the historic Jesus as promising, "If I go and prepare a place for you, I will come back and take you to be with me" (John 14:3), and presents the exalted Jesus as proclaiming, "Yes, I am coming soon" (Rev. 22:20).

Likewise, Paul asserts that it is "according to the Lord's own word" (I Thess. 4:15) that he is able to speak to the Thessalonians regarding Christ's return. Whether he means that he speaks on the basis of an actual statement made by Jesus that was not incorporated into our Gospels but continued within the tradition of the church (as I tend to believe), or on the basis of a revelation by the exalted Jesus to Paul or to the church (as in the Revelation of John), is impossible to say. In any case, however, it is important to note that Paul attributes his understanding of the return of his Lord to "the word of the Lord"—which in the Pauline vocabulary undoubtedly means "to Jesus." Perhaps, as many have suggested, we even have a précis of this "word" in I Thessalonians 4:16-17: "For the Lord himself will come down from heaven, with a loud command, with the voice of the archangel and with the trumpet call of God, and the dead in Christ will rise first. After that, we who are still alive and are left will be caught up with them in the clouds to meet the Lord in the air. And so we will be with the Lord forever."

Confirmed by the Resurrection and Ascension of Jesus

The reality of our Lord's return, however, is not only rooted in the covenant promises of God and expressed in the teaching of Jesus; it is also confirmed by the resurrection and ascension of Jesus. Thus, Paul can speak of Christ's resurrection as the "firstfruits" (*aparchē*) that guarantee the believer's own resurrection "at his coming" (I Cor. 15:20,23), and Peter can praise God for having "given us new birth into a living hope through the resurrection of Jesus Christ from the dead" (I Peter 1:3). From the perspective of Christ's resurrection, ascension, and living presence, the earliest believers viewed the covenant promises of God and the ministry of Jesus, and from that perspective they were assured of the return of their Lord. The earliest believers, in fact, began their relationship with the ascended Lord with the angelic words ringing in their ears: "This same Jesus, who has been taken from you into heaven, will come back in the same way you have seen him go into heaven" (Acts 1:11). And their lives and writings give evidence that they never relinquished this hope, for they had been witnesses of His resurrection and were experiencing His ascended presence.

Witnessed to by the Spirit

In addition to and stemming from the realities of which we have just spoken, the return of Christ is witnessed to by the Spirit—both to believers of the apostolic period and to Christians today. Paul therefore speaks in Romans 8:23-25 of the Holy Spirit as the "firstfruits" (aparchē) that guarantee God's continued working in our lives and sanctify all that follows:

> We . . . who have the firstfruits of the Spirit, groan inwardly as we wait eagerly for the adoption as sons, the redemption of our bodies. For in this hope we are saved. But hope that is seen is no hope at all. Who hopes for what he already has? But if we hope for what we do not yet have, we wait for it patiently.

And employing a slightly different figure of speech, he says much the same thing in Ephesians 1:13-14 in speaking of the Spirit as the "pledge" (arrabōn), "who is a deposit guaranteeing our inheritance until the redemption of those who are God's possession—to the praise of his glory."

Explicated in the Apostolic Message

Likewise, the Christian's hope for the future return of Christ bears the stamp of certainty because it has been explicated in the apostolic message. F. J. A. Hort succinctly characterized the Christian attitude toward matters of belief and practice:

> Our faith rests first on the Gospel itself, the revelation of God and His redemption in His Only begotten Son, and secondly on the interpretation of that primary Gospel by the Apostles and Apostolic men to whom was Divinely committed the task of applying the revelation of Christ to the thoughts and deeds of their own time. That standard interpretation of theirs was ordained to be for the guidance of the Church in all after ages, in combination with the living guidance of the Spirit (*Epistle of St. James*, p. ix).

Hort's words not only provide an apt conclusion and summation of the above discussion, but they also furnish an appropriate bridge leading into the discussion of the apostolic message that follows.

The Biblical Portrayal of Christ's Return

The biblical portrayal of the return of Christ is contained in such major didactic passages as Mark 13:1-37; Luke 17:22-37; I Thessalonians 4:13–5:11; II Thessalonians 2:1-12; I Corinthians

15; II Peter 3; and the Apocalypse of John, together with various other passing references and allusions in the New Testament. In these passages, at least seven themes stand out.

The Manifestation of His Glory

Throughout the New Testament, the return of Christ is referred to in terms of the manifestation of Christ's glory. His first coming fulfilled the prophecy concerning the Servant of the Lord who "will not cry or lift up his voice, or make it heard in the street" (Isa. 42:2 RSV; Matt. 12:19). Indeed, during His ministry, Jesus repeatedly commanded His hearers and those He healed not to make Him known. Even at such high points in His ministry as Peter's confession and the transfiguration, it is recorded that He ordered His disciples to keep silent regarding who He was and what they had seen—at least until after He had been raised from the dead (Mark 8:30 and 9:9). And though He was openly proclaimed as Messiah, Lord, and Son of God after the resurrection—or, more accurately, *because of* the resurrection (cf. Acts 2:36; Rom. 1:4)— and though this proclamation is destined to reach "all nations" (Mark 13:10; Matt. 24:14) and "the ends of the earth" (Acts 1:8), only in the return of Christ will His true glory be manifested visibly, irresistibly, and universally.

Jesus' own description of His Second Coming is in terms of an open and universal manifestation of power and glory:

> As the lightning comes from the east and flashes to the west, so will be the coming of the Son of Man. . . . At that time the sign of the Son of Man will appear in the sky, and all the nations of the earth will mourn. They will see the Son of Man coming on the clouds of the sky, with power and great glory" (Matt. 24:27,30; cf. Mark 13:26-27; Luke 17:24; 21:27).

And His words are echoed, at least in part, in the proclamation of the apostle Paul:

> The Lord himself will come down from heaven, with a loud command, with the voice of the archangel and with the trumpet call of God (I Thess. 4:16);

and in the announcement of John the seer:

> Behold, he is coming with the clouds,
> and every eye will see him,

154

even those who pierced him;
and all the peoples of the earth
will mourn because of him (Rev. 1:7).

The Consummation of His Presence

The return of Christ is presented in the New Testament also as the consummation of Christ's living presence in each believer's life and in the church. Matthew records Jesus as promising: "Where two or three come together in my name, there am I with them" (18:20), and, "Surely I will be with you always, to the very end of the age" (28:20). Christians testify to having experienced the reality of Christ's presence in their lives, not only personally and individually but also corporately in worship, witness, and fellowship. To be "in Christ," they have inevitably found, means also to have Christ by His Spirit living in them. But the reality of a present relationship with the living Lord, whether in the individual or the corporate experience, in no way diminishes the Christian's longing for a future consummation. Rather, it enhances it. The more meaningful and relevant that relationship is here and now, the more eagerly the Christian looks forward to future consummation. Thus, after enumerating the great truths of the believer's present life in Christ, Paul turns his eyes toward the future and declares: "We ourselves, who have the firstfruits of the Spirit, groan inwardly as we wait eagerly for our adoption as sons, the redemption of our bodies. For in this hope we were saved" (Rom. 8:23-24). And he can express the confidence that "he who began a good work in you will carry it on to completion until the day of Christ Jesus" (Phil. 1:6). Likewise, John rejoices in the wondrous relationship that God has established, yet he lifts his eyes as well to the time of final consummation when he says:

> How great is the love the Father has lavished on us, that we should be called children of God! And that is what we are! The reason the world does not know us is that it did not know him. Dear friends, now we are children of God, and what we will be has not yet been made known. But we know that when he appears, we shall be like him, for we shall see him as he is (I John 3:1-2).

The return of Christ, then, is the consummation of that relationship established by Christ and experienced in part here and now by the Christian through the ministry of the Holy Spirit. It is the living presence of Christ now experienced that shall be brought to full and final completion. Or, to employ the biblical imagery, it is the marriage of Christ and His Bride that consummates an earlier betrothal.

The Revelation of Reality

Not only is Christ's return depicted as the manifestation of His glory and the consummation of His presence, but it also appears in Scripture as the revelation *(apokalupsis)* of reality. It is for this reason that the last book of the Bible is called the "Apocalypse," for it is an unveiling of "what must soon take place" (Rev. 1:1)—— and within this unveiling are matters concerning "what is now and what will take place later" (Rev. 1:19).

With regard to Christ, the Second Coming will make clear to everyone what His first coming was all about, what His ministry, death, and resurrection really meant, and what has actually been taking place because of His living presence in and through individual believers and His church. It will unveil, as well, the true nature of His person for "every eye will see him" in all His power and glory. To the Christian, the return of Christ will demonstrate the genuineness of the believer's faith (I Peter 1:7) and reveal the quality of the believer's works (I Cor. 3:13). Finally, for those who stand in opposition to God's provision of redemption and reconciliation in Christ, it will also be a time of unveiling: the unveiling of motive, attitudes, and actions, with the result that "all the nations [peoples] of the earth will mourn" (Matt. 24:30; Rev. 1:7). Then will be fulfilled our Lord's statement, "There is nothing concealed that will not be disclosed, or hidden that will not be made known" (Matt. 10:26; Luke 12:2), for then will be revealed to all the state of things as they are known before God in reality—whether matters concerning Christ, concerning Christ's own, or concerning those apart from Christ.

The Resurrection of Believers

Intimately connected with the return of Christ in all the biblical portrayals is the resurrection of believers in Christ, whether deceased or then living. Jesus' promise regarding the Son of Man who will come "with power and great glory" is that "he will send his angels

156

with a loud trumpet call, and they will gather his elect from the four winds, from one end of the heavens to the other" (Matt. 24:31; cf. Mark 13:27). Paul's proclamation "by the word of the Lord" is that: "The Lord himself will come down from heaven, with a loud command, with the voice of the archangel and with the trumpet call of God, and the dead in Christ will rise first. After that, we who are still alive and are left will be caught up with them in the clouds to meet the Lord in the air. And so we will be with the Lord forever" (I Thess. 4:16-17). So intimately connected are the return of Christ and the resurrection of believers that Paul in II Thessalonians 2:1 can speak in one breath of "the coming *(parousia)* of our Lord Jesus Christ and our being gathered *(episunagōgē)* to him," and in I Corinthians 15:20-23 can relate the two events in both causal and temporal fashion by insisting: "Christ has indeed been raised from the dead, the firstfruits of those who have fallen asleep. . . . But each in his own turn: Christ, the firstfruits, then, when he comes, those who belong to him."

The major didactic passage on the resurrection of believers is, of course, I Corinthians 15, dealing as it does with (1) the relevancy of a future resurrection of believers for Christian faith and life today (15:12 ff.), and (2) the possibility and nature of such a resurrection (15:35 ff.). The passage builds up to a climax in the great affirmation of 15:51-57:

> Listen, I tell you a mystery: We shall not all sleep, but we shall all be changed—in a flash, in the twinkling of an eye, at the last trumpet. For the trumpet will sound, the dead will be raised imperishable, and we shall be changed. For the perishable must clothe itself with the imperishable, and the mortal with immortality. When the perishable has been clothed with the imperishable, and the mortal with immortality, then the saying that is written will come true: "Death has been swallowed up in victory.
>
> "Where, O death, is your victory?
> Where, O death, is your sting?"
>
> The sting of death is sin, and the power of sin is the law. But thanks be to God! He gives us the victory through our Lord Jesus Christ.

Such a conviction not only comforts and encourages believers in their sadness (I Thess. 4:18; 5:11), but also challenges them to faithful continuance and a full expenditure of energy in their service "because you know that your labor in the Lord is not in vain" (I Cor. 15:58).

The Assumption of His Prerogatives

Included in the biblical portrayals of Christ's return is the theme of our Lord's assumption of His rightful prerogatives. Paul alludes to this in I Corinthians 15:24-28 when he declares:

> Then the end will come, when he hands over the kingdom to God the Father after he has destroyed all dominion, authority, and power. . . . When he has done this, then the Son himself will be made subject to him who put everything under him, so that God may be all in all.

But it is the Book of Revelation that stresses this motif repeatedly in its imagery and symbolism, enunciating it with particular emphasis in connection with its depiction of the seventh angel with the seventh trumpet and the loud voices in heaven who proclaim:

> The kingdom of the world has become the
> kingdom of our Lord and of his Christ,
> and he will reign for ever and ever (Rev. 11:15).

Having brought to culmination the progressive outworking of God's redemptive program, and having climaxed it with His Second Coming and its associated events, our Lord presents His completed work to the Father and together with the Father reigns eternally in the full exercise of His rightful prerogatives.

Cataclysmic Phenomena Within the Cosmos

Associated with the return of Christ in the biblical accounts are a number of cataclysmic phenomena that are predicted to take place within the cosmos. In the Olivet discourse, our Lord refers to a build-up of events that will precede "the end of the age" (Mark 13:5-13; Matt. 24:4-14; Luke 21:8-19), to a satanic personage identified as "the abomination that causes desolation" of Daniel's prophecy, who will inaugurate from a satanic perspective the climactic events of "the end of the age" (Mark 13:14; Matt. 24:15; cf. Luke 21:20), and to a period of great distress that will result from the presence and activity of this satanic personage (Mark 13:15-23; Matt. 24:16-28; Luke 21:21-24). But most directly associated with the coming of the Son of Man in Jesus' teaching are certain cosmic occurrences, which are described poetically by Mark and Matthew (in words probably drawn from Isaiah 13:10 and 34:4) as follows:

The sun will be darkened,
and the moon will not give its light;
the stars will fall from the sky,
and the heavenly bodies will be shaken
(Mark 13:24-25; Matt. 24:29).

Luke records essentially the same thing, but puts it more prosaically:

There will be signs in the sun, moon, and stars. On the earth, nations will be in anguish and perplexity at the roaring and tossing of the sea. Men will faint from terror, apprehensive of what is coming on the world, for the heavenly bodies will be shaken (Luke 21:25-26).

Further references to such cosmic phenomena in association with our Lord's return appear elsewhere in the New Testament as well. And often the validation for such an expectation is related in some manner to the teaching of Jesus, whether as given historically during His earthly ministry or by the ascended Lord. Paul, for example, not only speaks "by the word of the Lord" of Christ's return as being "with a shout, with the voice of an archangel and with the trumpet call of God" and of believers being caught up "in the clouds to meet the Lord in the air" (I Thess. 4:16-17), but he also discusses in more apocalyptic fashion such satanic features as "the apostasy" and "the man of lawlessness" (II Thess. 2:3-5, 8-12), and such heavenly or heavenly inspired features as "that which restrains" and "he who restrains" (II Thess. 2:6-7). From his description of "the man of lawlessness" (vv. 4, 8-10) and his insistence: "Don't you remember that when I was with you I used to tell you these things?" (v. 5), it is not too difficult to identify the satanic personage of II Thessalonians 2 with "the abomination that causes desolation" of Daniel's prophecy and Jesus' teaching nor to postulate that the contents of II Thessalonians 2:1-12 stem in some manner from the common apostolic proclamation and go back ultimately to Jesus Himself.

Peter's words in II Peter 3 also are significant in this regard. The eschatological portion of this chapter begins with the statement: "I want you to recall the words spoken in the past by the holy prophets and the command given by our Lord and Savior through your apostles" (v. 2). Then, after a discussion of God's promise for the future and its apparent delay, the climax is reached: "But the day of the Lord will come like a thief. The heavens will disappear with a roar; the elements will be destroyed by fire, and the earth and

159

everything in it will be laid bare" (v. 10). And John's portrayal in the Apocalypse is even more graphic, both in its description of the heavenly Son of Man through whom the revelation comes (Rev. 1:13-19) and in its symbolic depiction of the cataclysmic phenomena associated with His coming. It may be possible to read the Apocalypse without any idea of what the cryptic symbols and rather grotesque images signify exactly, but one can hardly read the book without gaining a decided impression of awe and without being assured that cataclysmic phenomena will accompany God's wrapping up of the world's history in the Second Coming of His Son.

Exhortations to Watchfulness and Preparedness

The concluding element in the Olivet discourse—and, judging by the amount of space devoted to it (at least in Matthew's Gospel), a major reason for Jesus' eschatological teaching—has to do with exhortations to watchfulness and preparedness. Mark presents Jesus as concluding:

> No one knows about that day or hour, not even the angels in heaven, nor the Son, but only the Father. Be on guard! Be alert! You do not know when that time will come. It's like a man going away: He leaves his house in charge of his servants, each with his assigned task, and tells the one at the door to keep watch. So you also must keep watch because you do not know when the owner of the house will come back—whether in the evening, or at mid-night, or when the rooster crows, or at dawn. If he comes suddenly, don't let him find you sleeping. What I say to you, I say to everyone: "Watch!" (Mark 13:32-37).

Matthew, of course, expands this exhortation considerably, principally by the inclusion of a number of parables urging preparedness (Matt. 24:36–25:46); and Luke condenses it into the more prosaic warning: "Be always on the watch, and pray that you may be able to escape all that is about to happen, and that you may be able to stand before the Son of Man" (Luke 21:36). But all three synoptic Gospels, each in its own way, present as a major theme in the eschatological teaching of Jesus the exhortation to watchfulness and preparedness.

And this is true for all of the eschatological teaching of the New Testament. Again, to take the apostle to the Gentiles as a chief example, having set out the Christian's hope regarding the return of Christ in I Thessalonians 4:13-18, Paul goes on immediately to say:

160

Now, brothers, about times and dates we do not need to write to you, for you know very well that the day of the Lord will come like a thief in the night. While people are saying, "Peace and safety," destruction will come on them suddenly, as labor pains on a pregnant woman, and they will not escape. But you, brothers, are not in darkness so that this day should surprise you like a thief. You are all sons of the light and sons of the day. We do not belong to the night or to the darkness. So then, let us not be like others who are asleep, but let us be alert and self-controlled. For those who sleep, sleep at night, and those who get drunk, get drunk at night. But since we belong to the day, let us be self-controlled, putting on faith and love as a breastplate, and the hope of salvation as a helmet (I Thess. 5:1-8).

Theological and Practical Implications

The Christian life, according to the New Testament, is lived between the polarities of "realized" eschatology and "futuristic" eschatology—that is, between being presently "in Christ" and in the future "with Christ." The old age has been judged and is passing away, but the new age has not yet been fully brought about; the condemnation of sin has been dealt with and the compulsion of sin broken, but sin still is present to tempt and to frustrate; the tyranny of death has been crushed, but mortality and depravity still remain; the domination of the law is ended, but forms of legalism and our perverted desire to gain in divine favor by our own endeavors still exist; the supernatural antagonistic powers have been disarmed and defeated, but they are not yet destroyed. Indeed, those who have become righteous still await righteousness, those who have been received as sons still await sonship, those who have been raised to newness of life still await resurrection, and those who have known Christ's coming still await His return. It is this temporal tension between the "no longer" and the "not yet" that lies at the very heart of the gospel and that contains the key to the understanding of the entire New Testament.

A problem with all this, however, is that often those who profess themselves to be Christians tend so to emphasize one of the polarities as to virtually exclude the other from their thought and practice. On the one hand, there are those who have so stressed the aspect of present fulfillment—either because of some type of spiritual ecstasy or, conversely, because of secular complacency—that they

161

have lost any real expectancy regarding the future. The church at Corinth seems to have been of this nature, or at least to have had a group within it that took such a position. And probably so was the church at Laodicea, with its boast: "I am rich; I have acquired wealth and do not need a thing" (Rev. 3:17), though for far less "spiritual" reasons than at Corinth. Although in its more spiritual forms such an orientation may seem eminently satisfying, Christians of this sort have in reality lost their pilgrim consciousness and renounced the note of joyous expectancy that is inherent in the gospel. And, sadly, despite their possible lofty declarations to the contrary, they all too often sink into a state of self-congratulation and self-sufficiency. On the other hand, there are those who so stress the expectation of future salvation and get so wrapped up in spelling out the details of that future that they have little inclination to appreciate what God has done and desires to do in and through them here and now. The church at Thessalonica seems to have been of this type. But to base one's hope for salvation only on the future activity of God is to turn Christianity into one of the many "utopian" religions of man. And to view the apex of Christian theology as the proper identification of cryptic symbols and the proper detailing of temporal relationships in the eschatological message of the New Testament is to turn Christianity into something of an esoteric Gnosticism.

The proclamation of Christ's future return is not just a bit of pious speculation carried over from the church's Jewish heritage or some ossified tradition of ecclesiastical dogma that can safely be treated in rather passive fashion. Nor, on the other hand, is it a utopian hope or some new form of gnostic speculation that should consume all our passion. Rather, the return of Christ for the Christian is the consummation of God's redemptive program that was conceived in the eternal counsels of the triune God, unfolded progressively in the history of Israel, epitomized in the work and person of Jesus the Messiah, and experienced in that relationship of being "in Christ" and Christ, by His Spirit, being in us. It is that which brings to a climax all of God's redemptive purposes, and it carries important implications for Christian living today.

As the Christian lives between the "already" and the "not yet," he lives with the confidence that "he who began a good work in you will carry it on to completion until the day of Christ Jesus" (Phil. 1:6). And with the sure prospect of Christ's return before him, he

162

lives expectantly (Rom. 8:18-25) with a sense of "inexpressible and glorious joy" (I Peter 1:8) and with the realization that his "labor in the Lord is not in vain" (I Cor. 15:58). He also seeks to live a life of purity and holiness, for "everyone who has this hope in him purifies himself, just as he [Christ] is pure" (I John 3:3; cf. II Peter 3:11-14). And he considers whatever delay there may seem to be in his Lord's return as an opportunity for the further extension of God's redemptive purposes among all men (II Peter 3:9,15).

The Christian does not fear the future nervously, for he knows the Lord of the future and rejoices in His company. Therefore, Christians are exhorted "not to become easily unsettled or alarmed" by reports regarding the future (II Thess. 2:2), but to be "alert," "clear-minded," "self-controlled" (I Thess. 5:6-8; I Peter 4:7), and "dressed ready for service" (Luke 12:35)—"putting on faith and love as a breastplate, and the hope of salvation as a helmet" (I Thess. 5:8). And, therefore, Christians of every age have joined with the sentiments of what is probably the earliest extant prayer of the first-century church (I Cor. 16:22) and the last recorded prayer in the New Testament (Rev. 22:20), crying out in thankfulness, expectancy, and sheer delight: "Come, Lord Jesus!"

11

Times and Seasons

J. Stafford Wright

It is often said that the early Christians mistakenly believed that the Lord Jesus Christ would return in their lifetime. No doubt many of them did believe it, as have many other Christians all down the ages. Individual Christians never have been immune from error.

The Imminency of the Second Coming

Our concern is whether the writings that form the New Testament teach that the Second Coming must be imminent. If they do, then they also were mistaken, and we rightly should be suspicious of other things that they say about the Second Coming.

We readily admit that there is much in what is said that must be held in balance. Therefore, a Christian must live responsibly as though his Lord will return today. He cannot claim the expectation of a long life, with time to become an enthusiast for Christ when he retires. Suppose the Lord *were* to return today. This was the atmosphere in which the early Christians lived, and in which we, too, should live. This is what Jesus Himself taught in His analogy of servants who are to be ready constantly for their master to come back. "You also must be ready; for the Son of man is coming at an hour you do not expect" (Luke 12:35-40).

This expectancy is balanced by the unfolding of certain events before the Lord returns. Again Jesus said that "this gospel of the

165

kingdom will be preached throughout the whole world, as a testimony to all nations; and then the end will come" (Matt. 24:14). There will be a heading up of evil under a depraved person, "the man of lawlessness" (II Thess. 2:1-12), and there will be an outburst of spiritual evil directed against the teachings of Christ (I Tim. 4:1-3; II Tim. 3:1-9). There will be signs both in heaven and on earth (Matt. 24:21-30).

The Teaching of Paul

In striking the Christian balance, we find considerable help in Paul's attitude. In I Thessalonians 4:17, he expectantly uses the first person plural when he speaks of the Second Coming. "We who are alive, who are left, shall be caught up." Yet in II Corinthians 4:14 he includes himself among those who have died. "He who raised the Lord Jesus will raise us also with Jesus." In a later letter he again speaks as though he will be alive. "From [heaven] we await a Savior, . . . who will change our lowly body to be like his glorious body" (Phil. 3:20-21). By these statements, Paul reflects the proper Christian attitude, and he makes this even clearer in II Corinthians 5:1-10; he longs to be alive when the Lord returns, so that he need not pass through the intermediate state of nakedness, i.e., without his present material body and without his promised resurrection body. Certainly, he will have the joy of being "at home with the Lord" (v. 8), but he will still be incomplete, since God made man to be body, as well as mind and spirit. Meanwhile, not knowing when to expect his Lord, his one steady aim is to please Him (v. 9).

Unfortunately, many of the more excitable Christians could not be content with this attitude of expectant service. In Thessalonica the church was in confusion because of some prophets and a forged letter with the message that "the day of the Lord has come" (II Thess. 2:2). Probably, this idea was encouraging the withdrawal from work that Paul rebukes in the same letter (3:6-13). Obviously Jesus Christ had not yet returned, but it was maintained that the unfolding of the final events had already begun. Therefore Paul had to put the brakes on the idea that Christ was coming so soon that Christians could renounce all worldly obligations. He reminded the church that they had not yet seen the full outburst of the forces of evil. Anti-Christian forces already were at work (2:7), but their efforts would crescendo under a satanically dominated leader, the personification of blasphemy, evil, and supernatural wonder-working.

Other Events Prophesied in Addition to the Second Coming

There are, however, a few other texts that in isolation might appear to teach that the Lord would return during the lifetime of the first believers. One cannot attempt to interpret them without noting that there are three crisis events, in addition to the Second Coming, that may be referred to in very similar terms, and it is important to discover which is spoken of in any individual passage.

The Last Days of the Old Testament Preparation for the Coming of Jesus the Messiah.

Without the historical appearance and acts of the Messiah, the Old Testament would be no more than a description of one more world religion. Because the first Christians lived while the period of Jewish revelation was being wound up, they could say that "in *these last days* God has spoken to us by a Son" (Heb. 1:2), and that upon them "the *end of the ages* has come" (I Cor. 10:11).

The Destruction of Jerusalem

This is seen as God's visitation in judgment, and marks the parting of the ways for those who accepted and those who refused the Messiah. It is the final ending of the old era.

Pentecost, the Founding of the Christian Church to Start the New Age.

The Holy Spirit came to form the body of Christ on earth and to make real the kingship that Christ exerted from the place of authority and power, the right hand of the Father (Eph. 1:20-23). Christ Himself is not visible on earth yet, but He is the executor of the kingdom of God (Acts 28:31; Col. 1:13).

None of these three, important as they are, can be the fulfillment of the promises of the Second Coming, since, even when they have taken place, the New Testament still looks forward to the personal return of the Lord Jesus Christ. Yet, they could be relevant for the interpretation of texts that at first sight may seem to speak of the Second Coming.

Turning first to the Gospels, there are three passages that require examination.

1. *Matthew 10:23: "You will not have gone through all the towns*

167

of Israel, before the Son of Man comes." This does not make sense if it refers to the Second Coming, since Judea was evangelized before this Gospel was written. We must compare Scripture with Scripture. The verse takes up the command of verses 5 and 6 that the Twelve should not preach in any Samaritan or Gentile town, but concentrate on the Jews. The passage therefore has a primary application to this particular mission, not to post-Pentecostal preaching when the command was to go to both Samaritans and Gentiles.

Comparison with Luke 10:1 shows that Jesus sent disciples to prepare the way for His own arrival in various towns and villages, "[He] sent them on ahead of him, two by two, into every town and place where he himself was about to come." Hence, the words in Matthew mean in effect, "Concentrate, for now, on Jewish towns only. You will not have time to visit all of them before I come along to the place where we are to meet."

2. *The comment before the Transfiguration (the words vary slightly in the three synoptic Gospels): "There are some standing here who will not taste death—*

before they see the Son of man coming in his kingdom (Matt. 16:28)
before they see the kingdom of God come with power (Mark 9:1)
before they see the kingdom of God (Luke 9:27)."

Assuming that these are extracts from what Jesus said, we can see a reference to Pentecost and to the events that followed. Pentecost brought Christ in all His sovereign power into world history. Many of the disciples would live to see the gospel not simply at work but established as a real force in the world.

3. *Matthew 24:34: "This generation will not pass away till all these things take place."* There are several possibilities here. The Greek word, *genea,* could be translated "nation," and the reference would be to the Jewish nation, who would survive the tribulations that they have suffered down the ages. This translation is recognized by lexicons as acceptable, but the New Testament elsewhere uses a different word for "nation," viz. *ethnos.* Another possibility is that the generation that sees the beginning of the final signs will see their climax in the Second Coming. The end will not be drawn out for long.

A third possibility lies in the double question and consequent double answer of this chapter. Jesus said that the temple would be destroyed, and the disciples asked, "When will this be, and what will be the sign of your coming and of the close of the age?" (Matt.

168

24:3). We must therefore disentangle the answers, and see which refer to the destruction of Jerusalem and which to the Second Coming. The following is a reasonable attempt to do this:[1]

	Matthew 24	Mark 13	Luke 21
Occasion of the address	1-3	1-4	5-7
Warnings against being led astray by false prophets or calamities	4-8	5-8	8-11
Persecution foretold and help promised	9-14	9-13	12-19
Destruction of Jerusalem and dispersion of Jews	15-28	14-23	20-24
The coming of Christ	29-31	24-27	25-28
Watching for events of this generation leading to the judgment on Jerusalem	32-35	28-31	29-33
Watching for the coming of Christ	36-51	32-37	34-36

These passages are the only ones in the Gospels that might appear to teach an imminent Second Coming. By contrast, we also note the following: "This gospel of the kingdom will be preached throughout the whole world" (Matt. 24:14). "Wherever this gospel is preached in the whole world, what she has done will be told" (Matt. 26:13). In Matthew 24:48 and Luke 12:45 the master delays his coming, as does the bridegroom in Matthew 25:5. These latter passages are not conclusive, but at least they make provision for a considerable lapse of time before the Second Coming, of which no one knows the exact date (Matt. 24:36).

Although we already have looked at Paul's attitude, there are several other relevant verses in the Epistles. The sentence in Philippians 4:5, "The Lord is at hand," or "near," most naturally is a reminder of His presence. Romans 13:11-12 tells us to wake from sleep, "for salvation is nearer to us now than when we first believed; the night is far gone, the day is at hand." Although this might allude to the Second Coming, it is equally possible to see it as an exhortation to sleepy Christians not to drift into old ways (v. 13) but to press on into the light, knowing that final salvation is the goal. Every day brings us nearer to the day of accountability and deliverance.

Similarly, in I Corinthians 7:29, the New English Bible is justified in its translation, "The time we live in will not last long." Paul refers to the days of our life, whether they are terminated by death or by the Lord's return. There is the same sort of reference in I Peter 4:7: "The end of all things is at hand." Here the Jerusalem Bible translates, "Everything will soon come to an end," and Peter probably intends the same as James 4:14: "What is your life? For you are a mist that appears for a little time and then vanishes." Life, even at its best, is brief.

Finally, there are several references in the Book of Revelation. John is shown "what must soon take place" (1:1) and is told that "the time is near" (1:3). If one assumes that the whole book deals only with events at the time of the end, then these verses constitute a difficulty. But it is likely that the book is a symbolic unfolding of troubles, persecutions, and error that will affect the church, in whole or in part, all through its history, although they will reach their climax shortly before the Lord's return.[2]

When the risen Lord says more than once, "I am coming soon," in the letters to the seven churches, this clearly refers to a visitation of judgment or vindication (2:16; 3:11). The other three occurrences are in the closing chapter (22:7, 12, 20). Here, too, the context allows a reference to a visitation of judgment that will not be indefinitely postponed, but, since the whole church and not the local congregation is here in view, some other interpretation is preferable.

The words may be taken as a watchword and a comfort to the church down the ages. One might compare them to the promise of a mother as she tucks her child in bed. "You'll come up soon, won't you?" says the child. "Yes," says mother, "I'll be coming to see you again soon." The "soon" will vary according to the circumstances. If the child is feverish, the mother may come in half an hour. If the child needs to go to sleep without being disturbed again, "soon" may be two or three hours. To mother and child "soon" becomes a relative term, reassuring to both and well understood by both. In fact this thought is expressed definitely by II Peter 3:1-13, where scoffers laugh at the Lord's delay, but "with the Lord one day is as a thousand years" (v. 8).

Indications That the End Is Approaching

Having tried to strike a balance between a coming at any moment and a coming preceded by certain signs, we must obviously look at such indications as the Bible gives that the end is approaching. There are different types of signs.

1. Unique Signs

Signs in the heavens culminate in "the sign of the Son of man in heaven" (Matt. 24:29-30). Although it is possible to spiritualize the former signs, it is reasonable to take them as literal in view of the reality of the latter sign. The Bible is emphatic that Jesus will return in visible form as He went into heaven at the ascension (Acts 1:11). Thus "the sign of the Son of man" must be the appearance of Christ Himself. He Himself is the sign. We need not be afraid of the literality of this if we believe in the literality of the ascension from the Mount of Olives.

One cannot speculate over what form the other signs will take. When Jesus Christ was born, a strange star hung in the sky, and at His crucifixion the sun was blacked out, although the moon was full at the Passover and could not have caused an eclipse. There was also a great earthquake. Peter probably refers to these heavenly and earthly phenomena when he quotes from Joel in his sermon in Acts 2:19-20. His hearers would have experienced them. Down the years, comets and meteor showers have been hailed as signs of the Lord's imminent return, and in our own day unidentified flying objects have been claimed as signs in the heavens. One would, however, expect something more than this. Meanwhile, man's own behavior may well produce the droughts, famines, and wars that will cause men's hearts to faint with fear (Luke 21:10-11, 26).

2. Intensified Events

We have regarded the Book of Revelation as designating troubles that the church must face down the ages. These include natural disasters, plagues, droughts, famines, and wars. Christ also spoke of these not as signs in themselves, but as part of the sad state of a fallen world (Matt. 24:6-8). These things may, however, be intensified on a much wider scale in the final days. More important are the satanic attacks. The Book of Revelation describes the repeated attempts by Satan to wreck the church either by persecution or by injecting strange doctrines (see especially chap. 13). Christ Himself also warned of savage persecutions and of false messiahs (Mark 13:9-13, 22).

In the light of this, we note the teaching about Antichrist. Antichrist has his tentacles in every generation of the church. The anti-God movements that he fosters are always at work underground (II Thess. 2:7). This means that there are many antichrists. In a passage that we have deliberately left untouched until now, John says that we know it is the last hour because there are many antichrists (I John 2:18). These took the form of false prophets who denied the full deity of Jesus Christ (2:22; 4:1-3). Scholars such as Westcott point out that since there is no definite article before "last hour,"

171

"a last hour" may refer to an hour of crisis currently faced by the church to which John was writing. Or, as in Hebrews 1:2, the reference may be to the end of the former period. The overlapping Christian era had introduced a form of attack that had not been possible before, namely, a denial of the meaning of the Incarnation. It still seems, however, from II Thessalonians 2, that there will be a more devastating single figure at the time of the end. Similarly, the false teachers, possessed and directed by evil spirits, will become more prominent still (I Tim. 4:1-3; II Tim. 3:1-9; II Peter 3:3-7; Jude 18-19).

3. Intricate Calculations

These have bedeviled Christians for well over a century. People have used such passages as Daniel 8:14 and 12:7-12 to fix the date of the Lord's return. One of the most significant projections was that of William Miller, who calculated that 1843 was the date, subsequently moving it on to October 22, 1844. Pastor Russell and other leaders of the Jehovah's Witnesses, have also calculated various dates.

The rise of some powerful figure, such as Napoleon, Hitler, or Mussolini, always has produced a spate of attempts to identify him with one of the figures in Daniel. One line of interpretation has treated the fourth (Roman) empire of Daniel as perpetuated in the Roman Church, and this church has been regarded by many Protestants as the fulfillment of the Antichrist prophecies. This identification is coupled often with what is called an historicist interpretation of the Book of Revelation, tracing a step-by-step movement from secular Rome to ecclesiastical Rome.

Actually, Daniel is concerned with the Roman Empire only as the power that would be dominant when Christ should be born and found His church, which would increase into a worldwide force (Dan. 2:35, 44-45).

Signs in Our Day

Are there any specific signs belonging to our own day? The possible significance of the state of Israel in the light of Luke 21:24 is discussed in chapter 14. We have a more accelerated moral decline today than in the past. Fresh outbursts of the occult and the demonic disturb our society; Christians of our time are persecuted for their faith; adherents of both old and new religions are campaigning throughout the world; and Christian denominations constantly must

172

resist alien doctrines that strike at the heart of the New Testament revelation.

There is one entirely new sign. Today, modern methods of communication insure that the Gospel can indeed be taken to all peoples, and Jesus said that when this has been done "the end will come" (Matt. 24:14). It seems, therefore, that the time of the Second Coming lies partly in our hands, and this is what we are told in II Peter 3:12. We are to be "waiting for and hastening the coming of the day of God," or, as the New English Bible puts it, "Look eagerly for the coming of the Day of God and work to hasten it on."

Notes

1. This reconstruction is based on an article in *The Princeton Theological Review* of 1928.

2. For this view see *More Than Conquerors* by William Hendriksen (Grand Rapids: Baker, 1940).

12

The Millennium

John Warwick Montgomery

The word *millennium* is a Latin word (from *mille*, "thousand," and *annus*, "year"), which has been taken over into English and used to indicate a time of penultimate divine triumph over the forces of evil on earth prior to God's final conquest of all His enemies and the establishment of everlasting righteousness. Strictly speaking, there is only one passage in the Bible that speaks of the "millennium" or thousand-year reign of Christ, and that is Revelation 20:1-10, though other passages in the Old and New Testaments speak of the general concept of a millennium. The Greek expression used in Revelation 20 is *chilia etē* and is an exact equivalent of the Latin. From this comes the term *Chiliasm*, properly a synonym for *Millennialism*, but not infrequently employed in a pejorative sense to designate especially gross and sensual conceptions of spiritual bliss on earth.

The Biblical Data

Many passages in the Old Testament speak of a future condition of earthly blessedness for the Jewish nation (Isa. 9:6; 11:1-12:6; 40:9-11; 52:7-12; Jer. 33:17-22; Ezek. 37:25; Hos. 3:4-5; Joel 3:20; Amos 9:14-15; Zech. 9:9-10; etc.). There are, however, no time-limits connected with this experience of blessing for God's people. Thus it must be admitted that although these prophecies are compatible with a time of millennial bliss they do not expressly require it. The messianic kingdom is described as an "everlasting" or "eternal"

175

kingdom in such key prophetic books of the Old Testament as Daniel (2:44; 7:27), and this has led millennial interpreters to understand the history of Israel's restoration and blessing as extending across the millennial age into the age of the end, the ultimate eschaton, when "God shall be all in all."[1] Therefore, in spite of attempts such as those presented in *The Millennium Bible* by W. E. Biederwolf to find the doctrine of the millennium clearly set forth in the Old Testament, it is impossible to locate its biblical foundation there.

An examination of certain New Testament texts is, however, more fruitful. There are Paul's comments in I Corinthians 15:22-28, for example:

> For as in Adam all die, so also in Christ shall all be made alive. But each in his own order: Christ the first fruits, then at his coming those who belong to Christ. Then comes the end, when he delivers the kingdom to God the Father after destroying every rule and every authority and power. For he must reign until he has put all his enemies under his feet. The last enemy to be destroyed is death. "For God has put all things in subjection under his feet." But when it says, "All things are put in subjection under him," it is plain that he is excepted who put all things under him. When all things are subjected to him, then the Son himself will also be subjected to him who put all things under him, that God may be everything to every one.

Even those who oppose the doctrine of a millennium recognize that this passage, which seems to indicate three stages in the victory of God's kingdom (Christ's resurrection—His coming—the end), gives a foothold for millennial expectations. Other passages occasionally appealed to as teaching the doctrine of Christ's millennial reign are Matthew 19:28; 25:31-46; Luke 14:14; and I Thessalonians 4:13-18. Nevertheless, the real case for the doctrine rests squarely on the exegesis of Revelation 20, the one place in the New Testament that speaks explicitly of a period of a thousand years.

Revelation 20 informs us that after Messiah's victory over "the beast," "the false prophet," and all their followers, Satan will be confined to a "bottomless pit" for one thousand years. During this period, Christ will reign with His martyred saints, brought to life in the "first resurrection" at the outset of the millennial (thousand-year) period. At the end of the thousand years, Satan will be loosed for a short time, the final battle between God and His adversaries will occur, and the final resurrection and the last judgment will take place, followed by the "second death" of all evil forces and the establishment of everlasting righteousness.

The issues disputed by Bible scholars in regard to this passage are: (1) whether the text is to be taken literally (millennialism) or figuratively (amillennialism); and (2) if the millennium in Revelation 20 is literal, whether the Second Coming of the Lord is to precede (premillennialism) or follow (postmillennialism) the time of millennial victory.[2]

The Millennium in Christian Church History

Those who regard millennialism as an alien import into the Christian faith have been much embarrassed by its entry and widespread acceptance in the church during its earliest history. S. D. F. Salmond, for example, who considers millennial conceptions totally foreign to Christ's teachings, has to admit that "the dogma of a Millennium . . . took possession of Christian thought at so early a date and with so strong a grasp that it has sometimes been reckoned an integral part of the primitive Christian faith."[3]

Papias (ca. A.D. 60-130), who had personal contact with those taught by Christ and His apostles and who may well have been a disciple of John, asserted that "the Lord used to teach concerning those [end] times" that "there will be a period of a thousand years after the resurrection of the dead, and the kingdom of Christ will be set up in material form on this very earth."[4] Though Papias fleshes out his reference to the millennium with details from the apocryphal writing called the Apocalypse of Baruch, his account is a weighty testimony to early Christian beliefs concerning eschatology.

The author of the so-called Epistle of Barnabas (written no later than A.D. 138) was a millennialist. The six days of creation are interpreted by him as representing a period of six thousand years, because a thousand years are as one day in the sight of God (Ps. 90:4). In six "days" (six thousand years), everything will be completed, after which the present evil age will be destroyed and the Son of God will come again and judge the ungodly and change the sun, moon, and stars, and will truly rest on the seventh day. This will lead to the dawning of the sabbath of the millennial kingdom.[5]

Justin Martyr (ca. 100-165), an important Christian apologist of the second century, while granting that "many who belong to the pure and pious faith and are true Christians think otherwise" than he on the millennial issue, explicitly declares: "I and others are right-minded Christians in all points and are assured that there will be a resurrection of the dead and a thousand years in Jerusalem, which will then be built, adorned and enlarged."[6] Of Justin's testimony, Harnack declared in his article on the millennium in the great ninth and eleventh editions of the *Encyclopaedia Britannica*: "That a philosopher like Justin, with a bias towards an Hellenic construction of the Christian religion, should nevertheless have accepted its chiliastic elements is the strongest proof that these enthusiastic [sic] expectations were inseparably bound up with the Christian faith down to the middle of the second century."

Other Early Fathers of millennial persuasion were Irenaeus (*ca.* 130-200); Hippolytus of Rome (*ca.* 170-236); Julius Africanus (*ca.* 160-240);[7] Victorinus of Pettau (died *ca.* 304), whose views were censored by Jerome, an amillennialist, who produced an edition of his commentary on Revelation;[8] Tertullian[9] (*ca.* 160-220); Cyprian[10] (died *ca.* 258); and Lactantius[11] (*ca.* 240-320). Irenaeus's defense of his millennial beliefs at the end of the second century probably remains the most eloquent statement of the case:

> It behooves the righteous first to receive the promise of the inheritance which God promised to the fathers, and to reign in it when they rise again to behold God in this creation which is renovated, and that the judgment should take place afterwards. For it is just that in that very creation in which they toiled or were afflicted, being proved in every way by suffering, they should receive the reward of their suffering; and that in the creation in which they were slain because of their love to God, in that they should be revived again; and in that creation in which they endured servitude, in that they should reign. For God is rich in all things and all things are his. It is fitting, therefore, that the creation itself, being restored to its primeval condition, should be without restraint under the dominion of the righteous.[12]

In taking a pro-millennial viewpoint, these Fathers ranged themselves on the side of orthodoxy in two particulars. First, they supported the apostolicity and canonicity of Revelation (over against those who combined amillennialism with a denial of its authenticity).[13] Secondly, they opposed both the Gnostics, those early heretics whose dualistic spiritualizing of Christian doctrine completely wiped out eschatological hope, and Christian Platonists such as Origen[14] (*ca.* 185-254), whose rejection of a literal millennium stemmed from an idealistic depreciation of matter and a highly dangerous allegorical system of biblical interpretation.

It is a moot point as to whether other early Christian writings, such as the *Shepherd of Hermas,* the Clementine epistles, the *Didache,* the *Apocalypse of Peter,* the Letters of the Lyon martyrs, and those of Methodius of Tyre, Melito of Sardis, and Commodian show traces of millennialism. Polycarp of Smyrna (*ca.* 90-155) and Ignatius of Antioch (*ca.* 35-107) certainly do not—but little can be derived one way or the other from an argument from silence.

Active opposition to chiliastic views arose from several sources. First, there was Origen's influence (thus Eusebius's later shift to amillennialism and his false attribution of chiliastic origins to the heretic Cerinthus).[15] Second, anti-millennial reaction was produced by Montanist excesses, e.g., their prophetess's claim that "Christ came to me in the form of a Woman . . . and revealed to me that this place [the insignificant village of Pepuza] is holy and that here Jerusalem will come down from heaven."[16] Third, rejection of the millennium seemed the best defense against attempts to calculate the date of the end—a practice that has brought discredit, through guilt-by-association, to millennialism in every age.

No theologian of the ancient church had a greater influence on its history during the medieval period than Augustine (354-430). Once a chiliast himself, but driven away from that position by the "immoderate, carnal" extremism of some of its advocates,[17] he followed the symbolical-mystical system of biblical interpretation of the fourth-century Donatist, Tichonius, in arguing that the thousand years of Revelation 20 actually designated the interval "from the first coming of Christ to the end of the world, when he shall come the second time."[18] In this way, "a new era in prophetic interpretation" was introduced, in which Augustine's conception of the millennium as "spiritualized into a present politico-religious fact, fastens itself upon the church for about thirteen long centuries."[19] Millennialism did not die, but under the pressure of the "medieval synthesis" it tended to assume aberrant forms, particularly after the year 1000 when Augustinian chronology (if literalized) ran out. Thus, as is not infrequently the case, polar extremes developed: mystical, spiritualistic millennialisms presupposing the end of the church age, as represented by Joachim of Floris's "third age of the Spirit," and by Cathari, Spiritual Franciscans, and Waldenses; and grossly materialistic millennialisms bound up with the crusading enterprise, as il-

179

lustrated by Pope Urban II's harangue at Clermont: "As the times of Antichrist are approaching and as the East, and especially Jerusalem, will be the central point of attack, there must be Christians there to resist."[20]

Though both the Renaissance and Protestant Reformation stood against the world view of medieval scholasticism, they did not oppose the accepted Augustinian amillennialism. The Renaissance was too favorable toward Neo-Platonic modes of thought to be chiliastic, and the Reformers were so (legitimately) preoccupied with correcting the church's errors concerning basic salvation doctrine that little energy was left for eschatology. Beginning, however, with the pre-Reformers Wyclif and Hus, and going on to Luther, Calvin, and the doctrinal affirmations of Protestant orthodoxy, the papacy is identified with the Antichrist of biblical prophecy. This conviction led many Reformation Protestants to believe that the end of the world was at hand.[21]

Had it not been for the outbreak of chiliasm in particularly offensive form at the city of Münster in Germany (1534), early church teaching on the millennium might have been recovered along with other doctrines obscured in the medieval synthesis. The speculations of radicals, however, as concretized in Thomas Münzer's "Zion," were so offensive to all that this was rendered impossible. The Augsburg Confession (Lutheran) and the Helvetic Confession (Reformed)[22] expressly rejected such "Jewish opinions" (although they did not reject millennialism *per se*).[23]

Nearly all of the Reformation commentaries on Revelation 20 followed the Augustinian line, even when other aspects of their eschatology seemed to cry out for a millennial interpretation of the passage. The same was true even of Anabaptists: with the exception of Melchior Hofmann, only a few fringe figures of the Anabaptist movement were millennialists. The oft-heard claim that the mystic Jacob Boehme was a millennialist is repudiated by his own writings. In contrast, many of the seventeenth-century divines of the Westminster Assembly, e.g., Thomas Goodwin, were decidedly premillennial in their theology,[24] and "Cambridge Platonist" Henry More believed in a chiliastic future when "all the goodly Inventions of nice Theologers shall cease . . . and the Gospel shall be exalted."[25]

New England Puritanism, Continental Pietism, and the evangelical revivals of the eighteenth century were sufficiently distant in time or place from the events of the Reformation that perspective on the Reformers' limitations became possible. Among the results were increased missionary outreach and more careful eschatological study. Millennialism revived, and it was generally of the premillennial variety.[26] Except for Jonathan Edwards (1703-1758), who was postmillennial, virtually all the Christian leaders of colonial America maintained premillennialism: John Davenport (1597-1670); Samuel (1626-1671), Increase (1639-1723), and Cotton Mather (1663-1728); Samuel Sewall (1652-1730); Timothy Dwight (1752-1817); and others.[27] The Father of German Pietism, Philipp Jakob Spener (1635-1705), hymnwriter Joachim Lange (1670-1744), and the distinguished New Testament scholar J. A. Bengel (1687-1752) held millennial views. The hymns of John Wesley (1703-1791) attest to his early premillenarian belief, though later he embraced Bengel's concept of a future double millennium (the first on earth, with Satan bound; the second in heaven, representing the saints' rule with Christ).

In conclusion, it can hardly be maintained, as some have commonly alleged, that millennial belief did not have serious influence in Christendom prior to the rise of Adventist sects and the Plymouth Brethren in the nineteenth century and the appearance of the Scofield Reference Bible and the Fundamentalist movement early in the twentieth. Certainly, J. N. Darby and the Scofield editors introduced the church to Dispensationalism[28] as a special brand of premillennialism; but a premillenarian view of Revelation 20 logically did not require a dispensational framework of theology, and has in fact existed independently of it since the early days of the church.

Secular utopianism is a theme in the history of ideas correlative with the millennial hope, and it is instructive to note that where Christian millennial expectation has been absent or down-played, its utopian counterpart has entered the breach.[29] Greco-Roman civilization conceived of history cyclically, with the "golden age" as a future hope. During the amillennial Middle Ages, the legend of a mythical, idealistic kingdom in the East—under the rule of a Christian, "Prester John"—captured the imagination, and directly prompted men to explore for mythological sites (e.g., Ponce de Leon's search for the fountain of youth and Pizarro's quest for a *ciudad de oro*). The Renaissance, similarly unsympathetic to millennial doctrine, marked the beginning of literary utopianism with the work of Thomas More (1478-1535). The rise of the modern secular era during the deistic Enlightenment offered a secular alternative to the Christian millennium in what Carl Becker perceptively termed

181

"the heavenly city of the eighteenth-century philosophers." The Marxist goal of a "classless society," the Nazi dream of the thousand year *Reich*, and aspects of the capitalist-materialist "American way of life" are all inversions of the millennial hope. Eric Voegelin, in his multivolume series *Order and History*, has seen them rightly as illustrations of "metastatic gnosis": the idolatrous effort of man to create a millennial kingdom for himself without God. It would appear that the loss of theocentric millennialism leaves a vacuum into which rush the monstrosities of anthropocentric utopianism. At the same time, man's perennial utopian dreams can be viewed as the groping of the human soul, individual and collective, for the truth embodied in Christian eschatology. In this respect, as in all others—to quote amillennialist Augustine—"God has made us for himself, and our hearts are restless until they find their rest in him."

Conclusion

It is not the purpose of this chapter to decide the millennial question. Equally devout Bible scholars and theologians in times past— all seeking to honor the Lord Jesus Christ and to submit themselves to the authority of the Word of God—have disagreed on the subject. In our own day, sincere students of Scripture have immersed their minds in the prophetic texts and have arrived at differing conclusions.[30] Some are amillennialists and therefore interpret Revelation 20 in figurative terms—representing the present, heavenly reign of Christ, or the final victory of Christ, or a special ministry of Christ to and with those who have sealed their witness to Him with their blood. Others find themselves compelled to understand such passages as Revelation 20:1-10 and I Corinthians 15:22-28 in a way that commits them to a belief in a penultimate period in which the Lordship of Christ is expressed on the earth prior to the end. These Bible students may be postmillenialists (fairly rare today, but some still hold this view) or premillennialists, the latter being divided into a number of varieties of dispensational and nondispensational (or classical) premillennialists.

An important point to emphasize is that differences in this area pertain to the interpretation of certain prophetic passages in the Scriptures, not to the reality of the Second Advent—which the Ecumenical Creeds (Apostles, Nicene, and Athanasian) set forth as one of the defining marks of Christian orthodoxy. Although among

Christian believers very real differences of opinion prevail concerning the *manner* of Christ's coming and the chronology of events immediately surrounding it, there is no significant divergence of opinion among Christians concerning the central *fact* of His coming. All who know Him and trust Him look for Him to come a second time to establish His kingdom, to judge the world, and to receive His people. They may not be entirely certain concerning the manner in which God will finally work out His ultimate program— perhaps it will take *everyone* by surprise!—but there is no uncertainty in their hearts concerning His faithfulness to His promise.[31]

Notes

1. See, for example, R. D. Culver, *Daniel and the Latter Days* (Chicago: Moody, 1954); W. M. Smith, *World Crisis and the Prophetic Scriptures* (Chicago: Moody, 1951), pp. 179-237; W. M. Smith, *Israeli/Arab Conflict and the Bible* (Glendale, CA: Regal, 1967).

2. See chapter 8, "Evangelical Alternatives."

3. *The Christian Doctrine of Immortality* (Edinburgh: T. & T. Clark, 1896), p. 312.

4. Eusebius, *Ecclesiastical History*, III. xxxix. 12; Irenaeus, *Against All Heresies*, V. xxxiii. 3-4.

5. *Epistle of Barnabas*, 15:1-9.

6. *Dialogue with Trypho*, 80-81.

7. Cf. L. E. Froom, *The Prophetic Faith of Our Fathers*, I (Washington: Review & Herald, 1950), pp. 268-82. Note especially his helpful tabular summary of patristic views, pp. 458-59.

8. See J. Quasten, *Patrology* II (Utrecht: Spectrum, 1953), pp. 411-13; Froom, *Prophetic Faith*, I, pp. 337-44.

9. *Against Marcion*, iii. 24: *Apology* 48; see also Quasten, *Patrology* II, pp. 318, 339-40.

10. See Froom, *Prophetic Faith*, I, pp. 331-36.

11. *Divine Institutes*, vii. 14, 24, 26.

12. Irenaeus, *Against All Heresies*, V. xxxii. 1.

13. For example, Dionysius of Alexandria, as cited in Eusebius, *Ecclesiastical History*, VII. xiv. 1-3; xxiv. 6-8.

14. *Treatise on First Principles*, II. xi. 2.

15. *Ecclesiastical History*, III, xxviii.

16. Epiphanius, *Refutation of all Heresies*, xlix. 1.

17. *City of God*, xx. 7.

18. *Ibid.*, xx. 8.

19. Froom, *Prophetic Faith*, I, p. 479; see also his tabular summary of medieval views, pp. 896-97. Cf. also R. C. Petry, *Christian Eschatology and Social Thought* (New York: Abingdon, 1956), pp. 321-36.

20. On both varieties of medieval chiliasm, see Döllinger's "Essay on the Prophetic Spirit," published with his *Fables respecting the Popes* (1872); R. A. Knox, *Enthusiasm* (New York: Oxford Univ. Press, 1950), pp. 110-13; and especially N. Cohn, *The Pursuit of the Millennium . . . in Europe from the 11th to the 16th Century* (New York: Har. Row, 1961).

21. See T. F. Torrance, "The Eschatology of the Reformation" *Eschatology: Scottish Journal of Theology Occasional Papers*, II, (Edinburgh: Oliver & Boyd, 1953), pp. 36-62.

22. Augsburg Confession, Art. 17; Helvetic Confession, Art. 11.

23. Cf. G. N. H. Peters, *The Theocratic Kingdom* I (New York: Funk and Wagnall, 1884), pp. 531-34; M. Reu, *Lutheran Dogmatics* (1951), pp. 483-87.

24. See P. Schaff, *The Creeds of Christendom* I (New York: Harper, 1877), pp. 727-46.

25. See A. Lichtenstein, *Henry More* (Cambridge: Harvard Univ. Press, 1962), pp. 101-2.

26. Cf. the tabular summary of seventeenth and eighteenth century interpretations of Revelation 20 in Froom, *Prophetic Faith*, II (1948), pp. 786-87.

27. Tabulation of views in Froom, *Prophetic Faith*, III (1948), pp. 252-53.

28. Dispensationalism is a form of evangelical theology which has its origins in the nineteenth-century revival of the study of biblical prophecy and which is widely known through the *Scofield Reference Bible* (1909; rev. ed., 1917; *New Scofield*, 1967) and through the writings of many influential Bible teachers (e.g., J. N. Darby, W. Kelly, C. H. Mackintosh, L. S. Chafer, E. S. English, and J. Walvoord). This theological position is presently promulgated by Dallas Theological Seminary and many Bible colleges and institutes in the United States. Its name comes from the practice of dividing up the history of God's dealings with mankind into a series of ages or "dispensations," usually seven in number (the last of which is the millennium). C. C. Ryrie, *Dispensationalism Today* (Chicago: Moody, 1965) offers a responsible defense of dispensational theology, while G. E. Ladd, *The Blessed Hope* (Grand Rapids: Eerdmans, 1956) and O. T. Allis, *Prophecy and the Church* (Nutley, NJ: Presbyterian and Reformed, 1945) offer critiques of Dispensationalism from the point of view of classical premillennialism and amillennialism respectively. See also chapters 8 and 9 of this book.

29. See S. Baring-Gould, *Curious Myths of the Middle Ages* (London: R. Wington, 1868); E. Sanceau, *The Land of Prester John* (New York: Knopf,

1944); F. R. White, ed., *Famous Utopias of the Renaissance* (New York: Hendricks House, 1946); S. B. Liljegreh, *Studies on the Origin and Early Tradition of English Utopian Fiction* (Folcroft, PA: Folcroft, 1961); K. Mannheim, *Ideology and Utopia* (New York: HarBrace, 1955); G. Kateb, *Utopia and Its Enemies* (New York: Schocken, 1972); *Daedalus* (Spring 1965); and especially C. Walsh, *From Utopia to Nightmare* (London: Geoffrey Bles, 1962), E. L. Tuveson, *Millennium and Utopia* (Magnolia, MA: Peter Smith, 1964), and T. Molnat, *Utopia, the Perennial Heresy* (New York: Sheed & Ward, 1972).

30. Chapter 8 seeks to discuss the various alternative views held by orthodox Christians.

31. For a more detailed treatment of the entire subject of the millennium, see my article of the same title in the new edition of the *International Standard Bible Encyclopedia* (Grand Rapids: Eerdmans, 1976), from which this chapter has been largely extracted.

13

The Last Judgment

James P. Martin

This chapter approaches the subject of the Last Judgment primarily from the point of view of its function and place in the New Testament in relation to the gospel. It begins with the essential background in Jewish apocalyptic thought and in the Old Testament. Within the New Testament itself, the Last Judgment is treated in accordance with its place in the theological interpretations and messages of the different New Testament writings. We shall attempt to indicate throughout what the various authors hold in common in eschatology while trying to do justice to the distinctiveness of their thought and the language used to express it. The major problem of interpreting New Testament eschatology is to resolve the relation of present and future so that neither is lost but both are seen as essential parameters of the gospel.

Old Testament and Jewish Apocalyptic

The Last Judgment is the most characteristic expectation of Jewish apocalyptic thought. It is *the* great event in which God will vindicate His righteous purpose for all creation. The universe moves toward the day when God's justice finally will be established and be done—visibly.

Two matters are of considerable importance in understanding the Last Judgment in Old Testament and Jewish apocalyptic thought, and these matters pertain also to the interpretation of the Judgment in the New Testament. One is the relation of the Judgment to the basic apocalyptic doctrine of the two ages. What is the place of the Last Judgment with respect to the end of history? Does it close the present age and open the age to come, or does it precede (at least in part) a messianic kingdom as the final act of *history*? In other words, is the Last Judgment the *end* of history or a *prelude* to the end of history? The other matter is the variety of images and models of the Last Judgment in the Old Testament and in Jewish apocalyptic literature. The images and models seek to express certain important aspects of one judgment and must be interpreted as aspects and not as totally separate judgments.

Old Testament

The origin of the idea of a Last Judgment in the Old Testament may be found in the prophetic expectation of the Day of Yahweh (i.e., Day of the Lord, Day). This is the Day of Yahweh's judgment upon His foes and the vindication and triumph of His kingly rule. As Yahweh had intervened in Israel's past so would He intervene again to bring to fruition His saving purpose. Israel at the time of Amos expected the Day of Yahweh in the near future as a time of national triumph, as a day of light; but Amos announced that God would judge Israel also; that His day would be darkness because of Israel's crimes against justice and against God's righteousness.

Prophets after Amos spoke of the Day of Yahweh as the day of His judgment upon the nations of the world, including sinful Israel (Isa. 2:6-21; Zeph. 1−2). Judgment was announced frequently as a historical calamity, such as the destruction by the Babylonian armies. Because the prophets did not give up faith in the promises of Yahweh, the prophetic word did not end with calamity. Beyond judgment, Yahweh would establish a repentant and purified remnant of His people (Hos. 2:14 f.; Isa. 1:9 f.; 10:20 f.; Zeph. 3:8 ff.; Jer. 31:31; Ezek. 37).

Although the preexilic prophets looked upon the Day of Yahweh as the day of His vengeance upon the nation for its sins, the exilic and postexilic prophets spoke of a new and final act of Yahweh that would overthrow Babylon and restore Israel (Isa. 13:1−14:23). There would be a national resurrection and a restored Davidic state (Ezek. 37), a community established around a restored temple (Ezek. 40−48). Isaiah views this deliverance as a new exodus (Isa. 40−

66); others see it as a final battle between Yahweh and those who oppose His rule (Ezek. 38; Zech. 14) and as the outpouring of Yahweh's Spirit upon His people (Joel).

The return from Exile did not bring with it the Last Judgment, and in succeeding centuries the hope for Yahweh's final judgment took on more suprahistorical forms as apocalyptic thinkers extended the frame of reference of Yahweh's action from the historical to include the cosmological. In doing this, they were faithful to the prophets' basic stance of faith in Yahweh's Word (promise). It is important, therefore, to distinguish between the constant of Yahweh's revelation and the historical shape in which it was expressed in the thought forms and images of the times of the prophets and seers. When Yahweh revealed His Word to the prophets, he did not give away His sovereignty and freedom. The constant in God's revelation is the promise of the triumph of His righteousness over the whole creation. Consequently, the expansion of the expectation from the form it has in the prophets to that in the apocalyptic thinkers corresponds to a correct theological awareness of the scope of God's promise.

Apocalyptic thought presents as its basic doctrine the idea of the two ages, according to which it proclaims the final victory of the purpose of Almighty God. The Last Judgment marks the end of the present (evil) age (or, this age), and, along with the resurrection of the dead, ushers in the power of the age to come (or, the new age). A variety of concepts express the form and character of the apocalyptic Last Judgment. The two basic models are the catastrophic and the forensic. The recipients sometimes are Gentiles or the "wicked," who may include Jews. The Judge is either God Himself or the Messiah (the Elect One or the Son of Man). The Judgment is universal and ethical in character. Even the picture of the destruction of the Gentiles has an ethical core to it since Gentiles were guilty of idolatry, the worst of all possible sins in Jewish eyes. Often, the sin of idolatry is specified in the objects of God's judgment (Assumption of Moses 10:7; I Enoch 91:9; 99:7, 9).

At times the nation (Israel) occupies the center of interest for the portrayal of judgment; at other times judgment is seen in more individual terms (e.g., II Enoch). This development of individualization leads to the notion of the Last Judgment as a Great Assize, where justice is interpreted in forensic terms unlike those of the Old Testament Scriptures. This is the origin of the familiar judgment-seat

189

image, which is found also in the New Testament (II Cor. 5:10; Rev. 20:11 ff; a throne designates the judgment seat since the offices of ruler and judge were combined in ancient society). Daniel combines catastrophic and forensic elements in a judgment that embraces the dead as well as the living. Sometimes two judgments are envisaged, first a catastrophic historical judgment followed by a forensic judgment on the Last Day. This view is sometimes allied with a scheme of weeks (e.g. the Apocalypse of Weeks). *The Testament of Abraham* portrays three different judgments and three different judges, probably to combine all possible forms of judgment and so exclude the idea that anyone would escape judgment. Nevertheless, the heart of all such speculations was the conviction that God's saving purpose would triumph, that He would save His people, and that all evil would be punished and the good rewarded. The whole universe finally would acknowledge His sovereignty.

The complex of ideas concerning the Last Judgment in Jewish apocalyptic thought indicates the unsystematic and varied forms of eschatological expectation in Judaism. Variety was also characteristic of judgment in New Testament times; and it is dangerous to try to control the interpretation of New Testament views on the Last Judgment by appealing to a few ideas or models in Jewish apocalyptic literature, even though this apocalyptic thought is vital for understanding New Testament eschatology. In neither Old Testament prophecy nor Jewish apocalyptic thought does God give a blueprint of the future, but, rather, He calls His people to have faith in the triumph of His saving purpose. The saints of the Most High will inherit the everlasting kingdom of God (Dan. 7) because God has so promised it. God's judgments are a fulfillment of the promise that His righteousness will triumph over all the wickedness and rebellion of mankind and angels and demons. In understanding the biblical view of divine judgment, faith and ethics must be kept together. The interrelation of faith and ethics varies in different theological perspectives. For the apocalypticists of Judaism, the Last Judgment was a comfort; for the rabbis it was used for exhortation to right living. Consequently, whereas the apocalypticists fled into the future to endure the present, the rabbis took the present seriously to endure the Last Judgment. The same patterns have been repeated in Christian thought as well. Saint Hilary summed it up well when he remarked that one day was hidden that all days may be observed.

New Testament

In Jewish eschatology, the dividing point marking the end of the present age and the beginning of the new lay in the future (either in a sudden end to history or an end inaugurated by the Messiah). For the New Testament writers, however, the division between the ages is Jesus Christ. The place of the Last Judgment in New Testament theology, therefore, can be understood only in terms of the inherited eschatology of the two ages and in terms of the life, death, and resurrection of Jesus Christ as God's eschatological event. The Last Judgment belongs to the subject matter of the whole gospel where everything is eschatological. Eschatology cannot be extracted and isolated as a doctrine in itself, existing in independent life alongside other doctrines. Our task, therefore, is to interpret the present and future reality of divine judgment so as to hold both in a common view, neither allowing the Last Judgment to fly loose into a far-off future nor to be totally absorbed—to disappear in some concept of present judgment by human decision.

All the New Testament theologians share the doctrine of the two ages and all embrace what we may call a double eschatology: not only the future but also the present is "eschatological." This is so not because of calculation of apocalyptic weeks or "times and seasons" (which is expressly forbidden in the New Testament—see Acts 1:7) but because of the central and common conviction that Jesus Christ marks the beginning of the age to come. In Him the end-time has already come—the eschatological future has appeared and claims the present. Thus, the resurrection of Jesus Christ from the dead is the first fruits of them that sleep.

The Last Judgment, therefore, can be spoken of in a traditional way as still future, as belonging to the end of history. As an end-event, it belongs also with the resurrection of the dead and the *parousia* of Christ. But because the Lord whose *parousia* ends history is already known as Jesus Christ, the final judgment is also described as a present event, inaugurated in Christ and therefore standing over the present world and encountering it in the word of preaching about Jesus Christ. The future-yet-present judgment may be understood better if we think of the two ages in a biblical way as two spheres of power and not merely as two lengths of chronological time. The power of the age to come enters with Jesus Christ into the power of the present age. The result is conflict: the church serves in the present under the Lordship of the Christ who continues to extend His Lordship until the consummation (I Cor. 15:24-28). The New Testament can speak easily of a real future consummation in time and of the present as real eschatological time. Usually we must use words such as *inauguration, anticipation, proleptic* in attempting to express the peculiar New Testament consciousness of time after Jesus' resurrection as eschatological time.

These considerations are important if we wish to understand the complex way in which the different New Testament writers speak of the eschatological judgment of God. In addition to the present-future complexity, a wealth of language describing the Last Judgment in the New Testament uses many associated terms that do not include the word *judgment.* Indeed, the term *Last Judgment* is not found at all in the New Testament. Thus, "wrath (of God)," "coming wrath," "day," "day of the Lord," "day of Christ," "destruction," and "justification" are some of the terms used as surrogates for the word *judgment.*

The expectation, taken over from Jewish apocalyptic thought, of a messianic kingdom preceding and preparing for the end is found in two basic forms in the New Testament. The dominant form is that of the present ongoing reign of Christ from resurrection to *parousia.* Paul uses this model in I Corinthians 15:24 ff. and generally elsewhere. The emphasis is on the subjection of all of God's enemies and the final victory of His rule through His Christ. This final victory is the positive side of the Last Judgment. The other model of a messianic kingdom is the millennial one found only in Revelation 20. The interpreters are sharply divided as to whether this image of a thousand-year kingdom represents Paul's view or stands in contradiction to it by placing the messianic reign totally in the future. The problem then becomes: When does this future reign commence? For our purposes, it is sufficient to note that the thousand-year kingdom, too, ends with final judgment.

With these preliminary observations behind us, we now turn to the theme of eschatological judgment in the New Testament. We shall proceed by commenting on various writers to show how their special emphases on the judgment relate to their understanding of salvation. For we must not forget that grace and salvation are primary and dominant in New Testament theology, and that judgment enters the world precisely because of the salvation offered in Jesus Christ. Therefore, we shall speak first of all about eschatological judgment in the synoptic Gospels—Matthew, Mark, and Luke, then in the Gospel according to John, the Revelation to John, and finally Paul and Hebrews. Acts will be mentioned along with our study of the Gospel according to Luke since both exhibit the theology of their common author.

Synoptic Gospels

According to the synoptic Gospels, the message of Jesus in both word and deed was the coming kingdom of God. The kingdom of God (heaven) is the eschatological rule of Yahweh associated, in Jewish hope as we have seen, with the end of this age. In the preaching of Jesus, the kingdom is announced as both *present* ("come"—Luke 17:20 f.; cf. 7:22) and *future* ("impending, at hand"—Mark 1:14-15). According to Matthew, John the Baptist also proclaimed the kingdom and explicitly announced the Last Judgment in connection with it (Matt. 3:7-12; cf. Luke 3:7-9) as an event already beginning: "already the axe . . ." (although John the Baptist represents Jewish, not Christian, expectation). In Jesus' proclamation, on the other hand, the emphasis is on the kingdom as God's power for salvation (Luke 4:18; cf. 7:22-23). The present, therefore, is the time of grace, and the Last Judgment is shifted into the future. Any idea of a present judgment in the proclamation of Jesus is attached to the call to repentance, to faith in God's decisive eschatological act in Jesus Christ (Luke 7:23). Faith in Jesus as bringer of the kingdom or rejection of God's offer of the kingdom in Jesus becomes, consequently, a form of self-judgment, which, in turn, is integrally related to the Last Judgment executed by the Son of Man (Luke 9:26).

Among the parables of Jesus, which are to be interpreted as "stories" (a narrative with a beginning and an end) of the coming, rule, and effects of the kingdom of God, we find some which do conclude with a warning of judgment (Luke 18:1-8). But it is not correct to generalize on this fact without giving special attention to the particular emphasis made by the writers of the Gospels. Whereas we may detect a common teaching of judgment (Last Judgment in the sense of God's final judgment, and also self-judgment through the decision of faith) in all three synoptic Gospels, there are differences within the three that must be noted. These differences have to do with the selection of the traditions about Jesus preferred by the evangelists for their inspired theological purposes. Furthermore, their selection is bound up with the historical situation out of which and for which they wrote. We must take seriously the fact that we have four Gospels in the New Testament and not one. It is therefore misleading to quickly harmonize all the Gospels with respect to their teaching on eschatological judgment (or any other matter).

Consequently, we observe that the Last Judgment appears much more sharply and prominently in the Gospel according to Matthew than it does in Mark and Luke. We must ask why this is so. Matthew specially emphasizes final judgment, both in the future sense of the end, and in the sense of the finality of the decision for or against Jesus Christ as God's offer of the kingdom. Matthew alone gives us the special parables of judgment, such as the Wise and Foolish Virgins (25:1-13) attached to his version of the parable of the Talents (25:14-30), followed by the unique parable of the Last Judgment by the Son of Man (25:31-46). Matthew gives seven references to Gehenna (5:22,29,30; 10:28; 18:9; 23:15,33); Mark has one (repeated three times in 9:43-47) and Luke has one (12:5, which speaks of the power of God). Matthew speaks more frequently of fire as a metaphor for the Last Judgment (3:10-12 in the teaching of John the Baptist; 5:22; 13:40,42,50 in the parables of the kingdom; 18:8-9; 25:41). It should be noted, however, that fire may be used as a metaphor of destruction because of uselessness in this life (Matt. 7:19; probably also 5:22).

The emphasis on judgment in Matthew no doubt reflects the Jewish-Christian milieu of the book. The contemporary Jewish coloration of God's destructive judgment upon the Gentiles is transmuted into judgment upon all those who reject the gospel. This judgment falls also upon those who, according to Matthew's view, pervert the gospel by a false use of it. Matthew always has two perversions in view, both of which arise from a basic misunderstanding of the place of the law in Christian life. These perversions are: complete rejection of any validity to law (antinomianism), and assertion that the law in the sense of casuistic legalism is absolutely central to Christian life (legalism). According to Matthew (Sermon on the Mount, especially in 5:16 ff.), the gospel saves us from both perversions. The church of Matthew was caught up in a severe struggle with the synagogue. This explains why the question of the law figures so prominently in Matthew and also why Jesus' pronouncement of judgment receives such emphasis. At the same time, Matthew is well aware of the universal claim and offer of the gospel and understands Jesus as the Son of Man who identifies Himself with the poor and wretched of all

194

history, just as He did in the days of His flesh. Consequently, the Last Judgment, portrayed most powerfully in the famous picture of Matthew 25:1-46, embraces all nations who, through their ministry to the poor or their refusal of it, are inevitably involved in the final judgment of and by the exalted Son of Man.

Matthew does not allow us to escape into futurism, either by forgetting the present or by calculation of times and seasons. Rather, the gospel calls us to present involvement in the world because of the Incarnation ("God with us," Matt. 1:23) and exaltation (the Great Commission, Matt. 28:18-20). All *will* face the exalted Son of Man in His future judgment; all *now* face His contemporary judgment in His call to love our neighbor. What we do under the present judgment will determine how we do in the future judgment.

Matthew calls believers to live under the Judge, not in fear or in little faith, but in confident watching. Watching (Matt. 24:45-51) does not mean calculating when the end of history will occur, but living every moment of one's life under God's promise for the future. The expectation of future judgment serves as a basis for exhortation to watchfulness. Watchfulness, nevertheless, is not retreat from the world into passivity, but a call to remember why we have been called and for what future.

Because response to the gospel is the standard of judgment, Matthew, like Mark and Luke, commonly uses the model of separation in some descriptive scenes of the Last Judgment (24:40 f.; 25:11, 46). The vividness of these scenes (cf. Luke 17:34-35) is not intended to portray temporal suddenness of separation, but the difference between appearance and reality. These texts, therefore, cannot be used for false comfort of a rapture with its escape from the cross, but are for warning and exhortation to take heed to the reality of faith in view of the coming final judgment. Whereas man looks on the outward appearance (i.e., religious experience), God looks upon the heart (trust and faith). The difference between appearance and reality belongs also to Matthew's frequent denunciation of hypocrisy as the worst of all sins (Matt. 23).

In the apocalyptic discourse of Jesus in Matthew 24, the present and future again are joined with the fall of Jerusalem (judgment upon contemporary Judaism) and the final judgment at the end of history fused in prophetic vision. As in Mark (chap. 13), the discourse in Matthew is designed to warn believers against a false expectation of the end of history that would lead them to abandon life under the sign of the cross in favor of either triumphalist Christian living or an apocalyptic fanaticism totally absorbed with the "when" of the end. In the present time, the preaching of the gospel throughout the whole world occupies the center of the stage of world history. This proclamation (Great Commission) takes place in the midst of the ongoing present evil age. The church is not removed before the end from the suffering of this present time into the glory of the age to come. Along with this warning of tribulation (the believers' equivalent of bearing the cross), rejection, and misunderstanding, the discourse speaks of the assurance of the end and the final victory of the Son of Man. The pattern of present-future tribulation and final victory of God over all His enemies with the consequent deliverance of His elect is a common pattern in Jewish apocalyptic thought. Here, however, the pattern is thoroughly Christian because the task of proclaiming the gospel and the vital matter of knowing just who God's Christ really is (24:23-24) is central. The discourse serves, therefore, as an exhortation to faithfulness and as a comfort for those persecuted because of their faith in Christ.

The apocalyptic discourse holds present and future together. We would, however, misinterpret it if we tried to spread it out along a time line to see a print-out of the future, because the heart of the discourse is faith in Jesus Christ, who went to His cross, commissioned His church to preach the gospel, and called it to take up the cross and follow Him. The church's preaching of the gospel to all nations is, therefore, the only genuine *sign* of the end of history. Wars, historical tribulations, and persecutions come and go; indeed the whole time between Christ's resurrection and *parousia* is characterized by such "worldliness." The church is called to obedience *in* such a world, not to seek escape *out* of it.

All three synoptic evangelists (Mark 13; Matt. 24; Luke 17 and 21) employ the apocalyptic discourse of Jesus as a rebuke to a triumphalist church, as a rejection of a theology of glory before the *parousia* and Last Judgment, as a call to live under the cross in the world, and as an exhortation to the church to persevere in mission as a sign that the end has come. The faithfulness of the church prepares the world for the Last Judgment and the unfaithfulness of the church brings it under divine judgment. The evangelists know of no church that is allowed to isolate itself from the world and observe the Last Judgment as a spectator. Rather, the gospel calls the church into the judgment of God because it calls the church to the *righteousness of God* (Matt. 5:6; 6:33; 7:1).

Mark and Luke do not give as much attention to the judgment as Matthew does for reasons mentioned earlier. Instead, they emphasize the time of salvation inaugurated in Jesus Christ. According to Luke, the present (time of Christ) is the "acceptable year of the Lord" (Luke 4:19), not the day of vengeance of our God. The day of vengeance lies at the end of history and is guaranteed by the resurrection of Christ from the dead (Acts 17:31). The criterion of the judgment of the last day is acceptance or rejection of the gospel about Jesus Christ (Acts 17:30; Luke 19:21; 7:47; 10:16).

With Mark and Luke too, we cannot view the Last Judgment as a disconnected far-off divine event, nor as an imminent event that preoccupies all our attention and anxiety. Instead, Luke announces the divine judgment in Jesus Christ that comes as grace, offer, and promise, as the kingdom of God. We are invited to enter this rule as the *present* center of Christian life because it is the future certainty of Christian life. Luke so employs the apocalyptic discourse of Jesus to warn the church that the Last Day is after all really in God's hands and time, not ours (Luke 17:22). The world continues much as before (Luke 17:20 ff.—"as it was in the days of Noah . . . "), yet divine judgment is certain (Luke 17:30; 18:7). In the assurance that God will vindicate His chosen, now is the time to pray and not faint (Luke 18:1), because in Jesus Christ the kingdom of God is in our midst (Luke 17:20-21).

Because grace has come in Jesus Christ beyond measure, the judgment of God will be most severe upon those who reject this grace. It will be more tolerable for Sodom on that day than for the city that rejects the gospel of the kingdom of God (Luke 10:12, cf. vv. 13-15). Both the queen of the South and Nineveh will arise and condemn the generation that refuses Jesus Christ (Luke 11:29-32). These severe warnings do not justify the church's pronouncing condemnation on everyone in sight who seems not to respond to the preaching of the gospel, but they are an invitation to the church to be faithful in manifesting the grace, love, and mercy of the kingdom of God in the present time.

We have observed that the Sermon on the Mount (in Matthew) spoke explicitly of judgment, probably because of the problem of the law in Matthew's Jewish-Christianity. The Sermon on the Plain (not Mount) as recorded in Luke, on the other hand, because it does not deal with the problem of the law, proclaims love and mercy as the two ethical realities of the Christian life. Both Matthew and Luke, however, end the Sermon with the famous parable of the Last Judgment, which employs traditional flood imagery to depict judgment. The parable exhorts the reader to do the words of Jesus, not just hear them. Once again, the evangelists call their readers into the process of divine judgment and do not allow any to escape into the role of an observer.

The scenario of darkness and earthquake used by the synoptic evangelists for the crucifixion of Jesus was traditional for the Last Judgment (Mark 15:33; Matt. 27:45, 51 ff.; Luke 23:44). Matthew heightens these features somewhat. The condemnation of Jesus to death becomes in the event of His crucifixion a judgment on the world, an anticipation of the Last Judgment. Thus, in a sense not spelled out in the first three Gospels, the death of Jesus is the judgment of the world. What is alluded to descriptively in the synoptic crucifixion stories is declared more openly and theologically in the Gospel according to John.

The Gospel According to John

The fourth Gospel maintains the same basic apocalyptic eschatology as the synoptic Gospels, but shifts more in the direction of the *present* as the decisive time of judgment. John does, of course, speak explicitly of the last day, particularly with reference to resurrection (6:39-40, 44, 54). But resurrection involves judgment and division: the resurrection to life and the resurrection to condemnation (5:28-29).

The origin of the present-ness of the Last Judgment is the death of Jesus. The hour of His crucifixion, which is paradoxically called the hour of His glorification (2:4; 7:30,39; 8:20; 12:27), is the judgment of this world, the casting out of the prince of this age (12:31). In the crucifixion narrative, John expresses this with fine irony. Pilate places Jesus on the judgment seat and then passes the sentence of condemnation on Him (19:12-16, especially the variant reading in v. 13). Thereby Pilate condemns himself.

Jesus' death as the judgment of the world not only opens up the salvation Jesus brings through His own resurrection from the dead (which fulfills in a present sense the signs of His ministry), but it also brings judgment upon the whole world so that the word and deed of

Jesus becomes the absolute criterion of judgment. Indeed, Jesus Himself is the Judge, along with the Father (12:47-48; 5:22, 27, 30; 8:15-16). The apparent contradictions between these references are actually paradoxes that preserve the tension between present and future judgment. So certain is the divine judgment given to the Son by the Father that John can summarize his entire story of Jesus in terms of final judgment: "And this is the judgment, that the light has come into the world, and men loved darkness rather than light, because their deeds were evil" (3:19). Also, "he who does not obey the Son shall not see life, but the wrath of God rests upon him" (3:36). Nevertheless, John will insist that the purpose of the sending of the Son is not condemnation, but salvation (3:17; 12:47). Men bring condemnation upon themselves by their refusal to believe. This refusal becomes an anticipatory Last Judgment (3:18, 36). The present judgment, then, is not so much an external divine sentence, but a revelation of the secret of the heart. The last day will reveal these secrets. Jesus now stands in the world as the True Light, to lighten everyone (1:9), to give sight (8:12, 9:39), and thereby judge the hearts of mankind.

Finally, the sending of the Spirit by the risen Christ is for the purpose of convincing the world of sin, righteousness, and judgment. The Spirit convicts the world, because the ruler of this world is judged (16:8,11). Accordingly, the Jesus who was condemned to death in His trial is present in the *Paraclete* (the RSV's "Counselor") after His passion, and the fact that Jesus stands justified before the Father means that Satan has been condemned and has lost his power over the world.

The Gospel of John and the First Epistle of John emphasize the inaugurated or present form of the eschatological event, which the Book of Revelation presents in terms of final (future) eschatology. The task of interpretation is to know how to hold together both the present and future of the Last Judgment. This is not possible in terms of calculating times and seasons; it is possible only in terms of the past and future of Jesus Christ and His present-ness through the Word of proclamation, the testimony of the Spirit, and the hearing of faith.

The Revelation to John

Judgment in the Apocalypse of John is not sheer future event. The

Book of Revelation is intensely concerned with present judgments of God. Our conclusions concerning the Gospel of John apply equally to the Apocalypse of John: judgment, both present and future, is thoroughly Christocentric. Take Christ out of the Apocalypse and the result is not even a reasonable Jewish apocalypse, but a jumble of meaningless symbols.

Christ, the "one like unto a son of man" (1:13), exercises present judgment upon the churches, which are judged with respect to their fidelity, or lack of it, to their Lord. These judgments are not retributive and final, but educative and preliminary. This is indicated by the call to repentance and the promise attached (2:5, 16, 22; 3:19). Faithfulness to Christ is shown by the churches' works (2:2, 19, 26; 3:1, 8, 15). The author of the book intends his readers to take seriously these judgments against the churches. They go on throughout the course of history until the end and cannot be relegated to any narrow past or future period of time, e.g., apostolic age, or after a rapture.

Equally important is the fact that the preliminary and educative judgments also come upon the pagan world. The series of plagues, symbolized in seals, trumpets, woes, and vials, represent these preliminary judgments of God. Their partial character is emphasized (8:7-12), which reinforces the educative intent of the judgments. They are not always successful (16:9-11). The plagues in chapters 6–19 do not, therefore, portray the final and irrevocable judgment, but preliminary ones that call the pagan world to repentance, just as Christ's preliminary judgments on the churches call them to repentance. In the case of the churches, the call to repentance is a call to return to the Christ whom they know, or have known. In the case of the pagan world, it is a basic call to repent, that is, to turn to Christ for the first time. It is wrong interpretation to apply these preliminary judgments on the world in a mechanical way to Jews of a future time, as many interpreters in the so-called prophetic schools do. This interpretation fails to distinguish between the preliminary and the final judgment. More seriously, this interpretation loses sight of the truly dominant Christocentric character of all portrayals of judgment in the Apocalypse. "Prophetic" interpretation removes Christ out of present history, dissociates Him from the churches in any living way, and relegates His judging activity to some unknown future. In this way judgment becomes always retributive, catastrophic, even unethical. The active Lordship of Christ over present history is dissolved into an abstraction.

The entire picture of judgment in the Apocalypse is Christocentric, beginning from the judgments on the churches to the judgment on the pagans (1:7), the dragon (12:9; 20:2, 10), the beasts (13:1, 11), and their followers (14:9-10; 19:19-21). Faith in Christ or rejection of Christ is the criterion of all judgment. The reason for this is that judgment is a dimension of God's righteousness and His righteousness has been revealed in His Messiah, Jesus. The predominant symbol of Christ the Judge is the Lamb slain (chap. 5). The vision of the slain Lamb is the key to the Christology of the whole book. The Lamb is worthy to fulfill God's saving purpose for history and this task carries with it the activity of judgment. This is why judgment is such a central feature in the Book of Revelation. Judgment is God's action in finally overcoming the opposition to Himself and His Christ and so actualizing His perfect righteousness.

The picture of final judgment in the Apocalypse, which marks the end of all educative preliminary judgments, is symbolized in the great white throne scene (20:11-15). Here the scope of final judgment is universal: it includes the dead. This judgment confirms the verdict men have passed on themselves by their attitude toward God and His saving work in Jesus Christ. The final judgment is necessitated by man's unceasing rebellion, not by any vindictiveness in the nature of God. The wrath of God, which is the negative experience of His holy love, nevertheless serves His love (saving purpose). Finally, therefore, the Last Judgment in the Apocalypse of John throws us all into the mystery of God's holy love and brings us ultimately to God Himself. This is the vital reality that never should be lost or obscured by the apocalyptic symbolic forms of the representation of the Last Judgment.

As does the rest of the New Testament, the Book of Revelation confronts us *now* with God's enactment of His judgment in history through Christ. The educative judgments reveal God's long-suffering. The gospel of Christ crucified and risen still is the heart of the eschatology of the Book of Revelation, and judgment must be interpreted as a Christological matter.

Paul

Formally, Paul holds to the same duality of future and present judgment as do the other theologians of the New Testament. Materially, his terminology is different, and his solution to the relation between present and future judgment, though thoroughly Christ-ocentric, is expressed in terms of the gospel of the righteousness of God and the justification of the ungodly.

Unlike Jewish apocalyptic literature and that of the Qumran community and Gnosticism, there is nothing in man, according to Paul, that is of itself redeemable at the Last Judgment. The whole person stands under condemnation: there is none righteous, neither Jew nor Greek (Rom. 1:18–3:20). Paul's argument against religious man (both Jewish and Greek types) is predicated on the certain expectation of the Last Judgment. This expectation is "according to the gospel," which Paul preaches (Rom. 2:2, 5, 11-12, 16; 3:6, 9, 19-20; cf. also Acts 17:30-31). Confronted with the judgment of God, against which there is no excuse and which exposes all as ungodly, how can anyone escape condemnation? Only in Jesus Christ!

Justification, that is, freedom from condemnation in anticipation of the Last Judgment, comes through faith in Christ. Faith in Christ means total surrender of my future to the future of God promised in the resurrection of Jesus from the dead (Rom. 3:21; 5:9, 11; 8:1, 31-39). Also, through the Spirit there is freedom for life *now,* justification *now* (Rom. 5:9), right relation to God *now* (Rom. 3:21; II Cor. 5:21), reconciliation *now* (Rom. 5:11; II Cor. 5:17-21); freedom for work that is pleasing to God and freedom to fulfill the law through love of the neighbor (Gal. 5:13 f.).

Justification is a proleptic Last Judgment in that the sentence of condemnation is removed. Grace has encountered the ungodly and has conquered in love. The law of the Spirit of life in Christ Jesus has freed the believer from the law of sin and death (Rom. 8:2). This essential relation between justification and judgment (condemnation) is drawn by Paul in many passages where he combines the terminology of radical judgment ("wrath," "condemnation," "death") with the terminology of justification ("righteousness," "faith," "justified"). Some examples that merit study are: Romans 1:17-18; 4:13, 15; 5:9-12, 16; 8:2; II Corinthians 3:9-16; I Corinthians 1:18; II Corinthians 2:15; Romans 8:13. This confrontation of present/future terminology is found wherever Paul interprets the saving event of God in Jesus Christ. The peculiar Pauline emphasis, wherein he differs from traditional Jewish apocalyptic thought, is on the "already," the "now" (Rom. 3:21; 4:15; 5:11; 8:3; 10:4; I Cor. 15:21), even though death is the last enemy to be destroyed.

The differentiation of justified and nonjustified is related to proclamation (I Cor. 1:18; II Cor. 2:15 f.). The gospel announces life in Christ to the ungodly and therefore releases them, through faith, from condemnation. Nevertheless, in Christ, believers know that the Last Judgment has not disappeared from the history of the world or off the face of the future, but manifests its condemnation everywhere in that the wrath of God is revealed against all ungodliness (Rom. 1:18-32). The paradox of this present revelation of wrath and the last day as the future day of wrath, is known only in Christ and in faith.

If Paul has solved, in terms of his justification in Christ, the problem of how the ungodly may stand in God's judgment, he has at the same time posed another problem for the believer by holding fast to the judgment according to work. How can the believer be justified by faith and free from condemnation and also subject to a final judgment according to his lifework? The work is the life built upon the one foundation, Jesus Christ. The Day of Judgment will test this work and may destroy it, but without destroying the believer thereby. He will be saved even though he suffer the loss of this work when the fire of that Day reveals it to be wood, hay, and stubble (I Cor. 3:11-15). All must appear before the judgment seat of Christ to receive good or evil according to what each has done in the body (II Cor. 5:10).

The solution to this apparent contradiction is that for Paul the Last Judgment is not simply an event of condemnation (with the only problem then being how to avoid it), but it is, above all else, the event of the triumph of God's righteousness over the world. Therefore, it must include the manifestation of the good and the right, the work that corresponds to God's work. In this positive sense, judgment is correlative to salvation. Resurrection and judgment cover between them the entire religious destiny of mankind. Mankind is to be healed and transfigured, justified and set right ethically and morally. Through judgment, God vindicates and finishes His saving purpose.

The basic theological term in Paul's vocabulary is, then, *righteousness of God.* God's righteousness is the righteousness by which He makes the sinner righteous and the world "right." The scope of the saving action of God's righteousness embraces the entire creation (Rom. 8:18 ff.). The believer, knowing that no power in heaven or on earth (Rom. 8:38-39) can destroy him, and through faith being freed from condemnation, lives in Christ for the world, for the love of the neighbor. In this life the believer shows that he knows the judgment of God.

It is important to remember that Paul's letters deal primarily with churches of believers and not with mankind in general terms. In Romans, however, he does consider the world of mankind, and here we may expect to find clearer statements on the destiny of the unbeliever faced with the present call to faith and with the Last Judgment. In the present time, the wrath of God is revealed (Rom. 1:18) to frustrate and disappoint man's idolatries and his suppression of the truth in unrighteousness. Through this frustration, God seeks to lead man to repentance. God is long-suffering in this (Rom. 2:4). Rebellious man cannot forever elude the final wrath of God, however, and he will be brought face to face with God in the last day (Rom. 5:9-11). The wrath of God is the expression of God's holy love, which finally exposes man's rebellion for what it is. Wrath is future and eschatological in this sense. Paul does not speculate about this final confrontation. He is too overwhelmed with the present power of God's love in Christ as the way out of rebellion and the way to live with God.

The basic frame of thought of Paul, as well as the other New Testament theologians, is the apocalyptic doctrine of the two ages. This framework is filled with the saving work of God in Jesus Christ. The gospel calls man to repentance, to faith, and offers reconciliation, justification, freedom, life in Christ. The gospel forms the heart of Pauline eschatology. The Last Judgment is therefore not a separable element to be isolated from the gospel and relegated to a remote future. Rather, the Judgment is an eschatological event brought near in the word of preaching (I Cor. 1:18-25; 2:1-5). Paul "sits loose" to the question of "How long?" or "When?" He looks back to the historical revelation and forward to the last day, but the center of his vision is the living God revealed in Jesus Christ, the Judge of the Last Judgment.

Hebrews

The eschatological exhortation of the Epistle to the Hebrews exhibits the same concern as the rest of the New Testament for present and future judgment. The Day is the last day of condemnation and salvation, but the emphasis throughout is on the eschatological *now*, qualified by a warning against realized eschatology (triumphalism and perfectionism).

14

ISRAEL AND THE CHURCH (TWO VIEWS)

The New Israel

Edmund P. Clowney

"For we are the circumcision, who worship by the Spirit of God, and glory in Christ Jesus, and have no confidence in the flesh" (Phil. 3:3).

To grasp the full meaning of that amazing sentence we must remember the author. The apostle Paul makes that easy, for in the following passage of his letter to the Philippians he describes himself— "circumcised the eighth day, of the stock of Israel, of the tribe of Benjamin, a Hebrew of Hebrews . . . " (v. 5).

Can an Israelite aware of his genealogy call those who are, like him, circumcised, the "concision"[1] and declare that the *true* circumcision is found among uncircumcised Gentiles in Greece? Or, if it is conceivable that a Jew should say such a thing, must he not be a renegade who has broken with the faith of his fathers and despised his inheritance in Israel?

But Paul does not speak as a renegade. When he was accused before the governor Felix of profaning the temple as "a ringleader of the sect of the Nazarenes" (Acts 24:5), he replied, "But this I confess unto thee, that after the Way which they call a sect, so serve I the God of our fathers, believing all things which are according to the law, and which are written in the prophets . . . " (v. 14).

The "Way" proclaimed by Paul among the Gentiles is the way by which the true Israel serves "the God of our fathers." Paul's accusers

Scripture quoted in this chapter is from the New International Version unless otherwise indicated.

call it a sect, but for Paul it is the way of God, and therefore the way of the people of God. It is the path of obedient service and true worship followed by those who believe what is written in the Law and the Prophets, and confess their fulfillment in Jesus Christ.

The People of God

Who are the people of God? The Bible throughout gives one answer to this question. The people of God are those called, claimed, and redeemed by God in His salvation. Peter writes to the New Testament church: "But ye are an elect race, a royal priesthood, a holy nation, a people for God's own possession, that ye may show forth the excellencies of him who called you out of darkness into his marvelous light: who in time past were no people, but now are the people of God: who had not obtained mercy, but now have obtained mercy" (I Peter 2:9-10).

This statement of the nature and calling of the church is a composite of three Old Testament passages (Exod. 19:6; Isa. 43:20-21; Hos. 1:6, 9; 2:1). These passages draw together the sweep of Old Testament teaching about the people of God and proclaim their fulfillment in the New Testament church. The foundation passage is Exodus 19:6, which declares the realization of God's covenant as it is established at Sinai with His people. This covenant promise is the background for the prophetic declarations in Isaiah 43:20-21 (Septuagint) and in Hosea 1:6-2:1. The covenant relation of "your God/my people" has been disrupted by sin; Israel has been made *Lo-Ammi*, "not my people." But by God's grace, say the prophets, the covenant will be renewed and God's purposes realized with unimagined fullness.

Peter announces that this prophetic promise has been fulfilled. Gentiles, who are no people of God, and Jews, whose position has been forfeited through sin, are united in the church as the people of God. *Ammi*, "my people," is the name pronounced upon them.

In Paul's language, the Gentiles who were "separate from Christ, alienated from the commonwealth of Israel, and strangers from the covenants of the promise, having no hope and without God in the world" (Eph. 2:12) are strangers and sojourners no longer but now are "fellow-citizens with the saints, and of the household of God" (v. 19) built together as a temple of God's dwelling.

Neither Paul nor Peter conceive of Gentile Christians as remaining outside the ancient people of God. They *were* aliens, strangers, or at best sojourners (all terms used in the Old Testament of non-Israelites),

208

but presently they are citizens, saints, children of the household (all terms used in the Old Testament of Israelites).[2] To be outside the people of God is to be without God and without hope in the world. But to be joined to Jesus Christ is to be heir to all the covenant promises and a member of the commonwealth of Israel, for in Christ the old wall of partition that shut out the Gentiles has been broken down (v. 14).

Why is it that Paul describes Gentiles as without God, without hope, and separated from Christ just because they are Gentiles, aliens from the commonwealth of Israel? Certainly it is not because he thinks of God as the national God of the Jewish people— "Or is God the God of Jews only? Is he not the God of Gentiles also? Yea, of Gentiles also: if so be that God is one . . . " (Rom. 3:29-30). Rather, it is because God's promises to His people mark the bond of His covenant, the sphere of salvation. When Paul says, "They are not all Israel, that are of Israel" (Rom. 9:6), he is reflecting this same position from the other side: "It is not the children of the flesh that are children of God; but the children of the promise are reckoned for a seed" (v. 8). The true Israel are the children of God and to be called a child of God is to be included in the number of those "reckoned for a seed."

The beautiful terms applied in the Old Testament to God's covenant people are not being misappropriated when they are claimed by the apostles for the church in the New Testament. They are being fulfilled. The "elect race," the "holy nation," the "people for possession" are terms for the covenant relation that are deepened and intensified in Old Testament revelation until they are actualized through Jesus Christ.

This is enhanced by the context of Exodus 19. Those who are claimed as God's own people are those whom He has borne on eagles' wings unto Himself. Unlike the divine ancestor myths, so common in heathenism, God's relation to His people is established in history. In faithfulness to His promises to the fathers, God multiplies the descendants of Jacob in Egypt, delivers them from bondage there, and brings them to Himself in a rendezvous in the desert.

The Assembly of God

The people of God are constituted as a people by the covenant assembly at Sinai, the *ecclēsia* in the wilderness. The term *church,* it must be remembered, is an Old Testament word. The Greek word *ecclēsia* is common in the Septuagint; it is the term most often used to translate the Hebrew *qahal*. In the Old Testament as in the New, the term means "assembly" and may be used to describe assemblies that are not religious in their purpose (Ps. 26:5; Ezek. 38:7; Acts 19:39 ff.). Further, the term *ecclēsia/qahal* has an active meaning. It describes an actual gathering of people. It is more natural to speak of the assembly *(qahal)* of the congregation *(edhah)* than it would be to reverse the terms.[3] Some scholars have therefore argued that *ecclēsia* in both the Greek Old Testament and in the New Testament simply means "gathering," without any theological significance.[4] This, however, is to miss the definitive meaning of the assembly at Sinai for the whole Old Testament. In the history of Israel, there was one assembly par excellence in the great day when God made His covenant with His people. The Septuagint version puts the matter clearly in Deuteronomy 4:10: Israel is to remember and teach forever about "the day in which ye stood before the Lord our God in Horeb in the day of the assembly; for the Lord said to me, Assemble to me the people, and let them hear my words. . . ."

The Old Testament picture of the people of God as the assembly of the Lord of hosts comes to final New Testament realization in the festival assembly described in Hebrews 12. The point of the inspired author is to show the final and abiding fulfillment of this new covenant worship in the heavenly Jerusalem. "We have not here an abiding city, but we seek after the city which is to come" (Heb. 13:14). That coming city, sought by Abraham, the city with foundations (Heb. 11:10), is the city to which we come by faith, for it is the place of Christ's risen glory.

This final assembly brings together the Old and New Testament saints. By faith the saints of old awaited the fulfillment of the promise, for "apart from us they should not be made perfect" (Heb. 11:39-40). But they waited for Christ, endured the reproach of Christ (Heb. 11:26), and are now fellow citizens with us, "just men made perfect" by Jesus Christ.

The holiness of particular assemblies of the people of God reflects the heavenly assembly by which they are defined. Those who "call upon the name of our Lord Jesus Christ in every place" (I Cor. 1:2) are the holy ones (saints), the members of the assembly of the Lord. Like the Dead Sea community, the New Testament church looks back to the "church in the wilderness" [assembly in the desert] (Acts 7:38; cf. I Cor. 10:1-11). Like the message of the

Dead Sea covenanters, the gospel calls men to prepare in the desert a highway for our God. But the gospel announces the fulfillment of the coming of the Lord. The Lord has come and has ascended in triumph to Zion, leading captivity captive. Every assembly of His people on earth now celebrates His ascension to glory and awaits His return. Therefore, Paul challenges the Corinthians, "Despise ye the church [ecclēsia] of God?" (I Cor. 11:22). The gathering of the holy ones in Corinth now possesses a greater glory than the assembly at Sinai.

This theme of realization and fulfillment is strong particularly in the epiphany of the Holy Spirit at Pentecost. This feast is in itself a great assembly in the Old Testament pattern. It gained greater meaning through the pilgrimage of Jews of the dispersion coming to appear before the Lord with their brethren in Jerusalem. Jesus, in His ministry to the disciples after His resurrection, charges them to wait in Jerusalem for the coming of the promise of the Father (Acts 1:4). It was when the day of Pentecost "was being fulfilled" (Acts 2:1) that the Spirit was poured out. The Father, who holds the times and seasons in His authority (Acts 1:7), thus fulfilled the promise of the feast of the firstfruits, of ingathering. The disciples are themselves assembled together, and are made heralds as they praise God in the languages of the nations. The wind and the fire, as at Sinai, marked the coming of God with power to be present with His people. (Luke's description of the great assembly of those who heard reminds us of the account in II Chronicles 30:25 when the Jews and proselytes rejoiced at Hezekiah's restoration of the passover.)

Against the background of the Old Testament, Pentecost must be seen as the restoration of the people of God in one great assembly of fulfillment at Jerusalem. Joel's prophecy, quoted by Peter, describes the blessing of God poured out in the latter days upon the people of God. Peter's call to repentance recalls an earlier passage in Joel (2:15-17) where a solemn assembly for repentance is described by the prophet. The sign of the tongues points toward the reversing of the curse of Babel, and therefore to the blessing that must flow to the nations when the Spirit is poured out upon God's people. Preaching to the people, Peter declares that the promise is to them and to their children, but also to those who are afar off, as many as God shall call. It is the fulfillment of promised blessing, the coming of the Lord and His finished death and resurrection, that brings the blessing of the Spirit to both the people of God and the Gentiles. Pentecost remains as a positive witness to the fulfillment of the festival assembly of the Old Testament in the worship of the New Testament church. The symbolism of Old Testament worship is fulfilled in Jesus Christ; the blood of bulls and goats must no longer flow to depict the need of a sacrifice for sin. But the presence of God with His people in the assemblies of the Old Testament was not only in symbol. God revealed Himself, spoke to the fathers through the prophets, and declared His own presence in their midst. The saving relation He established with His people is fulfilled in Jesus Christ, and the assembly of praise in the presence of the Lord is the one assembly of all the saints.

The same theme of continuity and renewal applies to all the figures and descriptions of the people of God in the Old Testament. For example, we might compare the *dwelling* theme to the *assembly* theme. If the concept of the assembly stresses the active response of God's people to His immediate presence, the concept of the temple stresses the abiding of God in their midst. God sets His name in the sanctuary. The design of the tabernacle and of the temple symbolizes a double function of the cult of worship: first, the separation of a holy God, screened off by the veils of the sanctuary; second, the way of access opened into the holy of holies by God's appointed sacrifice. The dwelling of God in their midst demands that Israel be holy, a nation of priests, sanctified to live and serve in the presence of the living God. Israel is not only a priesthood, but even, figuratively, a temple, for God builds His people in blessing and will rebuild them in the latter days with the Messiah as the chief cornerstone (Ps. 118:22 ff.; Isa. 28:16).

The Elect of God

It is especially on the chosen people of God that the Bible focuses its teaching of restoration and renewal. God's people are His chosen, His precious possession, and the lot of His inheritance. "For thou art a holy people unto Jehovah thy God: Jehovah thy God hath chosen thee to be a people for his own possession, above all peoples that are upon the face of the earth. Jehovah did not set his love upon you, nor choose you, because ye were more in number than any people; for ye were the fewest of all peoples: but because the Lord loveth you, and because he would keep the oath which he sware unto your fathers . . ." (Deut. 7:6-8).

The electing love of God forges the bond of the covenant that claims the people of God as His. This is the theme throughout the

212

history of the patriarchs: God chooses Abel, not Cain; Shem rather than Japheth; Isaac, not Ishmael; Jacob, not Esau. The calling of the nation follows from the calling of the father—God's election of Abraham includes the calling of his seed, the promise that God recalls in His revelation to Moses at the bush (Exod. 3:6,16).[5]

The electing love of God for Israel is further expressed in the figures of a father's love for his firstborn son (Hos. 1:10; 11:1-3; Isa. 45:10 f.; 46:3 f.; 64:8; Jer. 3:14,19; 31:9), a husband's love for his wife (Hos. 1-3; Isa. 50:1; 54:5 f.; Jer. 2:2; 3:20; 11:15; 12:7; 31:3; Zeph. 3:17), the espousal of an unwanted infant (Ezek. 16:6; cf. Jer. 2:2), and many other poignant figures.

But what if the jealous love of Yahweh is spurned by an adulterous nation? God chose Israel, but Israel chose other gods (Judg. 5:8). The language of covenant choosing in the Old Testament has a negative side. The vengeance of the covenant falls upon the covenant-breakers (Lev. 26:25; Deut. 28:15-68). For the adulterous wife there is stoning (Ezek. 16:40). The rebellious son may be cast out (Hos. 12:14; 13:3). The pleasant vineyard can be laid waste (Isa. 5:5-6); and the planted vine uprooted and burned (Ezek. 19:10-14; Ps. 80:12-16). The glory of God that filled the temple (I Kings 8:11) can leave the temple (Ezek. 10:18; 11:23). Israel, who had been God's people, can be made no people (Hos. 1:9).

These dread prospects are realized in the outpouring of divine wrath in the Old Testament. A generation perishes in the wilderness through unbelief. Disasters of war, pestilence, and famine sweep over the land of the promise. Fiery destruction engulfs the city of God's dwelling, and God's people are swallowed up in captivity among the nations.

Does God choose in vain? Does His election fail? Are His promises of no effect? As the storm of judgment rises to a crescendo in the Old Testament, these questions become an overwhelming issue for the prophets.

Indeed, the prophets intensify the problem as they proclaim God's sovereignty. Since God is free to choose, He is free to reject. The potter who makes a vessel is free to smash it (Isa. 30:14). None can stay his hand or question his authority (Isa. 29:16; 45:9; 64:8).

Remnant and Renewal

But will God's word of promise then become void? Will His good pleasure be frustrated? The answer that the prophets give is repeated

213

and amplified by the apostle Paul in the light of God's full revelation in Jesus Christ (Rom. 9–11). Two distinctions need to be made: between the true and the false people of God, and between the present and future people of God. The first distinction appears in the motif of the *remnant*, the second in the motif of *renewal*. For these two reasons, God's election does not fail. A remnant is preserved, according to the election of grace. "But it is not as though the word of God hath come to nought. For they are not all Israel that are of Israel" (Rom. 9:6). The remnant becomes the center of a great renewal; God's promises will be realized in final fullness and "so all Israel shall be saved" (Rom. 11:26).

These distinctions acknowledge the sovereignty of God to choose and differentiate between an outward calling that may be void and an effective calling of God's Word that creates what it names (Isa. 46:10 f.; 55:11; Jer. 33:2). God's Word may seem to delay, but it is sure; at last, all that the Lord has spoken will be performed.

The principle of the remnant is widespread in the Old Testament. Joseph interprets his mission in this light (Gen. 45:7); Joshua and Caleb alone survive the Exodus generation; Amos pictures "two legs, or a piece of an ear" (3:12) rescued; Isaiah declares that "a remnant shall return" (7:3); and Ezekiel cries to God not to make a full end of the remnant (11:13).

The remnant, which comes to be identified with the Babylonian captives (Ezek. 11:14-21; cf. Jer. 24:4-10), is seen as chastened and purified (Hos. 5:15–6:3; Jer. 3:12-14). With those prophecies that speak of their restoration we are brought from the picture of a surviving remnant to the picture of renewal and a renewing remnant.

Covenant Renewal

The scattered remnant also will be regathered and renewed (Ezek. 11:17). Their recovery will be like the resurrection of an army from a valley full of dry bones (Ezek. 37:12). God will give them hearts of flesh for hearts of stone (Ezek. 11:19; 36:26) and make His covenant with them (Ezek. 11:20; 14:11; 16:60-62; 20:37; 34:25; 36:28; 37:26; cf. Jer. 31:31-37).

The mercy of God proclaimed by all the prophets will be shown to the remnant (Mic. 7:18). In the dispersal among the nations, the good grain will not fall to the ground (Amos 9:9). Those written in the book of life will remain, quickened from the grave (Isa. 4:3).

214

To this new Israel, God seals all the glories of His covenant. They are invincible (Mic. 5:7-9); they will enjoy the fruit of the land (Isa. 4:2); they will be planted of the Lord, taking root downward and bearing fruit upward (Isa. 37:31).

Although these great promises are repeated to the feeble remnant returning from captivity, the fullness of the restoration still is to come. God not only will restore the former glory but also bring the greater glory of the future. Indeed, the glory of the promised renewal becomes the climactic theme of the Old Testament. From the opening of the Book of Genesis (3:15), the promise of God shapes the history of redemption, and prophets thereafter point to the total and final fulfillment that the zeal of the Lord of hosts will accomplish in the "latter days." In those days, after the blessing and the curse, the final blessing will be given. Just as the pattern of the sabbatical years led at last to the year of jubilee when all debts were canceled, all prisoners freed, and every man restored to his inheritance in Israel; so in the history of God's covenant dealings with His people, there will come at last the jubilee of redemption, the year of the Lord's favor (Lev. 25; Isa. 61:1-3; Luke 4:17-19).

In the glory of God's blessing, a new Israel is to be raised up under the seal of a new covenant of peace (Isa. 54:10), an everlasting covenant (Ezek. 16:60). The new Israel is raised not only from the symbolical death of captivity but also from real spiritual death in sin (Ezek. 37:14). The new covenant is spiritual, bringing the covenant principle to its actualization (Jer. 31:31-37; Ezek. 36:24-28). Through the rich outpouring of the Holy Spirit, all the blessings of the covenant are sealed in the name of God (Isa. 44:1-5) and through the Word of God (Isa. 59:21; Ezek. 36:27; 39:29; Joel 2:28).

Restorative completeness describes the fulfillment of the promise. The temple will be reestablished (Isa. 2:2-4; Ezek. 40:2); sacrifices will again be offered (Isa. 56:7; Jer. 17:26; 33:18; Ezek. 43); the priests and Levites will be restored (Ezek. 44:9-31). Israel will resume its mediatorial position among the nations (Mic. 4:1-3; Isa. 66:23; 45:14; Zech. 14:16-19).

The very fullness of the blessing, however, transcends the form of the covenant that is restored, so that the spiritual realities symbolized in its ceremonial types are actualized. Therefore, the restoration is more than restoration; it is renewal. The old covenant in its final restoration becomes a new covenant.

215

It is thus not only a reunited remnant of both Israel and Judah that is redeemed (Hos. 1:11; Isa. 11:13; Ezek. 37:15-22). The Gentiles are included (Isa. 2:2-4; Mic. 4:1-3). The outcasts of other nations are brought in with Israel's captivity (Isa. 56:6-8) and their sacrifices will be acceptable on God's altar (Zech. 14:16-19). From the ingathered Gentiles, God will choose priests and Levites (Isa. 66:21). Indeed, so unthinkably great will be God's sanctifying blessing that God will be worshiped by sacrifice at an altar in Egypt, and Assyrians will pilgrimage there to worship, as well as Egyptians to Assyria, so that Israel's position as the covenant people will be shared by Egypt and Assyria, formerly her enemies (Isa. 19:19-25). Otherwise expressed, the heathen will be born in Zion and inscribed on the rolls of Zion's citizens (Ps. 87). The barrier between Jew and Gentile is broken down because God in mercy calls those His people who were not His people; both Jews and Gentiles are shut up in sin as "no people," that God might have mercy upon both. For this reason, even where Hosea spoke of Israel and Judah (Hos. 1:11) when he enunciated this principle (Hos. 2:23), Paul rightly finds a reference to the Gentiles (Rom. 9:25-26). The great figure of the festival assembly of the people of God to His place of dwelling in the midst of the nations will have its glorious fulfillment. The final feast on God's mountain is for all peoples (Isa. 25:6-8).[6] Many nations shall become His People, and He will dwell in the midst of them (cf. Zech. 2:11 and Ps. 47:9). The lips of the Gentiles will be cleansed to join in the praises of Zion: "For then will I turn to the peoples a pure language (lip), that they may all call upon the name of Jehovah to serve Him with one consent" (Zeph. 3:9).

The "remnant of men, and all the Gentiles among whom my name is called" will earnestly seek the Lord in that day, when He raises up the tabernacle of David that is fallen. (Cf. Amos 9:11-12 in the Septuagint with Acts 15:16-17.)

Eschatological Symbols

The outward symbols of the old covenant are so intensified with the fullness of the glory of the new covenant that they are transfigured and transformed. For example, the symbol of both the city and the temple are heightened to an apocalyptic degree. So holy will the city of God become that the inscription of the high priest's diadem will be found on the bells of the horses, and the very wash pots of the town will be as the holy vessels of the temple (Zech. 14:20; cf. Jer. 31:38 ff., where the boundaries of the New Jerusalem include all the unclean areas as holy places).

Ezekiel's vision of the new temple includes a new land. Note the allotment of tribes in equal strips, running east and west, regardless of terrain. So glorious will be the dwelling of God with all the remnant of the redeemed that the ark will not be missed (Jer. 3:16-17).

In the eschatological newness of the worship of "that day," the ceremonial is sublimated in absolute glory. It is not a restoration of Solomon's temple, but of the garden of Eden where the river of life flows, with trees whose leaves are for the healing of the nations. The finger of the Lord touches the worship, and the altar is consumed with the sacrifice. New Israel is a new humanity; the restoration of the covenant brings a new heaven and earth (Isa. 65:17; 66:22). Peace will prevail (Hos. 2:18; Isa. 9:4-7; Mic. 4:3-4), the animals are included (Isa. 11:6-9; 35:9), heavenly bodies have their light increased (Isa. 30:26), and there no longer is day and night (Isa. 60:20) because the sun and moon are replaced by God's glory.

The eschatological blessings in the latter days are not to be, and could not be, without the renewed manifestation of God's covenant presence. Just as it was God's call to Abraham and God's voice from Sinai that brought about the old covenant, so it must be God's new coming and calling that will renew the covenant and usher in the eschatological blessing. God's presence with His people is the heart of the covenant, and any covenant renewal must be with His presence manifested anew.

The Lord appears, amidst the rejoicing of His creation, to set up His kingdom on earth (Ps. 46:5-6,10; 98:7-9). In a second exodus, He leads forth His sheep as their Redeemer-Shepherd-King (Isa. 10:26; 35:1-10; 40:3,10; 52:12; Ezek. 34:11-16; cf. Jer. 32:21, 37-44). He Himself comes to dwell on Zion, and this is the source of the surpassing glory (Isa. 60:20) as He rules over all nations (Zech. 14:16), fills the new temple with His glory (Ezek. 43:2,7), shines as the light over the city of God (Isa. 60:19 f.), and is a fiery wall about it (Zech. 2:5).

The Lord is "waked up" out of His holy habitation (Zech. 2:13). The mount of the temple will rise above all mountains and hills (Isa. 2:2). God's truth will appear as a light to the nations (Isa. 51:4; 60:3).

217

God calls the nations: "God, Jehovah, hath spoken, and called the earth from the rising of the sun unto the going down thereof" (Ps. 50:1). "Assemble yourselves and come; draw near together, ye that are escaped of the nations. . . . Look unto me and be ye saved, all the ends of the earth; for I am God, and there is none else" (Isa. 45:20-22). The feast that God spreads for all nations in His holy mountain is a feast of covenant renewal (Isa. 25:6-8; cf. the feast of the Sinai covenant through which God revealed Himself to the elders of Israel, Exod. 24:9-11).

The Messiah in the New Covenant

The coming of God is identified with the coming of the Messiah. In Isaiah 40, it is God Himself who comes as the Shepherd of His people (verses 9-11 especially) to rule, judge, and deliver. In Isaiah 42, it is the Servant of the Lord who, in God's Spirit, sets justice in the earth (vv. 1-9). In Ezekiel 34:11, God Himself is the Shepherd; in verse 23, "my servant David" is the Shepherd (cf. the relation of the "angel of the covenant" and the Lord in Malachi 3:1-3). The messianic, Davidic King of Psalms 2, 45, 72, 110 exercises a divine rule. The Root of Jesse stands as an ensign to the peoples, and His resting place shall be glory (Isa. 11:10). The servant of the Lord restores the preserved of Israel and is a light to the Gentiles (Isa. 42:6; 49:6). It is the Messiah who exercises God's rule over all the nations (Zech. 9:10; Dan. 7:14; Isa. 9:4-7; 11:1-6).

In covenant renewal, God must come in power; and the focus of the Old Testament promises of God's coming are messianic in form. On the other hand, the Messiah will fulfill Israel's sonship. He is the Seed of the promise: not only the Seed of David (Ps. 89:35-36) and of Israel, but also the Seed of Abraham (Gen. 13:15; 17:8; cf. Gal. 3:16), and of the woman (Gen. 3:15). He is the true Israel (Isa. 49: 3-7), the Son of God (Ps. 2:7), and the Servant of God (Isa. 52:13), the true man—the second Adam.

In Him the role of Israel's sonship is fulfilled at last. He manifests the true distinctiveness of the holy Son of God (Isa. 11:3-5); in Him the covenant principle is realized: God with us—Immanuel (Isa. 7:14). He is anointed with the Holy Spirit without measure (Isa. 11:2 ff.; 61:1-3) as the Prophet (Deut. 18:15 f.), Priest (Ps. 110:4), and King (Ps. 2; Isa. 9:6-7), the mediating representative of all the people of God.

218

He not only fulfills the obedience of the Son of the covenant, but also appears as the righteous Sufferer, to make atonement for the sins of "the many" (Isa. 53; Ps. 22, 69). He suffers as the righteous King (cf. David in his rejection and suffering, Ps. 57, 59); as the Prophet (cf. the sufferings of Elijah, of Jeremiah, Jer. 15:10); as the Priest (who offers the sacrifice and *is* the sacrifice, Isa. 53).

The Messiah and Israel

As the coming Lord and as the promised Seed, the Messiah stands in the closest relation with the renewed Israel. The former deliverances under Moses, Joshua, and David become figures of the final deliverance, the last exodus, conquest and kingdom, and the images of these saviors of Israel foreshadow the final Savior. We have seen how the intensification and heightening of the figure of the temple and the cult carry it into a transcendent dimension of realization. So with the messianic figure, who is identified both with God and with Israel. The fluidity with which prophecy passes from the community to the Individual of the Servant Song, or from the Son of Man to the saints of the Most High in Daniel 7, has for its background the whole history of the covenant promise and the intimacy of the covenant bond. The Redeemer, who dwells with His people, is identified with them in His final work of salvation. The New Israel is the Messiah's people in the last day.

The Messiah and the Church

The New Testament proclaims in Christ and the church the fulfillment of all of these Old Testament prophecies. Luke says of the risen Lord that "beginning from Moses and from all the prophets, he interpreted to them in all the scriptures the things concerning himself" (Luke 24:27).

The Old Testament promises are realized in the advent of the Messiah and the gathering of Messiah's people, the true Israel of God. Christ comes as Immanuel, as the Lord of the covenant, and as the Son of the covenant. He thus completes both the promised work of God and the required response of His people. His work includes both redemption and ingathering. All the promises foreshadowed in the old people are gathered up—individually in Christ and corporately in His body, the new covenant people of God.

219

Who, then, can be called the Israel of God? If Christ is not only the Messiah but also the recipient of all the promises of God to Israel, then those united to Him by faith are recipients with Him of these promises. The remnant according to faith has become the true flock, whether gathered from the lost sheep of the house of Israel or from those who were formerly "No People" (Hos. 1:9 f.; Rom. 9:25 f.).

Paul makes it plain that those who are Christ's are the seed of Abraham and heirs according to the promise (Gal. 3:29). That this group includes the Gentiles is self-evident. This, for Paul, is the mystery of Christ (Eph. 3:6), that the Gentiles who were formerly "alienated from the commonwealth of Israel" have been united in Christ Jesus with the covenant people and become fellow-partakers of all the covenant promises made to Israel.

But it is not merely the inclusion of Gentiles in an otherwise Jewish nation that Paul has in view, but rather a renewed people of God. Paul is emphatic—there is neither hope nor promise nor inheritance for Israel outside of Christ. The present Jerusalem is in bondage (Gal. 4:25), whereas the new Jerusalem is the mother of all the people of God. But Paul is not condemning his people; rather, he is preaching the gospel to them. His heart's desire is that they be saved (Rom. 10:1), but first they must recognize God's judgment on their own nation and see the mission to the Gentiles as part of the new era. God has not cast His people away; rather, a remnant remains, according to the election of grace, renewed in Christ, and bringing blessing to the Gentiles (Rom. 15:27).

Paul's summary of the Old Testament prophecies is this: By the wonderful working of God's mercy, all the promises of God are being realized, but in ways we could not have imagined. The distinction between Jew and Gentile is removed, but not by the erection of a fellowship separate from both and foreign to the Old Testament covenants of promise. Rather, in Christ, Gentiles are united to the true Israel. They are one with Abraham, Isaac, Jacob, and all their true descendants (Eph. 2:12, 19; 3:6). What God has joined together, let not man put asunder.

Two Peoples of God

Paul E. Leonard

"I ask then, has God rejected his people? By no means . . . God has not rejected his people whom he foreknew" (Rom. 11:1-2). "These words are not spoken from the security of the shore, or from the safe refuge of a lifeboat as it approaches, or pulls away from, a wreck. These words are spoken from the deck of a ship—*as it sinks*" (italics mine).[1] Such a statement assumes a conclusion to the question of the relationship between Israel and the church. Israel has, according to this conclusion, sunk from sight (nearly without trace), her prerogatives and privileges now assumed by a new body, the church. But is this a probable conclusion? Has Israel disappeared forever? Has the church assumed the prerogatives of her "unworthy" forbearer? Has the church a special role to play, to be followed by the re-emergence of Israel in her destined place in the history of God's redemption of His people? In light of the contemporary re-emergence of Israel as a political entity, the above questions, which have broad implications both for theology and evangelism, cannot be ignored. And because the nature of Israel's role in biblical prophecy always has been the basis for any discussion, the subject is a fitting one for a volume like this.

First, we shall proceed to survey the evidence by examining the historical and prophetic question of Israel's place and expectations as God's chosen people. Second, we shall ask what features are shared in common by Israel and the church. Next, it will be helpful to survey the features that distinguish the two. And last of all, we must ask whether the church is in fact ever identified in the New Testament as the fulfillment of Israel.

221

The Historical Question

By *history* we refer to the place occupied by Israel prior to the time of Christ. This position is described succinctly by the apostle Paul in the following texts:

> Then what advantage has the Jew? . . . To begin with, the Jews are entrusted with the oracles of God (Rom. 3:1-2).

> They are Israelites, and to them belong the sonship, the glory, the covenants, the giving of the law, the worship, and the promises; to them belong the patriarchs, and of their race, according to the flesh, is the Christ (Rom. 9:4-5a).

In Ephesians 2:12, Paul reminds the Gentile Christians that prior to their conversion they were "alienated from the commonwealth of Israel. . . ." The Israelite is a descendant of Jacob to whom the name "Israel" had been given by God. As used by Paul, the term is distinctive. For Israelites were entrusted with the "oracles of God," commonly understood as the Old Testament Scriptures, though limited by some to the special messianic promises or the Law. Furthermore, "to them belong the sonship." Even before Israel's divinely superintended exodus from Egypt and her receipt of the covenant of Sinai, God had challenged Pharaoh with the warning "Israel is my firstborn son. . . . Let my son go, that he may serve me . . ." (Exod. 4:22-23; cf. Deut. 14:1; 32:6; Jer 31:9). Sonship, a new legal status, was conferred specially on this people Israel. Furthermore, to them was "the glory," certainly referring to the visible presence (*shekinah*) of God among His people (Exod. 16:10). This "presence" was considered to have sanctified Jerusalem and the temple, and thus set the "holy city" apart from any other spot on earth. The "covenants" refer to the repeated covenants enacted by God with His people, with a focus on the covenant enacted between God and Abraham (Gen. 15:18; 17:2-9) and that between Moses, as representative of the people, and God at Sinai (Exod. 24:3-10). The "law" was uniquely given to Israel, and this was a high privilege indeed, the law being in Pauline terms the school teacher (or custodian; some would argue "jailer") under whose authority she lived until the Messiah should come (Gal. 3:25). The "worship" of Israel centered in the temple, and there is little doubt that there were many messianic overtones in the details of worship, not to mention that when Messiah was to come the temple would figure prominently in His establishment of His rule. The "promises" of the Old Testament

222

are manifold, spread from Genesis to Malachi, centered in their earlier stages in the relationship between God and the "fathers" of the nation, and pointing toward the ultimate arrival of the Messiah, who would be an Israelite of Israelites, a son of Abraham and of David.

All of the past history of Israel, whether genealogical, political, theological, or social, had led up to the grand conclusion that it was this nation through whom God proposed to make Himself known in many ways, not the least of which was in the expected appearance of the Messiah. And now Messiah had appeared. Israel refused to recognize Him, and the tragic question is posed: Is she to be cast off by God, after all of her past glory and failures wherein God had shown Himself gracious to her? Will He now forsake her, literally at the altar, or is she absorbed somehow into the newer community, the church? How we answer this question will determine our interpretation of many Old Testament prophecies that pertain to Israel.

Features Common to Israel and the Church

Before we can answer the question of Israel's role in biblical prophecy, we must consider some preliminary matters. The first of these touch on characteristics common to Israel and the church. If the church, as visualized by the theologians of the New Testament, is so close to Old Testament Israel that there is little to distinguish the two, then the hermeneutical principle of the amillennial interpreter (see chapter 8, "Evangelical Alternatives") is strengthened.

Both Israel and the church are chosen by God as recipients of His grace. Paul suggests that this applies, in the case of Israel, only to that portion of the nation that responds in faith to the promise (Rom. 9:6-13; cf. Gal. 3:7 f.), whereas the church, by its very nature, is a community of faith. But prior to the faith is the promise, and nothing could be clearer than the fact that old Israel and the people of the New Covenant are both such because of the sovereign, electing promise of God. That the church was, even in the Old Testament prophecies, included in the promise, is argued by Paul with reference to such passages as Hosea 2:23 (cf. Rom. 9:25 f.): "I will say to NOT my people, 'You are my people'; and he shall say, 'Thou art my God.' " But the point at issue is whether Paul or any other New Testament writer intended us to believe that such a correlation be seen as a transfer of all the promises of election to the new body.

223

Second, both Israel and the church have a universal mandate to proclaim God's grace. Israel was open traditionally to proselytes joining her company, but implicit in the message of the prophets was the mission of Israel to proclaim the righteousness of God abroad. In the same context appealed to earlier by Paul (Rom. 9:19-21; cf. Isa. 45:9-15), a clear prophetic call invites the nations to turn to the God of Israel and be saved:

> Assemble yourselves together and come, draw near together you survivors of the nations! . . . Turn to me and be saved, all the ends of the earth! For I am God, and there is no other. By myself I have sworn, from my mouth has gone forth in righteousness a word that shall not return: "To me every knee shall bow, every tongue shall swear" (Isa. 45:20a, 22-23; cf. Rom. 14:11; Phil. 2:10).

The "servant" texts of Isaiah, although certainly messianic, also are clearly national in import. The servant has been appointed and provided with the Spirit so that justice may be brought forth to the nations (Isa. 42:1); He is given for "a covenant to the people, a light to the nations, to open the eyes of the blind" (Isa. 42:6b-7).

Paul points out, however, that whereas a few Israelites (a remnant) had achieved their goal, the vast majority had failed either in the reception of God's grace or the communication of it, or both. What is the significance of this, asks Paul, "Have they stumbled so as to fall?" His abrupt answer—"By no means! But through their trespass salvation has come to the Gentiles, so as to make Israel jealous" (Rom. 11:11)—seems to imply a continuing role for Israel as a people. What Israel failed to do has come about anyway, but now *through* their failure. The point is that the grace of God has been spread abroad to the nations. And in an important aside, the apostle continues, "Now if their trespass means riches for the world, and if their failure means riches for the Gentiles, how much more will their full inclusion mean!" (Rom. 11:12).

The mission of the church and its individual members to share the "good news" hardly needs arguing. The message of the great commission (Matt. 28:19-20) provides us with a strategic plan implemented in the early years of the church (see the developing witness as recorded in Acts), a central theme of much of the rest of the New Testament, and the marching orders of the church ever since. Here again, God's mandate to Israel is regarded as somehow fulfilled or realized in the church's proclamation of her Lord (cf. the "light to the nation" figure in Isaiah 42:6 and 49:6 with its use in Luke 2:32 [Christ], Acts 13:47 [Paul, Barnabas, *et al.*], and 26:23 [Christ]).

Third, both Israel and the church share the reality that true membership in either is a matter of spiritual and not primarily physical descent. This point has been touched on above, but is worthy of expanded comment. John the Baptist warned his audience to repent and not to count on their Abrahamic descent to save them from the coming wrath, because "God is able from these stones to raise up children to Abraham" (Matt. 3:9). Jesus, confronting another audience, made the same point when He said to natural-born Jews, "If you were Abraham's children you would do what Abraham did" (John 8:39). Paul has argued elsewhere that since even Abraham evidenced his faith response to God's call prior to his circumcision, that physical act served only as a "sign or seal of the righteousness which he had [achieved] by faith while he was still uncircumcised" (Rom. 4:11). The purpose, writes Paul, was "to make him the father of all who believe," whether circumcised (Jew) or uncircumcised (Gentile).

Closely related terminology is used to describe Israel and the church. Concerning believers, the apostle Peter wrote:

> . . . you are a chosen race, a royal priesthood, a holy nation, God's own people, that you may declare the wonderful deeds of him who called you out of darkness into his marvellous light. Once you were no people but now you are God's people; once you had not received mercy but now you have received mercy (I Peter 2:9-10).

Three salient facts emerge from this text: (1) Verse 9 consists of a series of allusions to Exodus 19:5-6, where God promises Israel that if she will obey His voice and keep His covenant she shall be "my own possession among all peoples; for all the earth is mine, and you shall be a kingdom of priests and a holy nation"; and to Isaiah 43:20, where Israel is called "my chosen people." (2) The call from darkness to light is reminiscent of Isaiah 42:6, where the prophet quotes the Lord's promise, "I have given you [my servant] as a covenant to the people, a light to the nations, . . . to bring out the prisoners from the dungeon, from the prison those who sit in darkness," a text almost certainly providing the apostle Paul with his personal operation order to evangelize the Gentiles (see Acts 26:17-18). (3) In verse 10, Peter, like Paul (Rom. 9:25 f.), draws

225

his symbolism from Hosea 2:23, to provide Old Testament background for God's call of the Gentiles to redemption.

Finally, the church (largely Gentiles) and Israel share the same messianic consciousness: Israel in prospect only, the church in retrospect and in present experience with the living, indwelling Christ. This common point, however, also provides the issue upon which the widest divergence occurs.

Features That Distinguish Israel and the Church

There are certain obvious differences between Israel as a nation and the church as an institution. First among these are their respective historic and ethnic backgrounds. It is Israel who can look back to Abraham as her father. It is Israel who was led out of captivity in Egypt by Moses, to whom was given the law by a holy God on Mount Sinai. The stories of Gideon, Barak, Samson, Jepthah, David, Samuel, Isaiah, Jeremiah, Daniel, and other prophets are stories of Israel and her victories and defeats. The Psalms are expressions of worship, discouragement, contrition, and exaltation of inspired Israelite poets, preserving for later ages the records of some of the most intimate moments of Israel's past.

It was through Israel that the Messiah arrived in the person of Jesus. He was born in Bethlehem (Mic. 5:2) and recognized as the Son of David (Luke 2:4) by virtue of His parents' genealogy. Later, He was hailed as the Christ, the Son of the living God (Matt. 16:16) by His Jewish followers who accompanied Him in life and were witnesses to His death, resurrection, and ascension.

Furthermore, it was to Israel alone that Jesus initially sent His disciples to declare the arrival of the kingdom of heaven:

> Go nowhere among the Gentiles, and enter no town of the Samaritans, but go rather to the lost sheep of the house of Israel. And preach as you go saying "The kingdom of heaven is at hand" (Matt. 10:5-7).

Although Jesus later claimed that He was sent "only to the lost sheep of the house of Israel" (Matt. 15:24) He had already exclaimed, in response to the request of a Gentile Roman centurion for healing for his dying servant, "Truly, I say to you, not even in Israel have I found such faith" (Matt. 8:10). This incident was followed by Jesus' promise that many others would one day "come from east and west and sit at table with Abraham, Isaac and Jacob in the

226

kingdom of heaven, while the sons of the kingdom will be thrown into outer darkness" (Matt. 8:11-12).

It might be argued that the distinction made here between Israelite and Gentile is of no significance in this discussion of the distinction between Israel and the church. But Paul does not see it that way. He insists on maintaining the distinction of a historical kind in his survey of God's purpose for His nation Israel. In response to the question "Has God rejected his people?" (Rom. 11:1) Paul cites his own conversion as conclusive proof that the answer is No! He then illustrates his point with reference to the experience of Elijah, who despaired of his own people but who was reassured by God that a remnant of faithful remained (seven thousand, possibly symbolic of a relatively large number, I Kings 19:10-18). However, having conceded a "mere" remnant to follow Christ, Paul goes on to speak of the restoration of the *whole* nation ". . . if their failure means riches for the Gentiles, how much more will their *full inclusion* mean!" (Rom. 11:12). The preservation of the distinction, although secondary in Paul's argument, is important for this discussion. The finale arrives when Paul writes that "all Israel shall be saved" (Rom. 11:26) in fulfillment of specific Old Testament prophecy (Isa. 59:20-21) and of God's elective choice (Rom. 11:28-32). Whatever else we may derive from this text, it is clear that Paul sees not only a present role for a "remnant"—those like himself who confess Jesus as Lord—but a future for the nation as a whole, in fulfillment of the promise of old given to the patriarchs and reaffirmed repeatedly in Israel's history. If the stumbling is national, so is the later restoration.

Further support for a distinction between Israel and the church as separate communities in the mind of the apostle is found in the language and argument of the Epistle to the Ephesians.[2] A clear distinction is made in this Epistle between the "we" (probably Paul and the early apostolic communities; cf. Eph. 1:5-14) and the "you" (the recipients of the Epistle). The emphasis in the following discourse of Paul is that both "we" and "you" are now made "alive together with Christ" (2:5). Therefore, continues Paul, you who were once far off, "separated from Christ, alienated from the commonwealth of Israel, and strangers to the covenants of promise, having no hope and without God in the world" (Eph. 2:12 f.), are now "fellow citizens with the saints and members of the household of God, built upon the foundation of the apostles and prophets [Christian prophets—cf. Eph. 4:11], Christ Jesus himself being the cornerstone . . ." (Eph. 2:19-20). Note that Paul speaks of the new community that had its beginning with the life of Jesus and the apostolic witness. This is impressive particularly when the context notes the separation of these Christians in their pagan state from not only the "promises" but also from the "commonwealth of Israel." If the church and Israel were now one and the same, it would have been the most natural thing for Paul to have emphasized the antiquity of the household into which the Ephesians had been initiated. Although there is no suggestion of the disappearance of the old Israel in the Epistle, nor changes in the careful teaching of Romans 9–11, neither is there any suggestion that Israel has now become the church or that Israel even is part of the church.[3] Rather, the reference is to the formation of a new humanity in Christ. From two distinct and quite separate people—Jew and Gentile—there emerges something new and greater—not merely new in point of time, but new in the sense that it brings into the world a wholly new kind of thing (Eph. 2:13-16).[4] It is intriguing to notice Paul's description of the Gentile side of this new creation who were "separated from Christ, alienated from the commonwealth of Israel, and strangers to the covenants of promise, having no hope and without God in the world" (Eph. 2:12). These words very nearly are the complete opposite of the description of Israelites in Romans 9:4.

A final feature that distinguishes Israel from the church is found in the character of the promises given to each. The expectations of the church, the body of Christ, are personal, spiritual, and heavenly in character—note Paul's personal expectation of transport to the presence of Christ at his death and emphasis on holy living with no reference to the physical aspects of Israel's expectation (Phil. 1:23; II Tim. 4:8). By contrast, Israel's expectations include a physical (though not less spiritual) earthly fulfillment of the promises in the restoration to her land and the inauguration of a time of bliss and universal supremacy under the reign of her returned Messiah-King (Gen. 17:3-8; II Sam. 7:12-13; Dan. 9:25; John 4:25; 12:13). In fact, it is with these very expectations that much of Old Testament prophecy is concerned.

Can the Name "Israel" Be Applied to the Church?

In only one text in the New Testament can the term Israel possibly be applied to the church, a text comprising the concluding words

228

of the apostle Paul to the Galatians: "And as many as walk according to this rule, peace be *on* them *and* mercy, *and upon* the Israel of God" (Gal 6:16 KJV, italics mine). However, Peter Richardson[5] is among the most recent to argue against such an interpretation. Richardson shows that in Christian literature the equation between Israel and the church is not made until the writings of Justin Martyr, A.D. 160. Turning to the text itself, he refutes the usual claim that this text equates Israel and the church. The argument centers on the italicized words "and" and "upon." Richardson contends that the "we" and "you" motif of Ephesians is being repeated—except this time the "we" is represented by "all who walk by this rule" and the "you" is really the "they" who should be connected with "us" but are not yet.[6] In a repunctuation of the sentence it reads, "Peace upon them, and mercy also upon the Israel of God." He further argues that the "Israel of God" represents those Israelites who will come to their senses and receive Christ, but have not yet done so.[7] It may also be of value to note that in Romans the concept of God's mercy is limited to the texts where Paul is discussing the place of Israel in God's plan (see Rom. 9:15-16, 18, 23; 11:30-32; 15:9). Furthermore, the restriction holds true for the rest of Paul's writings as well, with the possible exception of two references in II Timothy (1:16,18). The Galatian text therefore not only fails to equate Israel with the church but carefully distinguishes even those future believers who at the moment of Paul's prayer remain within the nation of Israel.

The one persuasion to emerge from our study is that Israel and the church are distinct entities. Although both share important characteristics, even more important differences prevail. Each has its own "place in the sun" of God's redemptive acts—past, present, and future. It is true that in Romans 9 to 11, Paul himself has said nothing about the restoration of an earthly Davidic kingdom or nothing directly about national reinstatement in the land of Israel. F. F. Bruce suggests in this regard that what Paul envisaged for his people was something infinitely better.[8] This statement, however, raises even larger questions: (a) the interpretation of the intent of the divine covenant promises to Israel; (b) the mode of their anticipated fulfillment; and (c) a study of the subsidiary but important questions as to why and how Judaism of the first century failed in its expectation of the Messiah and the kingdom of God. These are questions that students of biblical prophecy still ponder.

Notes

Section One

1. *Katatomé*, the excision, mutilation (Phil. 3:2).

2. For the Old Testament terms for *aliens* see Gustav Stählin in *Theological Dictionary of the New Testament*, Gerhard Kittel, ed. (Grand Rapids: Eerdmans, 1967), V, p. 8. For the other terms, note Jer. 31:34 (Septuagint, Jer. 38:24— "citizen"); Ps. 87:6; Num. 27:11 ("inheritance to members of the household"); Deut. 33:3 ("saints").

3. "All the assembly of the congregation," Num. 14:5; cf. Exod. 12:6.

4. J. Y. Campbell, "The Origin and Meaning of the Christian Use of the Word ΕΚΚΛΗΣΙΑ," *The Journal of Theological Studies* 49 (1948), pp. 130-142.

5. Many Old Testament passages link the election of the patriarchs and of the people. See H. H. Rowley, *The Biblical Doctrine of Election* (London: Lutterworth, 1950), pp. 19-23. Among the passages: Hos. 11:1; Jer. 2:2; Ezek. 20:5; Isa. 41:8 f.; Mic. 7:20; Ps. 105:5-10.

6. On the importance of this figure, see Joachim Jeremias, *Jesus' Promise to the Nations* (Naperville, IL: Allenson, 1958), pp. 59 ff.

Section Two

1. K. Barth, *The Epistle to the Romans.* E. T. (London: Oxford Univ. Press, 1933), p. 393, italics mine.

2. H. L. Ellison, *The Mystery of Israel* (Exeter: Paternoster, 1968), pp. 97-117.

3. Ibid., p. 117.

4. F. Foulkes, *Ephesians* (London: Tyndale, 1963), p. 83.

5. Richardson, P., *Israel in the Apostolic Church* (Cambridge: Cambridge Univ. Press, 1969), pp. 74 ff.

6. Ibid., p. 81.

7. Ibid., p. 82.

8. F. F. Bruce, *The Epistle of Paul to the Romans* (London: Tyndale, 1963), p. 221.

15

Living Between Two Ages

James Robert Ross

What is the most distinctive characteristic of Christian disciple-ship? It cannot be commitment to high ideals, for the Stoic and the Buddhist are committed to very high ethical principles. As the title of this chapter suggests, one of the most decisive and crucial aspects of the Christian life is that it involves the believer in the life of two ages, or in two radically different realms or kingdoms. And this dualistic involvement that characterizes Christian discipleship has most important implications for the correct understanding of ethical issues and for effective action in this present world. It is the purpose of this chapter to explore some of these implications.

The Purpose of Prophecy

One of the most serious distortions of prophetic studies, especial-ly by conservative expositors, is the separation of eschatological speculations from the concrete realities of human existence. When we study biblical prophecies simply to satisfy our curiosity about the future or to engage in titillating debate about how and when the prophecies will be fulfilled, then we have forgotten why the prophecies were delivered by inspired men.

The basic purpose of prophecy is redemptive and ethical. In the biblical covenants, God has shown Himself to us as a gracious, redeeming God. And that we might comprehend more fully what it means that God is our father and that we are His children, He has

231

raised up men to proclaim His Word to us. The prophetic Word recalls us to our covenantal obligations. It reminds us of the mighty redemptive acts that established the covenants, especially the liberation of Israel from Egypt and the death and resurrection of Christ. Therefore, the prophetic Word instructs us in the implications of the gift of grace, i.e., what it means to live as those who are now bound by God's love into His own family.

Finally, the prophetic Word includes warnings regarding the consequences of infidelity to our covenant commitment. But even in the midst of warnings of judgment there is sounded the note of grace, a confirmation of the purpose of God to redeem His people and to save His world from the ravages of the primal rebellion. These predictions about future judgment and salvation are rooted firmly in a basic ethical concern, viz., that God's covenant people understand and make effective in their lives the significance of the special love that they have received.

If the prophecies are indeed motivated by a basic ethical concern, as I am convinced a detailed study will demonstrate,[1] then it is our response that is the most crucial issue. If we should become experts in prophetic interpretation, if we have all knowledge of things future, yes, even if we know the day and the hour of Jesus' coming, but if our lives are not transformed by the expectation of what God will do, then we have turned prophetic study into a parlor game and our knowledge becomes a curse instead of a blessing.

Living Between Two Ages

The first point that needs to be made is that "living between two ages" involves the Christian in a unique tension between two spheres of loyalty and commitment. On the one hand, he is living in this present age, and he cannot escape the involvements that characterize this age. He fulfills the biological functions of all men— being born, eating, physical and mental maturation, sleeping, and reproducing. Furthermore, he participates in the various social, political, and economic orders that characterize this age. He marries and has a home. He goes to school. He is a citizen of some country. He works and buys and sells within some modern economic order, capitalistic or socialistic.

On the other hand, the Christian has been grasped by a higher loyalty. His more fundamental citizenship is in heaven, from whence he awaits his Savior (Phil. 3:20). And what makes the tension between his earthly and his heavenly citizenship all the more acute is that he has already begun to experience the life of the new age. He has "tasted . . . the powers of the age to come" (Heb. 6:5). The Christian is not one who simply wishes to go to heaven by and by but in the meantime has to make do in this world. Rather, he currently possesses eternal life (John 6:47), and by faith is striving already to make effective what will be fully completed only in the new creation.

The New Testament is full of references to this already-experienced dimension of the life of the age to come. The most significant aspect of the new life is the Holy Spirit now given by Christ to His church. According to the prophets of old, the new age was to be inaugurated by the out-pouring of God's Spirit upon man (Isa. 32:15; 44:3; Ezek. 36:25-27; Joel 2:28). And as Peter pointed out in his Pentecost sermon, these prophecies were fulfilled on that day when the risen Christ sent the "Comforter," the Holy Spirit, upon the band of disciples waiting in Jerusalem (Acts 2:14 ff.). And Paul speaks of the Spirit as God's down payment (*arrabōn*, "earnest") on our future inheritance[2] (II Cor. 1:22; Eph. 1:13 f.).

But the blessings of the age to come, which the Christian experiences now, do not solve the problems of living in this age. In a very real sense the problems become more acute, or at least they become more acutely perceived. The non-Christian can live his life with one concern only, to get along as best he can in this world. He has difficulties, of course, and he has alternative courses of action from which to choose. But the basic goal of life and the fundamental principles of this world are never seriously questioned. His life is lived out on one plane, and he can get along in this world using commonly accepted methods to gain status, wealth, and power.

But the Christian, although he is part of a social class, never can be satisfied with the alienation from his neighbor that such class distinctions imply. He is a citizen of a particular political order, but his higher allegiance to Christ as Lord calls into question the claims of his earthly government and often puts him in direct conflict with it. In every relationship the demands of the kingdom of heaven are in constant tension with the way this world operates. The Christian, as it were, has already been fitted with wings for the life of the age to come, but he has to learn how to use those wings within an alien, earthbound environment. Becoming a Christian does not automatically solve moral problems. It makes him more

233

conscious of them and of how serious they really are. It demonstrates how radical a transformation is required to overcome them and how nothing but the grace of God can make any real difference ultimately in our lives.

Temptations in Resolving the Tension of Living Between Two Ages

There is, however, a persistent temptation to resolve the tension between the competing claims of the kingdoms in which the Christian lives. The first temptation is to *deny* the reality of our involvement in this world's affairs. Sometimes, when a Christian becomes enthusiastic about the new creation in Jesus Christ, he denies or suppresses the continuing claims that this world makes on him. He simply may deceive himself into thinking that his political and social involvements are irrelevant to Christian discipleship. He continues to live much as other men do: raising a family, writing checks and using credit cards, paying taxes, and punching his time clock at the plant, but he resists the idea that these aspects of his life are relevant to being a Christian. (Others take more extreme measures to isolate themselves from the affairs of this age by retreating to the cloister or to some other sheltered community.) But inevitably worldly claims are made upon him or else he finds himself dependent upon society for the necessary amenities of life, such as sewage disposal or medical care.

If the first temptation is to deny this world, the second and probably more serious temptation is to dilute the claims of the kingdom of God. Examples of this approach may be seen in almost any Sunday school class studying the Sermon on the Mount. Most Christians seem to assume that there are no fundamental conflicts between Christian discipleship and old-fashioned patriotism, astute business practices, or participation in the local Chamber of Commerce. But the Sermon on the Mount offers no formula for success in a military, financial, or political career. Rather it describes a radically different kind of existence, an alternative to the secular ideology of achievement.

But modern Christians are able by the most ingenious explanations to show that Christ did not really mean that happiness is found in meekness and that turning the other cheek is not a viable option in relating to one's enemies. When Christian discipleship loses this vision of radical transformation by Christ, to be completed at His coming, it reduces and dilutes Christian commitment to the level of worldly ideals. This weakened brand of Christianity is no longer an alternative to this world, it is only a pious blessing pronounced upon it, as evidenced by invocations at sports events and political rallies. For most, civil religion certainly is not a recognition of the absolute claims of the King of kings.

A third temptation is to *divorce* the two realms in which the Christian lives. There is a recognition that the Christian lives in this world and cannot evade the responsibilities of involvement in its affairs. Christians, too, after all, must build houses, enforce the laws, raise corn, mine coal, collect garbage or taxes. On the other hand, Christians have their spiritual obligations: to worship God, to study their Bibles, to give money to missions, and to help neighbors. Thus Christians have their socio-political-economic life and they have their personal-spiritual life, but never the twain shall meet. From this distorted perspective, for example, a white Christian can "love" a black man by giving him last year's suit of clothes, but he does not involve himself in questioning the validity of discriminatory laws.[3]

Biblical Teaching Regarding Living Between Two Ages

Against these temptations to denial, dilution, and divorce, the Bible teaches, first of all, the reality of this world and of our involvement in it. Sometimes Christians ask, "Should we get involved in social and political affairs?" The question really makes no sense since to live in this world is to be involved inevitably in one way or another. The real issue is "*How* shall I be involved?" Second, the Bible also teaches that the claims of Jesus Christ are absolute. There is no way that Jesus will share the sovereignty with the chairmen of the million-dollar corporation or the president of the United States. This sovereignty is a reality. Jesus *is* Lord. And although His Lordship will not become universally effective until His Second Coming, the very essence of Christian discipleship is the recognition of the validity of His claims today. Finally, the Bible teaches that there is no such thing as earthly obligations as distinct from heavenly or spiritual obligations. There is only one obligation, and that is to make real the rule of Christ in every aspect of our lives—social, economic, political, and ecclesiastical.

The Influence of an Eschatological Hope

The New Testament repeatedly bears witness to the impact upon our lives today of the future appearance of our Lord. Jesus' own teaching emphasized the need to live in the light of this future. The difference between the five foolish and the five wise virgins was their perception of the future (Matt. 25:1-13). Numerous passages in the Epistles speak of the effect that the Christian's hope has upon his life in this world. To look forward to the "blessed hope" is the most effective motivation to sober, righteous, and godly living in this present world (Titus 2:12 f.). The hope of seeing Jesus face to face purifies the lives of Christians (I John 3:2-3); and because it so dominates their thinking, their feeling, and their decision-making, every other influence is simply overwhelmed. The girl who constantly hopes for the return of her absent lover has no time, no thoughts, no eyes for other suitors.

Citing passages that relate the influence hope has upon a Christian's life could be multiplied. The parables of the talents and the pounds (Matt. 25:14-30; Luke 19:11-27) teach faithfulness to a Lord who is absent but who will return for an accounting from His servants. The parable of the sheep and the goats (Matt. 25:31-46) shows how impossible it is to separate service to Christ from service to a neighbor in need and how future judgment will be concerned precisely with what we have done with Jesus when we meet Him in the person of a hungry child, a prisoner, or a cold and lonely traveler. The experience of present salvation and the confidence of a future salvation soon to be revealed invoke a unique sense of urgency in the Christian's life. Paul reminds us, "In all this, remember how critical the moment is. It is time for you to wake out of sleep, for deliverance is nearer to us now than it was when we first believed. It is far on in the night; day is near. Let us therefore throw off the deeds of darkness and put on our armour as soldiers of the light" (Rom. 13:11-12, NEB).

Because we have seen Jesus Christ we have a glimpse of what this world *can* and *will* someday be like. This hope in a coming new world order conformed to the image of Christ and to His will has both a critical and a creative function in relation to the circumstances now prevailing.[4] First, it is critical of both traditional and revolutionary programs. Hope in the new order, implicit in the resurrection life of Christ, hope for freedom, peace, and reconciliation— these all are causes for dissatisfaction with every arrangement humanly designed to meet human needs. Even the most sacred institutions (i.e., ecclesiastical and civil) are not immune from critical interrogation from the perspective of our future hope. Even if the present order is the best that ever has been, although such comparative judgments are always suspect, it is only a hint as to what shall be. Hope is the very opposite of defensiveness. It feels no need to preserve the present system simply because it has the sanction of history, human authority, or even relative success.

In this world, however, are structures that function well, with which a society can be content even if there is no vision of the future of Jesus Christ. Segregation has been one such arrangement, supported by the civil powers and often blessed by religious institutions. Its persistence resulted not only from the satisfaction of whites but to some degree of blacks also. The system specifically defined all forms of social contact—religious, economic, sexual, recreational—and provided a rather secure framework for interaction. Everyone knew his place. At times, even the oppressed party, by working within the system, could enjoy a modicum of security and on certain levels develop close ties with the oppressor. Thus the breakdown of segregation evoked considerable anxiety among many blacks. Where there was no hope there was no will to endure the pain of change. But the future hope in Jesus Christ calls this arrangement into question along with many others, no matter how comfortable they may be. Hopeful Christians must speak out against them, and they will endure gladly the suffering necessary for the light of the dawning day to break into the darkness of every dehumanizing activity.

Hope criticizes not only the *status quo* but also every revolutionary movement that is hostile to the past. While hope is not afraid of change, it nonetheless refuses to worship even the best imitators of the kingdom of God, no matter how bright their promises. Thus when the Christian withholds allegiance from a radical movement or when he refuses to contribute to the purchase of guns for distribution among revolutionaries, he need not act out of reactionary fear but rather out of the most revolutionary hope. Precisely because of this hope in God's promises, embodied at one point in time and space in Jesus, the Christian refuses to be satisfied with any other "messiah."

Although hope is continually critical, it never despairs. Paradoxically, because of its vision of the future, hope is a stimulus to creativity in the face of apparently insurmountable barriers. This is the hope that believes against hope and ventures the impossible, confident that the God who raises the dead is able to accomplish whatever He promises (cf. Rom. 4:18-21). Such hope has no attachment to the clay idols of tradition. It looks for new heavens and a new earth. And such a vision produces imaginative, compassionate, and daring action.

The conviction that Jesus Christ is man, as man shall one day be transformed by God's grace, kindles the hope that all men may share in His likeness. In the faces of the poor, the homeless, the lonely, the sick, and the oppressed, hope can see only Christ, and it acts accordingly. This does not mean that Christ is identical with a neighbor in need, as some modern distortions of the gospel would have it. Rather, hope expects the impossible. Men who are by nature so unlike Christ are those for whom He died and by His power may be conformed to His most glorious image according to the promise of God. Conversely, the negative side of this hope is the realization that wrath awaits those who persist in their rejection of the free gift of life in Christ. Hell is not an object of hope, properly speaking. But it is the inevitable consequence of persistent moral rebellion, given the fact that the moral creator of the universe cannot deny Himself. Hell is no arbitrary, spiteful vengeance by an ill-tempered deity; it is the ultimate expression of His moral character for those who refuse His grace.

The Christian's confidence in the fulfillment of God's stupendous promises means that we must search for new meanings for words such as "radical" and "revolutionary." What men call radical or revolutionary often is merely a superficial reworking of a very old and corrupt system. By way of illustration, a black revolution that only repaints an old order black rather than leaving it white is no revolution at all. A truly radical approach to the situation requires more than a frustrated reaction by an oppressed minority, no matter how socially or psychologically understandable or justifiable such a reaction might be. A truly radical approach calls for (1) a redemption from the sin and guilt weighing on the oppressors; (2) a transvaluation of the social and political norms in terms of the single criterion of humanness as defined by Jesus Christ without regard to the worldly criteria of race, class, or culture; and (3) the acceptance of one fact as the model for all human relations: "God was in Christ reconciling the world to Himself" (II Cor. 5:19).

238

The ones who act upon these truly revolutionary principles will ignore or negate every social structure that might interfere with the realization of these biblical principles. They have no need to cling to their own lives––physically, socially, or politically. Their reliance upon and hope in a resurrected God enables them to affirm their own death, and that includes the death of the social or institutional structures with which they would identify ordinarily as citizens of this world. Indeed, in baptism, the Christian already has affirmed his death in union with Christ (Rom. 6:3-4). Such audacious action is possible only because of the Christian's firm assurance that death already has been conquered in Christ and that some day he will share in that victory.

This approach to the "life between two ages" argues that vital Christian hope does not motivate one to withdraw from the arena of social and political conflict. But a word of explanation is in order here since many conservative Christians with the most fervent hope in Christ's appearing have taken a different position. According to their view the world is a sinking ship and it is futile to polish the brass or trim the sails. Better to spend their time getting the lifeboats under way and warning their fellow passengers of the impending doom. There is some plausibility to such a view, for it is of the utmost importance that the Christian not forget the judgment that stands over this world and that he not become so entangled in its affairs that he loses sight of his ultimate allegiance. Christians are pilgrims and strangers in a land that is most definitely not their home.

Nevertheless, quietistic or pietistic religion taken to its extreme forgets the importance of both the Incarnation and the Second Coming. When Christ became flesh He demonstrated to man the intention of God to save the world, not by ignoring it but by becoming most concretely involved in it. And if the redemption to be revealed at Christ's appearing is a real redemption of the world God has made and loves, not merely a rejection of it for something more ethereal, then those of us who hope in Christ must be no less concerned with the world today while still awaiting that future world that will see the fulfillment of all God's promises. Even Paul speaks of the creation waiting "for the revealing of the sons of God" (Rom. 8:19). Apparently, the curse that fell on the world at Adam's rebellion (Gen. 3:17-18) is removed only at the final redemption of Adam's sons.

It is true that there are almost no prescriptions in the New Testament for the Christian's participation in the larger problems of society. But social involvement is a fact of human existence in this age, and no biblical author in any dispensation was so naive as to suggest otherwise. A Christian slave in the first-century Roman Empire had almost no opportunities for involvement in the wider social and political problems of his community. But the opportunities and responsibilities of a free citizen in a modern, democratic state are something entirely different.

How the Christian uses political techniques cannot be prescribed, and they can never substitute for his witness to Jesus Christ. Political processes, like everything else in this world, are *temporary means by which some proximate good may be accomplished.* They are not the method by which the kingdom is inaugurated, and political parties and goals never should be allowed to compete with the Lordship of Christ. In passing, it is well to point out that political activity is not something limited to the processes of civil government. It occurs whenever power is exerted to achieve the goals of any human institution, including the church. The person who wishes to stay out of politics should never become an elder, bishop, deacon, or pastor in the church. And when he does accept an office in the church, he should not forget that the kingdom of God is not accomplished by ecclesiastical politics any more than by civil politics. If there is a word to guide us in these difficult matters it is this: "I do all things for the gospel's sake" (I Cor. 9:23 A S V).

The Realism of Christian Love

The ultimate effect of hope on our life today is to prompt us to make every decision in the light of the future. But this does not imply a naive idealism or a wishful fantasy that things will be better by and by. Hope begins with the most realistic fact of history, the cross of Christ. And, therefore, it does not delude itself about the risks of living in this world according to the rules of another world. God loved, and the cross was the key expression of His love. And when we accept the call of Christ the only hand with which He leads us is the one scarred by nails.

Precisely because of the element of hope within it, the realism of Christian love does not degenerate into cynicism. The cynic is one who is too conscious of present limitations of human existence. The Christian commits himself in the present moment to his neighbor in need, but he does so in hope of the resurrection. Thus, the cross and the resurrection are inextricably bound together so that one cannot hope for the resurrection without the anguish of the cross, and one does not endure the cross without the hope of the resurrection. If "heaven" is love, then love today is a sign of heaven on earth. As Moltmann puts it, "Love creating new life out of nothing, is resurrection in this life."[5]

Notes

1. Following are only a few of many references to the ethical intent of the prophetic messages: Isa. 1; Jer. 2; Ezek. 20; Hos. 14; Joel 2:12-17; Amos 3:1-2; 5:21-24; Mic. 3; Zeph. 3; Hag. 1; Zech. 8:8-14; Mal. 2:10-17; Matt. 25; I Cor. 15:58; I Thess. 5:1-11; Titus 2:11-13; II Peter 3:14; Rev. 2-3; 16:9,11.

2. This is the grain of truth in the "realized eschatology" of C. H. Dodd and others. But in order to develop a completely realized eschatology one simply has to ignore or explain away by arbitrary means the references to a *future* eschatology in the Gospel of John as well as elsewhere throughout the New Testament.

3. Slavery is the closest New Testament parallel to today's racial problems. The approach of the early Christians to slavery, which is a blatant contradiction of the new life in Jesus Christ, was not to seek a political solution, i.e., legislation or revolution. Rather, they simply ignored the fundamental social conventions which buttressed slavery and ultimately, as the proportion of Christians grew relative to the whole population, slavery fell under its own weight.

When Paul urged Philemon, the master, to treat Onesimus, the slave, as a *brother* (Philem. 16) he introduced an absolutely subversive element into the master-slave relationship. Philemon could not possibly treat Onesimus like a brother and as a piece of property at the same time!

4. At this point I am indebted to many of the insights of Jurgen Moltmann's theology. Cf. *Theology of Hope*, James W. Leitch, trans. (New York: Har-Row, 1967); and *Religion, Revolution and the Future*, Douglas Meeks, trans. (New York: Scribner, 1969).

5. *Religion, Revolution and the Future*, p. 58.

16

Of This We Can Be Sure!

W. Ward Gasque

The hope of the Second Coming of our Lord Jesus Christ is an essential part of the historic Christian faith.

No early Christian would have doubted the truth of this statement for a moment, since every time he partook of the Lord's Supper he was reminded of this event (I Cor. 11:26; 16:22b), and every time he listened to the reading of Scripture in church he heard reference to this hope from every second or third page of the New Testament. In addition, the doctrine is affirmed by all the early church fathers and creeds.

Tertullian, for example, writing in the second century, quotes a creedal statement, current in the church of his day, which speaks of Jesus Christ, who "sitting now at the right hand of the Father, will come to judge the living and the dead" (*De Virginibus Velendis*). An early form of what we today call the Nicene Creed, adopted by a church council in A.D. 325 but certainly reflecting earlier doctrinal statements, contains these words: "I believe in one God the Father Almighty. . . . And in our Lord Jesus Christ . . . [who] shall come to judge the living and the dead." The traditional form of the Nicene Creed that is recited in many churches today, dating from A.D. 341, affirms faith in "Jesus Christ His only Son our Lord, who . . . sits at the right hand of God the Father Almighty; from thence He shall come to judge the living and the dead. . . ."

And so one could continue to leaf through the creeds of Christendom and find this basic Christian hope affirmed and reaffirmed time and again. Although some modern theologians — and, of course, many non-Christians—have expressed their doubts concerning the doctrine of the Lord's return, these doubts have not found their way into any of the church's creeds. And we can rest assured that they will not, since the ordinary Christian believer knows that this hope of the Second Coming is an essential element of his faith. And this rightly so!

However, having affirmed the united conviction of the church down through the centuries that the Lord Jesus will come again, we must hasten to recognize—as has already been noted in several of the previous chapters—that the subject has been the basis of controversy among believers and also the focus of fruitless, not to say ridiculous, speculation by doubtlessly sincere but misguided students of the Bible. The controversies that have arisen and the all-too-obviously wrong-headed speculations are no doubt partially responsible for the doctrine being discredited in some circles and neglected in others.

Therefore, we need to remind ourselves of certain basic principles that will enable us to avoid the pitfalls of the past and the dangers of the present, and thus enable us to maintain a biblical and balanced perspective concerning this important doctrine.

Some Positive Affirmations

First, it is important for us to emphasize the aspects of the biblical teaching concerning the Lord's return that unite Christians rather than those that divide. That is to say, we should focus on the great truth of the Second Coming—a truth that all Christians affirm— rather than on the details, concerning which equally sincere students of Scripture are disagreed.

As in the case of other doctrines, we should conclude that if devout and orthodox men of God cannot agree concerning what the Bible teaches on any particular subject, it must be that the Bible is not all that crystal clear in this regard (and perhaps it is not all that important to the Holy Spirit that there be agreement, since He is the One who both inspired the biblical writers and illuminates the interpreters). Above all, we should be extremely wary of sectarian views of the subject, of taking an approach that has not been a part of the historic Christian faith but that has been advocated by only a small section of the Christian community and at only one particular time in history. Interpretations that could make sense only in our time, or that have only recently come to light, or that are held by only a small group of Bible students in contrast to the majority of the teachers that God has given as gifts to His church, must be considered suspect.

Second, we must strive to live in the tension of two biblical truths: our Lord Jesus Christ may come very soon—and we work and pray to that end—but He may not. He may, according to the divine purposes that we do not understand, delay His return. And if He does, then we must be faithful in these circumstances, too, and work to build for the future, so that the next generation of Christians will be able to carry on an effective witness for Christ during the interval between the two comings.

Thus the church must guard always against the twin temptations to attempt to place a date on the Lord's return (even when this is expressed in general terms) and to live in a manner that might seem to imply that we would be very surprised if He *did* come within our lifetime. Much harm has been done to the cause of Christ by Christians yielding to either of these temptations, as the history of the church has so often demonstrated. The Golden Mean may be a more difficult course, but it is the biblical perspective. Here the apostle Paul is our great example. He certainly lived his life expectantly in the light of the hope of the *parousia,* but he also planned for the future of the churches that he founded (by stressing teaching and faithfulness to received doctrine, by ordaining elders, and by training leaders for the next generation).

Third, we must remember the practical orientation of what the New Testament teaches in the area of eschatology. That is to say, the Bible is never speculative concerning the events surrounding the End, nor is the Lord's return conceived of as an abstract doctrine. Rather, whenever the Bible touches on these subjects, it is within the context of dealing with some ethical or practical problem facing the believers who are addressed.

For example, I Thessalonians 4:13-18 deals with the distress felt by the early church when some of its members had died before the expected return of the Lord. Thus Paul concludes: "Therefore comfort one another with these words." And in Mark 13 our Lord prepares His disciples for the impending crises of their generation by warning them about the destruction of the city of Jerusalem with

245

its temple, their persecution in and eventual expulsion from the synagogues, false messiahs and false prophets who would wrongly predict the End, and by telling them of the need for faithfulness in the task of world evangelism.

Second Peter 3:9-12 places the subject in its proper perspective:

> The Lord is not slow about his promise . . . ,
> but is forbearing . . . , not wishing that
> any should perish, but that all should
> reach repentance. But the day of the Lord
> will come like a thief, and then the
> heavens will pass away with a loud noise,
> and the elements will be dissolved with
> fire, and the earth and the works that
> are upon it will be burned up.

> *Since all these things are thus to be
> dissolved, what sort of persons ought
> you to be in lives of holiness and
> godliness,* waiting for and hastening
> the coming of the day of God. . . .

In this way, the end of the present age, which will be inaugurated by the return of Christ, is seen as a challenge to godly living and ministry rather than an occasion for speculation or theological discussion (cf. I Cor. 15:58).

The Christian Hope

What will happen at the Lord's return? What are the central features of the hope that is ours and in light of which we live expectantly? When we focus on the fundamental aspects (which are clear) rather than on the details (which are debated), three affirmations may be made.

First, the return of Jesus Christ will mean the full experience of salvation for the people of God. The biblical emphasis is on the resurrection of the body (I Cor. 15) at the return of Christ rather than on the salvation of the soul in conversion or at death, though orthodox theology rightly emphasizes union with Christ both in conversion and at death. But although we have experienced a foretaste of salvation in the present and look forward to being "with Christ" when we die (unless Christ comes first), we also can be assured that we will be resurrected at His coming. Because Christ has

246

been raised from the dead, those who belong to Christ also can confidently expect to be resurrected at the *parousia* (I Cor. 15:20-23).

Second, the return of Jesus Christ will issue in the final judgment on evil. The influence of evil, which has been a part of human experience since the fall of our first parents, will be excluded from the new world which is coming. The *parousia* will spell condemnation for all demonic powers and for all men who cooperate with them (Acts 17:31; I Peter 4:17-18; Rom. 1:18; 2:16; etc.). This, above all, is the message of the Book of Revelation: the kingdom of Christ finally will triumph over the kingdom of this world, regardless of the external appearance of current events at any given time in history. At the Lord's return, a new age will be ushered in, in which all sin and unrighteousness will be excluded (Rev. 21:8, 27; 22:3). To affirm this truth is not to give license to speculation concerning the nature of the punishment experienced by those who remain outside of Christ's kingdom. It is rather a call for us to cooperate with God in the fight against evil, and to warn people to "flee from the wrath to come" by finding their refuge in Christ.

Third, the return of Jesus Christ will mark the establishment of His universal lordship. True, He is presently "Lord of all" (Acts 10:36; Rom. 10:12) by virtue of His person and the work that He accomplished at the cross; but this sovereignty has yet to be fully realized by the world. At His coming, the One who "came unto His own home, and His own people received Him not" (John 1:11), who has been rejected by the majority of people but believed on by a growing number in whose lives the Holy Spirit is at work, will be acknowledged to be the One to whom universal homage is due. To Him every knee will bow and every tongue confess that He alone is Lord (Phil. 2:10-11). In this way, the scene of His rejection at His first advent will become the scene of His exaltation at the second. This is the truth of the doctrine of the millennium, however one conceives of the details being worked out historically. As the hymn writer puts it,

> Jesus shall reign where'er the sun
> Does his successive journeys run;
> His kingdom spread from shore to shore
> Till moons shall wax and wane no more.

Each of these elements contained in the New Testament teaching concerning the *parousia* has profound implications for contemporary

Christian life and witness. As we reflect upon them, we are motivated to mission, to share the gospel with the whole world; we are challenged to be concerned for justice in the world; we are moved to minister to the needs of the whole man, body as well as soul, since it is the resurrection *of the body* that we expect; and so on and on.

Thus the hope of the Lord's return has—or should have—a profound effect on the lives of believers, and through them on the world.

Of this we can be sure: our Lord Jesus Christ will certainly come again! This is our hope. This is our faith.

Even so, come, Lord Jesus!
Maranatha!

Study Guide

Riley B. Case

Chapter 1: The Age of Aquarius

What a curious phenomenon—in a time of sophisticated technological advance, our nation is experiencing a rebirth of astrology, fortune telling, and prophetic (in the non-biblical sense) speculation! "The Age of Aquarius" deals with this phenomenon and argues that it exists because we face in our day a spiritual crisis. Because we don't know who we are and why we are here, we are easy targets for those views which claim assurance for the future. Unfortunately, part of this is because Christianity has ceased for many to be a vital principle of living.

Whether we think we are interested in "history" or not, we desperately want to know if there is hope for the future, and what is the basis of that hope. Is history going some place? Are things getting better or are they getting worse?

There are several different responses to these kinds of questions:

1. There is no "plan" or direction to history, except such as we furnish ourselves (secularism).

2. The course of history is predetermined, and there is little we can do about it (astrology and various forms of fatalism).

3. A personal and loving God directs the course of history and has acted decisively in Jesus Christ, who stands at history's end. This gives meaning for living.

Questions

1. What is fatalism and why is it not a Christian view?

2. How widespread is the interest in astrology and fortune telling in the area in which you live? Give examples. What is the reason for this interest?

3. What does the author mean by the phrase: ". . . our Western view of progress has been secularized" (middle of p. 21)? Do you agree?

4. How would you describe your own view of history? What do you understand history to be?

5. The statement is made near the bottom of page 23: "But we must be careful that our longing for Christ's return is not motivated by a desire to escape responsibility." Why is such a statement made? Is it possible that some Christians would rather spend time talking about the return of Christ than in the difficult business of witnessing, caring, and addressing the problems of the community? Why?

6. What is the meaning of this sentence: "Prophecy is not merely prediction; it is judgment and it is promise" (p. 23, line 4)?

7. The chapter refers several times to an "identity crisis" or a "spiritual crisis." Deal with this by responding personally to the following questions: Who am I? Why am I here? Who loves me? How do I know? Does God have a plan for me? What is it? Does God have a plan for the world? What is it? What are five important beliefs that give me direction for life?

Chapter 2: The Danger of Mistaken Hopes

Sometimes, new Christians "discover" prophecy and wonder why the church has neglected to preach and teach truths concerning the return of our Lord. There has been neglect. On the other hand, it may be that down through the history of the church there has been more teaching about the return of our Lord than we realize. Sometimes, unfortunately, there have been excesses. A look at a few of the "mistaken hopes" of the past should help to keep us humble in our own study of biblical prophecy.

1. Montanism, from the teachings of Montanus in Phyrgia (second century), preached the near approach of the millennial reign of Christ. Speaking in tongues, prophetic utterances, asceticism, and severe discipline were linked with the movement, as well as disinterest in efforts to change the present order of things. When the expectations proved false, the movement died.

2. Joachim of Fiore (twelfth century) used prophecy in his linking of the pope with the Antichrist. He anticipated a New Age of the Spirit, starting in the year 1260, in which the world would be given to contemplation and would become like one vast monastery. Like others, he was mistaken.

3. Later, the followers of Francis of Assisi built new hopes on the ideas of Joachim and the example of Francis. The Golden Age would represent the victory of the spiritual order of things. This Golden Age, however, did not come.

4. Johann Heinrich Alsted fired the hopes of many Protestants in the seventeenth century. Alsted took special interest in the books of Daniel and Revelation to project a premillennial coming of Christ in 1694.

5. Leonard Sale-Harrison is a more recent interpreter who saw prophetic meaning in the events that took place on the world scene between World War I and World War II. Like others during this period, he was particularly fascinated by the rise of Mussolini. And, like others, his interpretations proved to be false.

Study of biblical prophecy should always be undertaken with the knowledge that sincere Christians have interpreted the Bible incorrectly in the past.

Questions

Christians are asked to live in the tension between watchfulness for the Lord's return on the one hand, and the knowledge that no one knows the time or season of the Lord's return on the other hand. We are always to be ready, but we are also to avoid date setting.

Theoretically, we agree on the importance of "balance." But practically, there are differences of opinion. What appears to be balanced to me may appear to be an extreme to someone else.

1. In the following passages is the emphasis on "being ready," or is it on the avoiding of undue speculation?

Mark 13:3-8   James 5:7, 8
Mark 13:32-37   Acts 1:6, 7
II Peter 3:3-13

2. Among Christian people you associate with, is it possible there is too much of an obsession with the possibility of prophetic fulfillment taking place in our day? Or is the opposite true—is teaching on the Lord's return too much neglected?

3. How are our Christian lives affected if there is too much emphasis on the expectation of the immediate return of the Lord?

4. How are our Christian lives affected if there is very little or no emphasis on the expectation of the return of the Lord?

5. What was the most recent sermon you heard on the Lord's return? What did this sermon say?

Chapter 3: Nineteenth-Century Roots
of Contemporary Prophetic Interpretation

In understanding the different approaches to biblical prophecy, it is helpful to look a the historical development of several of these points of view. While historic Christian faith is in basic agreement on many major teachings, present-day evangelicals are not in agreement on prophetic interpretation. Much of the way we think and believe today about biblical prophecy has been influenced by thinkers and developments in the late nineteenth century.

The prophetic understanding of the Middle Ages was primarily amillennial, after the example of Augustine. The optimism of the Puritans and the Great Evangelical Awakenings did much to enhance the position of post-millennialism, which was primarily the position of the evangelical church in American before the Civil War.

Various forms of premillennialism have been in existence from the earliest days of the church, but not until the nineteenth century did premillennialism become widespread. Some nineteenth-century premillennialists expected the return of Christ in the 1840s. Signs to support this view were the increasing conversion of Jews, the preaching of the gospel throughout the whole world, evidence of apostasy in the church, and upheaval and chaos in society.

A new form of premillennialism developed with John Nelson Darby in the 1820s. Darby stressed a more literal approach to Scripture, and the 1260 days of Daniel became literal days set during the Great Tribulation (which is not to take place until the Rapture of the Christians). Darby held to the futurist approach to Revelation and to the concept that Old Testament prophecies concerning Israel refer to a literal Israel and not to the church. This position, which became known as dispensational premillennialism, spread to America and strongly influenced the faith missions movement, the Bible school movement, and fundamentalism. It is the point of view which dominates much of present-day preaching and writing on "prophecy," including Hal Lindsey's best seller, *The Late Great Planet Earth*.

Questions

It is not necessarily true that most evangelicals hold the position of dispensational premillennialism. However, it must be said that much of the preaching on the Second Coming of Christ and many of the books on biblical prophecy that are being published today are from the perspective of dispensational premillennialism. For this reason, a serious study of biblical prophecy should include an understanding of dispensational premillennialism.

Perhaps the best way to do this is by becoming acquainted with key concepts and phrases and persons associated with dispensational premillennialism.

1. Identify and explain the significance of the following (page numbers in the text are given where material can be found):

Scofield Reference Bible (p. 59)
Historicist approach to Revelation (p. 44; cf. p. 54)
Futurist approach to Revelation (p. 51)
Literal-day theory (pp. 51-54)
Tribulation (p. 51)
Secret Rapture (p. 51)
Dispensational premillennialism (pp. 50ff.)
Literal Israel (p. 52; see also chapter 12)
John Nelson Darby (pp. 50ff.)

2. Dispensational premillennialism stands or falls, for the most part, as a system. One of the key features of the system is the concept of a literal Israel. Examine the following passages from Isaiah:

4:2-6	25:6-12
11:10-16	27:12-13
14:1-2	30:19-33
19:16-24	

Have these passages already been fulfilled? If so, how? If not, how will they be fulfilled in the future? Literally? Or in a way that defies literal description?

Chapter 4: Prophecy in the Old Testament

"Prophecy in the Old Testament" is a summary of how God used prophets and prophetic utterances during different time periods of the Old Testament. It contends that prophecy has a much broader scope than "the predicting of future events," and that "futurology," the obsession with what is going to happen in the twentieth century, was not the primary concern of the original biblical writers.

The earliest prophets in the Old Testament were political counselors. Later prophets were preachers who called the people to faithfulness and to the ethical demands of the covenant. These prophets proclaimed God's sovereignty and interest in human affairs. On the one hand they spoke of judgment upon sin; on the other hand they spoke of God's redemptive activity and of hope.

The nation of Israel played the prominent part in the prophet's message concerning the future. One prophetic theme pictured a day of universal peace and justice over all the earth.

How do these utterances relate to events in the twentieth century? Different interpreters are divided on answers to that question. Much of the division revolves around the understanding of what is meant by "Israel." More important than this question is the assurance that God is a God of power and love, whose purposes will result ultimately in the fulfillment of history.

"Prophecy in the Old Testament" offers some helpful guidelines for the interpreter of prophecy. The chapter stresses the importance of the historical and cultural context in which the message was spoken. It cautions us to be aware of various kinds of language in prophetic utterance (such as poetry), of the nature of symbolic actions, and of the extent and nature of predictive elements.

The chapter also speaks of "multiple fulfillment" and "indirect fulfillment" of prophecy, concepts which guard, on the one hand, against the view that the only legitimate meaning of a prophetic passage comes out of cultural and historical settings (liberalism), and, on the other hand, against the mechanical one-to-one view which sees predictive prophecy as a series of newspaper reports written before the event (extreme literalism).

Questions

Note the story on page 61 of a student who, immediately following a study of the prophetic book of Amos, asked his Bible professor, "When are we going to study prophecy in our Old Testament course?"

1. Read Amos 1 and 2. Why is this passage (and the entire book of Amos), a favorite among those who stress the social application of the gospel? Why is this passage (and the entire book of Amos), often neglected by those interested in what the author calls "futurology"? What is your understanding of the meaning of Amos 1 and 2?

2. Read Zechariah 14. Why is this passage (and the entire book of Zechariah) often neglected by those who stress the social application of the gospel? Why is this passage (and the entire book of Zechariah) a favorite among those interested in what the author calls "futurology"? What is your own understanding of the meaning of Zechariah 14 for today?

3. A section of the chapter, "Guidelines for Interpreting Prophecy," is found on pages 69 and following. Look up all the Bible references mentioned in this section and summarize in your own words the "special rules for prophetic Scriptures" which the author suggests.

4. What does the author call the "dual focus" to which all prophetic themes move with increasing clarity?

5. What is meant by "multiple fulfillment" and "indirect fulfillment" of prophecy (p. 70)?

Chapter 5: Messianic Prophecies in the Old Testament

"Messianic Prophecies" constitute one theme within the overall subject of Old Testament prophecy. They are of particular interest to Christians, because Christian faith centers on Jesus, and Christians believe that Jesus is the Messiah, or Christ, the One who fulfills the messianic prophecies.

How are we to understand the nature of messianic prophecies? Are they prediction or promise? Are they to be seen separately or cumulatively? Do they speak of matters temporal or eternal? Are they to refer to a national messiahship or a cosmopolitan messiahship? Do they refer to one who is primarily a messiah or a servant?

The chapter answers these questions by concluding that the prophecies are promises, interrelated, and part of a single, unified plan of God. They are at the same time fulfilled and yet to be fulfilled. They include a future for Israel—nationhood, land, king, worship, and riches—yet point to an eternal covenant in which all nations will be blessed.

Because the promises are not to be considered as separate or unrelated to one another, they are part of the whole of biblical teaching that includes the doctrine of salvation, and the kingdom of God. They speak of the direction of history and eternal destiny, both for individuals and for creation.

The promises can be traced from the Garden of Eden. They include the words spoken to Abraham, the authority given to priests and prophets, and the kingship of David. They come to fuller expression in Isaiah's vision of a Suffering Servant and Daniel's vision of "The Son of Man."

Questions

One of the values of this chapter is its stress upon the larger scope of biblical prophecy. The focus of biblical prophecy is not on isolated events, whether past or future, but in the great plan of God, accomplished in history through the person of Jesus Christ. To study these prophecies one ought not read individual Old Testament verses, but the whole Old Testament! It is in the feel and movement of the entire Bible that one comes to an appreciation of the plan of God and purpose of messianic prophecies.

1. The best way to appreciate the messianic prophecies is to go directly to the Bible. Read the following passages and then match them with the messianic subthemes that the passages best illustrate. (To check your answers, the references are listed in the discussion of each of the subthemes.)

II Samuel 7:12-16	_____	A. Roots of the Promise
Genesis 12:1, 7	_____	
Daniel 7:13, 14	_____	B. The Promise of Abraham
Micah 5:2	_____	C. The Everlasting Priesthood
Genesis 3:15	_____	
Isaiah 42:1-4	_____	D. The Prophet Like Moses
Deuteronomy 18:15, 18	_____	
Genesis 12:3, 7	_____	E. The Sure Mercies of David
Isaiah 53	_____	
Genesis 17:2, 7, 9, 19	_____	F. The Servant of the Lord
I Samuel 2:35	_____	
Zechariah 6:12, 13	_____	G. The Son of Man

2. What does the author mean when he speaks of the "distributive sense" on page 84?

3. For further study, answer in your own words: Is the nature of messianic prophecy separate or cumulative? Is it temporal or eternal? Is it cosmopolitan or national?

Chapter 6: When the Time Had Fully Come

Chapter 6 looks at New Testament events as the fulfillment of Old Testament prophecy. More specifically it looks at New Testament writers and seeks to understand how those writers used the Old Testament in their effort to give meaning to New Testament events, specifically those events surrounding the life, death, and resurrection of Jesus Christ.

The findings of this chapter are important for the study of biblical prophecy. On the one hand, they counter the charge made by some liberal interpreters that the New Testament writers forced meanings into Old Testament passages that were never intended by the original writers. The assumption behind the charges is that New Testament writers sometimes misused the Old Testament (and need to be corrected by the "scholarship" of today). The result is the de-emphasis on the importance of biblical prophecy, and in some cases the denial of the interpretations that have been a part of the tradition of the church for many years.

On the other hand, the conclusions of this chapter argue effectively against a kind of extreme literalism which holds that if a literal fulfillment of a passage was not accomplished at the time of Christ, the passage must then refer to events that are still future. The chapter, by implication, also argues against those who make use of a kind of midrash interpretation today, which would find contemporary events (whether in the Middle East or elsewhere) hidden in various prophetic passages of the Bible.

The chapter operates with these assumptions: 1. Jesus himself furnishes the impetus for the New Testament interpretation of the Old Testament. 2. Not all the Old Testament is fulfilled in New Testament events. There is some fulfillment that is as yet future.

A summary of the chapter's conclusions is as follows:

1. Events may have more than one meaning. A deeper, more significant meaning of an event may be contained within and alongside the primary or contemporary meaning.

2. Typological correspondence—in which the meaning and significance of persons or events are prefigured or anticipated in earlier events or persons—is used by New Testament writers and has some significance for us today.

3. The New Testament writers, for the most part, refrain from fanciful allegorical use of the Old Testament.

4. The use of midrash, or the discovery of hidden meanings relevant to present circumstances, was employed by many non-New Testament writers in biblical times. This method was, for the most part, avoided by the New Testament writers and should be avoided by us today.

257

Questions

1. What is the difference between "realized eschatology" and "inaugurated eschatology" (p. 90)?

2. The issues addressed by this chapter are better understood by examining biblical passages.

In the following pairs of Scripture references, read first the Old Testament passage. Make an effort to understand the context in which the words were spoken. Check commentaries and background material if it is available. What was the meaning of the passage to the original hearers? What deeper meaning was given the passage by the New Testament writer?

Isaiah 7:10-17	Isaiah 53	Matthew 2:18
Hosea 11:1	Matthew 1:20-25	Matthew 8:17
Jeremiah 31:15	Matthew 2:15	1 Peter 2:24, 25

Check these once again with the discussion in the text on pages 91-93. What do these passages say about how literally the New Testament writers interpreted the Old Testament?

3. What is the difference between "allegory" (pp. 94-95) and "typology" (pp. 93-94)?

4. What do you understand the midrash interpretation to be?

Chapter 7: Guidelines to the
Interpretation of Daniel and Revelation

Daniel and Revelation are the best examples of apocalyptic literature in our Bible. Special care is needed to avoid extremism in the interpretation of these books. On the one hand, liberal interpreters find little value in apocalyptic literature. They see it as strongly influenced by the events of the writer's day and limited by the historical situation. These interpreters see the significance of apocalyptic literature in the "faith" that the literature inspired in the first hearers. They study the books from the point of view of biblical times, but overlook the content and message relevant for today.

On the other hand, there are some who interpret this literature as a literal historical outline for the immediate future. It is predictive prophecy which can be directly related to current events.

The chapter contrasts the prophecy of Daniel with the prophecy of Isaiah and Jeremiah. Daniel is different in that the message looks beyond history to the ultimate and transcendent solution of God to the problems of the times.

Both Daniel and Revelation share in common with "futurists" of today a looking forward in history. The literature is able to penetrate the limits of space and time to give us a view of the cosmic-wide struggle between God and the forces of evil. As a result, believers are encouraged in their own times of difficulty.

In addition to the message of the books, the chapter stresses the books' value for worship.

The imagery and symbolism of the books need also to be noted, since they have enriched the thought of believers through the centuries.

Questions

1. Have you ever read the books of Daniel and Revelation? If so, describe your feelings after reading them.

2. Do you remember sermons preached from the books of Daniel and Revelation? What was the thrust of the sermons?

3. Define "apocalyptic."

4. Define "eschatology."

5. Matthew 24 is a well-known apocalyptic passage found in the Gospels. Without benefit of commentaries, read Matthew 24. How would you explain the meaning of this passage to someone in your church? How would you explain the meaning to an unbeliever?

6. Are Daniel and Revelation underemphasized or overemphasized in our day?

7. The overriding message of the Book of Revelation is that Jesus Christ will be the ultimate victor. Within that framework, and in your own words, outline some of the basic ideas presented in the Book of Revelation.

Chapter 8: Evangelical Alternatives

Chapter 8 should be read in conjunction with chapter 3, "Nineteenth-Century Roots." Both deal with schools of interpretation of biblical prophecy. Chapter 3 traces the historical development of the schools. Chapter 8 describes the major features of each school.

It should be mentioned that the word "evangelical" is being used in this chapter to describe those who accept the full authority of the Scriptures. The approach of "liberalism," in contrast, sees the Bible prophecy as limited by historical and cultural considerations and therefore relevant only in an indirect sense for today. (For example, some interpreters might emphasize that the significance of the prophetic message is in the faith it inspires rather than the truth of that message.)

Within the evangelical movement, three schools of interpretation can be defined: premillennialism, amillennialism, and postmillennialism. The schools can be characterized by their views of the millennium (see chapter 12) and their interpretation of Revelation 20.

Premillennialism is divided into two schools of interpretation: historic, or traditional premillennialism, and dispensational premillennialism. The latter is the view most often presented in popular books on prophecy and in prophetic conferences. This perspective features the Rapture of the church before the Great Tribulation (pre-Tribulation premillennialism), seven years of judgment and chaos on the earth (the Great Tribulation), a final battle of Armageddon, and a victorious return of Christ leading to a millennium of peace. It is this understanding of biblical prophecy which sees great significance in events taking place in the Middle East today. One of the assumptions of dispensational premillennialism is that "Israel" in the Bible always refers to the political entity Israel and never to the church or a spiritualized Israel (see chapter 14).

Amillennialism takes a less political and more of a nonliteral approach to biblical prophecy. While believing strongly in Christ's Second Advent, amillennialism considers as spiritual or poetic or symbolic many of the biblical passages which refer to the millennium or a time of peace and righteousness on earth. This position holds that many of the prophetic passages have been fulfilled already in Christ's birth, life, death, and resurrection, and the establishment of a new age at Pentecost. It allows for future consummation of all Bible promises in ways not necessarily comprehensible to us today.

Postmillennialism, the view of most American Protestants before the Civil War, is not widely held today. It holds that the rule of Christ, already established in the events of the New Testament, will enlarge and influence the world until a time of peace and justice (the millennium) comes on earth. At that time Christ will come personally to claim His Kingdom.

Questions

The following questions may be answered from material in the text or from your own experience. Answer with one of the following choices: (A) traditional premillennialism, (B) dispensational premillennialism, (C) post-millennialism, (D) amillennialism.

1. Which views have the strongest interest in prophecy? Why?

2. Which views expect a more complete fulfillment and a more literal fulfillment upon this earth of the biblical prophecies?

3. Which view insists that "Israel" in the Bible is always a literal, political Israel?

4. Which view is most optimistic about the possibility of the gospel in our day to change the course of history?

5. Which view speaks of the "Rapture"?

6. Which view believes the church has nothing to do with God's prophetic designs for Israel?

7. Which view believes that many of the prophecies have already been fulfilled in the First Advent of Christ?

8. Which view holds that the church will endure the Tribulation, and that Christ will appear on earth only after the Tribulation?

9. Which view makes a distinction between the "first appearance" of Christ to rapture the church, and the Second Coming of Christ?

10. Which view does not necessarily believe in a literal millennium?

11. Which view speaks most frequently of "apostate Christendom"?

12. Which view often speaks of Pentecost as the beginning of Christ's reign?

13. Which view is sometimes known as a "Jewish" approach to prophecy?

14. Which view sees the church as the fulfillment of many of the Old Testament prophecies?

15. Which is your own position?

Chapter 9: The Kingdom of God

One of the important—perhaps the most important—themes of biblical prophecy is that of the kingdom of God. While this theme does not lend itself to that which is spectacular or sensational in prophecy, its study is basic for proper understanding of the Old and New Testaments. Within the

Old Testament there are several diverse kinds of prophecies concerning the "King," or "Messiah," and the way the kingdom will be accomplished. The New Testament sheds light on the understanding of these prophecies.

It is the teaching of Jesus that there is to be a new eschatological order—the fulfillment of the vision of the prophets—established by divine revelation. These teachings assume the existence of a spiritual world beyond this world in which the forces of good and evil are in conflict. What takes place in this transcendent world beyond the world of our experience influences the present course of events. God ultimately will be victorious. With the coming of the heavenly Son of Man, God's power will be established, evil will be defeated, this world will be redeemed, and the relationship between God and his creation will be restored. This victory is already inaugurated in the mission of Jesus Christ. Its consummation, however, is still to come.

Questions

1. How does the author interpret the meaning of Hebrews as it relates to prophecy (p. 131)?

2. What three distinct messianic personages appear in Old Testament prophecy (pp. 131-33)?

3. Summarize three constant features of Old Testament prophetic expectations (pp. 132-33).

4. What is the theme of Jesus' teaching (p. 133)?

5. What does Jesus mean by the "kingdom of God" (p. 133)?

6. What does the chapter teach about the significance of "the two ages" (p. 134)?

7. Who or what are the ultimate enemies of God (p. 134)?

8. How and when are they ultimately overcome (p. 134)?

9. How and when is the new age of God's kingdom inaugurated (pp. 134-35)?

10. According to the chapter, what did God accomplish in the mission of Jesus (p. 136)?

11. What is the relationship between the death of Jesus and the coming of the kingdom (pp. 140-41)?

12. Who are the people of God according to the Old Testament? According to the reinterpretation of the New Testament (pp. 141-42)?

Chapter 10: The Return of Christ

The futuristic message of the New Testament centers on the Second Coming of Christ. The return of Christ (and not obsession with the Rapture or the Tribulation or signs of the times or the millennium or the battle of Armageddon) should be the focus of our attention in matters of prophetic teaching and the future.

This chapter makes a distinction between "prophetism" and "apocalypticism" and discusses the importance of keeping both in proper perspective. Prophetic truth has ethical relevance for today, but also offers hope for the future. The message of the New Testament has a two-advent structure—there is a sense of fulfillment already and yet there is a sense of watchfulness for more that is to come. Christ has come already—but at the same time is still to come again.

This hope of Christ's coming is:
1. Rooted in the covenant promises of God
2. Expressed in the teachings of Jesus
3. Confirmed by the resurrection and ascension of Jesus
4. Witnessed to by the Spirit
5. Explicated in the apostolic message

This hope is not based on human speculation but on the promises of God given in His Word.

Seven biblical pictures or themes portray Christ's return:
1. The manifestation of Christ's glory
2. The consummation of Christ's presence
3. The revelation of spiritual reality
4. The resurrection of believers
5. The assumption of the prerogatives that belong to Christ
6. The accompaniment of cosmic phenomena
7. Exhortation to watchfulness and preparedness

One implication of this is that Christians must learn the importance of living in two ages: the age that is and the age that is to come. Redemption is now, yet it is also future. The believer lives confidently in the present, and expectantly for the future.

Questions

One of the purposes of chapter 10 is to make a case for balance in the doctrine of the Second Coming. Some see no relevance in the doctrine of the Second Coming of Christ. Other persons put such emphasis on the doctrine and the events surrounding it that they have lessened commitment to the problems of the present age.

1. Do you see a need for this kind of balance among the Christians with whom you are acquainted?

2. Do you see an imbalance in the church today, either on the side of too little emphasis on Christ's return or too much emphasis on that teaching?

3. Does the approach offered in chapter 10 offer this balanced view, or is it itself one-sided?

4. What emphases have been neglected by the church today in its approach to the doctrine of the Second Coming of Christ?

5. What is the distinction between "prophetism" and "apocalypticism"?

6. What is meant by the "Two-Advent" structure?

7. What is your own understanding of the Second Coming of Christ?

Chapter 11: Times and Seasons

Can the Second Coming of Christ take place at any moment? Or, are there certain events—signaled by "signs"—that must first come to pass before the return of the Lord? Are these signs in evidence today? Were the disciples mistaken in believing the return of the Lord would take place in their own lifetime? These are questions being asked by persons interested in biblical prophecy today. How they are answered affects our attitude toward the world and the work of the church.

Numerous biblical texts must be compared in the process of deciding about the imminency of the Lord's return. These texts must be understood in the light of several other important New Testament events: the first advent of Christ, the destruction of Jerusalem, and Pentecost (the establishing of the new age). The apostle Paul urges a view which looks for Christ's coming at any moment, yet which understands that life must continue as normal and believers have obligations to fulfill in this world.

The following are categories of "signs" which some persons identify in the Bible with the return of Christ:

1. Unique signs: heavenly appearances, or strange phenomena in the heavens have been considered as a type of sign. The birth of Christ is a unique event which can be seen as a sign.

2. Intensified events: troubles such as disasters, plagues, droughts, famines, and wars may be intensified as the final days appear before the return of Christ. Satanic attacks, the work of the Antichrist, and the persecution of the church are also mentioned in the Bible.

3. Intricate calculations: Adventists, Jehovah's Witnesses, and others believe it is possible to calculate the time of Christ's return on the basis of a link between Bible passages and personalities and events of the present day.

Extreme care must be taken in the discussion of "signs." Many have misinterpreted what they thought were signs of the End. Still, it is possible to point to intriguing data in our day which seem to confirm the state of affairs mentioned in the Bible linked to the End. This should encourage us to be watchful for "the coming of the Day of God."

Questions

There is danger in building our understanding of the return of Christ on an effort to interpret "signs and seasons." So many have been so wrong so many times in the past! Persons and events which seem significant in one age pale to insignificance in another. Still, the Bible does refer to "times and seasons." On the basis of Matthew 24, Mark 13, Luke 21, chapter 11 of the text, and your own reading of other sources and biblical material, respond to the following questions.

1. Is the return of Christ imminent? Why? What does the idea of "imminent" mean to you?

2. How do you interpret the words, "This generation will not pass away till all these things take place" (Matt. 24:34)?

3. Are there "signs" which must first appear before the return of Christ?

4. Is there significance in the existence today of the political state of Israel?

5. Is it possible to put too much emphasis on "signs and seasons"?

6. How does the idea of an imminent return of Christ affect the way we live today as believers?

7. What "signs" in our present day do you see in evidence that correspond to "signs" mentioned in the Bible (see pp. 172-73)?

265

Chapter 12: The Millennium

Millennium (from Revelation 20) is an English word that has been used by Bible interpreters to refer to the time of peace and blessedness on earth after the forces of evil have been conquered by the power of God. Among those who take biblical prophecy seriously, there are differences between the view that the millennium is to be taken literally (premillennialism and, to a certain extent, postmillennialism) and the view that the "millennium" is to be understood figuratively, or spiritually (amillennialism). Among those who look for a more literal millennium, there are differences between those who see the millennium as preceded by the Lord's return (premillennialism), and those who believe the Lord's return follows the reign of peace (postmillennialism).

The concept of a literal millennium was very much a part of early church thinking. However, with the writings of Augustine, the millennium was spiritualized and became a symbol of the present church age, referring to the time (the present time) between Christ's resurrection and the end of the age. "Millennialism" for much of church history has been identified with extremist views and the sects. Secular views of progress and the concept of a "golden age" or "utopia" sometimes correlated with Christian millennialism. Despite this, however, belief in a millennium in some form has continued to have support, even in our present day.

Questions

Chapter 12 should be studied in conjunction with chapters 3 and 8, since all three chapters deal with a major issue among evangelical interpreters of prophecy—the issue of pre-, post-, or amillennialism.

Chapter 12 discusses background that is basic to this debate. It asks whether passages that speak of future peace and blessedness are references to the millennium, and whether such passages are to be interpreted figuratively or literally.

Read the following passages:

Isaiah 11:1-6	Jeremiah 33:17-22
Isaiah 52:7-12	I Corinthians 15:22-28
Isaiah 65:17-25	Revelation 20:4-6

1. Which, if any, of the passages suggest a literal millennium?
2. To what do the passages refer if not to a literal millennium?

On the basis of these Scripture passages, the chapter in the book, and other readings . . .

3. What are the arguments for a "literal" millennium?

4. What are the arguments for a "spiritual" millennium?

5. How does the issue of the millennium relate to events in the Middle East today?

6. Which view has the strongest support in the tradition and history of the church?

7. Do you look for a time of earthly peace and blessedness under the reign of Christ?

8. What do you believe about the millennium?

Chapter 13: The Last Judgment

The Last Judgment is another theme that must be considered as a part of biblical prophecy. Jewish apocalyptic thought gives witness to a final judgment in which God will vindicate His righteous purpose for all creation.

However, interpreters differ whether judgment is the end of history or the prelude to something that is beyond (and thus the issue of the millennium is related to this question).

Judgment in the Old Testament is within the course of history and is often related to historic events (such as the Fall of Jerusalem), but it points to a larger cosmological "Day of Yahweh" (the Lord) as well. Judgment is often upon nations, but is also upon individuals.

While judgment in the Old Testament is futuristic, judgment in the New Testament is both present and future. It is present in that Christ has inaugurated the New Age and has defeated the power of evil in His death and resurrection. Still, the New Testament gives witness to a future consummation and final victory over sin.

The New Testament does not present a single, clear, systematic, detailed picture of the shape of the Last Judgment. Rather, different New Testament writings—the synoptic (first three) Gospels, John, Revelation, the Epistles—present partial views and emphasize different facets of this great event, the depth of which may be too great for full human comprehension.

Questions

1. What does the author mean by "double eschatology" (p. 191)?

2. What is the major difference between judgment as it is viewed in the Old Testament, and judgment as it is viewed in the New Testament (p. 191)?

3. How does the emphasis on judgment in Matthew differ from the emphasis in Mark and Luke (pp. 193-96)?

4. How does the emphasis on judgment in John differ from the emphasis in Matthew, Mark, and Luke (pp. 198-99)?

5. What does the author mean in this sentence: "The evangelists know of no church that is allowed to isolate itself from the world and observe the Last Judgment as a spectator" (p. 196, bottom)?

6. How does the chapter understand the teaching on judgment in the Book of Revelation (pp. 199-201)?

7. According to Paul, how is it that believers escape condemnation in Last Judgment (pp. 201-4)?

8. What is "the apocalyptic doctrine of the ages" (p. 204)?

Chapter 14: Israel and the Church (Two Views)

Chapter 14 is addressed to one of the major issues dividing evangelicals interpreting biblical prophecy. The issue has to do with the identity of "Israel" in the Bible. It is of special significance for those who are wondering if there is a connection today between events in the Middle East and biblical prophecy. When the Bible (mostly the Old Testament) speaks of God's promises to "Israel," or "His people," are we to interpret the passages "spiritually," as references to a spiritual Israel or to the church? Or, do we interpret "Israel" literally, as the Jewish people, specifically the Jewish people who claim the nation Israel as their homeland?

The section, "The New Israel," argues that since the coming of Christ, "Israel," or the "people of God," are those who claim Christ as Savior. Believers in Christ are the inheritors of Old Testament promises. The New Covenant has fulfilled the Old Covenant. Those who live by faith represent the "New Israel," or the "people of God." The symbolism associated with Pentecost, the arguments of Paul, and the way New Testament writers interpret the Old Testament support this view. The biblical themes of remnant and renewal argue further for this position. Old Testament visions of a new temple, a new land, and of a coming Messiah speak of a transfigured and transformed kind of reality, a future consummation bestowed upon all who walk by faith, not just to Jews alone, but to the entire people of God.

A second and opposing view of "Israel" is set forth in the section, "Two Peoples of God." The argument of this section is for Israel and the church as separate entities. They share features in common: they are both chosen by God as recipients of God's grace; they have a universal mandate to proclaim that grace; they share the truth that membership in either is a matter of spiritual and not primarily physical descent; they share the same messianic consciousness.

However, there are differences. Israel and the church have distinct historic and ethnic backgrounds; Israel and the Gentiles are discussed in Scripture as separate entities; the language used by Paul in Ephesians implies a distinction; the character of the promises given differ. Therefore, "Israel" is not to be confused with "the church." Each has a special place and purpose in God's plan.

As with several of the issues of biblical prophecy, prayerful study is needed to help the believer sort out the varying points of view within Christian tradition and come to a mature and responsible position.

Questions

The issue behind the discussion in chapter 14 is that of scriptural interpretation. Is the Bible to be interpreted literally, so that "Israel" is always "Israel"? Or, is it possible to interpret the Bible "spiritually" or "poetically," so that the "people of God" who are the church are now the recipients of the promises once made to the "people of God" who were once called Israel? Does the cross of Christ bring a different kind of fulfillment from that anticipated by Jews before the time of Jesus? The issue is addressed in another way in chapter 6, "When the Time Had Fully Come."

The best way to study the question further is to look at several specific biblical passages.

1. Study Jeremiah 31:31-34. Is there a way in which this passage has already been fulfilled? Or, does it refer primarily to an age that is to come? If an age that is to come, will it be fulfilled by the "people of God" who have faith in Christ? Or, is it a reference to the nation Israel, that is, the Jews? Is it possible it is both fulfilled in a certain sense and yet to be fulfilled in another sense?

2. Refer to Galatians 6:16. Who is the "Israel of God," the church or the Jewish people?

269

3. Study Galatians 3:6-29. Who are the sons of Abraham? Does this passage preclude the possibility of a separate plan for Jews?

4. Study Romans 9-11. Does this passage suggest a special purpose of God for Israel apart from that accomplished by Christ in the new covenant?

5. Study Ezekiel 36:22-38. Has this passage been partially fulfilled in the New Age inaugurated by Jesus Christ? Or, is it a reference to a different kind of fulfillment? Is it to be fulfilled literally?

Chapter 15: Living Between Two Ages

If the study of biblical prophecy does not affect how we live, then we have turned its study into a game and have misused it for a purpose other than how it was intended. The basic purpose of prophecy is redemptive and ethical.

A key to how our lives should be lived in the light of prophecy is in the concept of "Living Between Two Ages." We live and move in the present age and are citizens of this world. Yet we also have a loyalty to a world that is beyond this one. There is continual tension between the two worlds. The ethics of the Sermon on the Mount (Matthew, chapters 5, 6, 7) are not the ethics that usually operate in the nation's marketplace.

How to live in the midst of this tension between the two ages is the problem that faces the believer. Eschatological hope encourages us with what this world can and will someday be like. It gives a more realistic outlook about the possibilities of peace through social and political movements. It keeps us from despair in the midst of the most serious of problems.

At the same time, this hope ought to make us better citizens of the present world. Instead of causing us to withdraw from the arena of social and political conflict, it should involve us more concretely in the world, as we seek to give expression to the peace that comes from God.

Such a hope saves us from cynicism and pessimism on the one hand, and from naive idealism or wishful fantasy on the other.

Questions

In some ways chapter 15 is the most important chapter in the book: it focuses on the tension that comes from living in two radically different realms or kingdoms. We are citizens of this world and also of the world that is to come (the spiritual kingdom inaugurated by Jesus Christ). It is not easy to live as a Christian! The study of biblical prophecy should have impressed us of that by now.

One way to deal with the practical implications of this tension is in the discussion of personal ethics and lifestyle. One of the clearest biblical passages on ethical teaching in the realm of the kingdom is the Sermon on the Mount. In the light of the ideas expressed in the text, read Matthew 5.

1. Is there a conflict between the demands of the Kingdom and . . . participation in the local Chamber of Commerce (p. 234)?
old-fashioned patriotism?
astute business practices?
involvement in a labor union?
interest in latest clothing fashions?
running for political office?
spending three hours a day watching television?
In what way is your lifestyle different from the people you live near or work with who are not Christians?

2. Is Matthew 5 meant to be taken literally or "spiritually"?

3. Do you agree or disagree with the author's statement, "The Christian's confidence in the fulfillment of God's stupendous promises means that we must search for new meanings for words such as 'radical' and 'revolutionary' " (p. 238). What does it mean to you to be "radical" or "revolutionary" in the Christian sense?

4. What is the "sinking ship" approach to the world (p. 239)?

5. Should the Christian be involved in politics? Why? To what extent? Does God often use politics to accomplish His purposes?

Chapter 16: Of This We Can Be Sure!

Biblical prophecy is not to be considered as an idle curiosity. The Second Coming of Christ is an integral part of biblical faith. Certain basic principles can help us avoid the mistakes of the past and the excesses of the present while incorporating this hope into our Christian experience.

There should be an emphasis on the aspects of the teachings that unite, rather than divide, Christians. We should beware of interpretations that have not been a part of the major Christian traditions of the past and present. We should recognize the tension of the "two ages" idea—Christ has come and yet is to come. The New Age is inaugurated but also yet is to be consummated.

Could evangelical Christians agree on several central features of the return of Christ? That the full experience of salvation is related to Christ's Second Coming? That this coming will result in the final judgment on evil? That Christ will, at His return, establish His universal Lordship?

While there is room for various interpretations within these themes, they suggest broadly based affirmations that we can claim as important essentials in the faith.

Questions

The following are affirmations that have been made either in the past or in the present that relate to the Second Coming of Christ.

1. In the space before each affirmation put a plus ($) before the affirmations that you agree with and a minus (-) before the affirmations that you do not agree with. Leave blank those about which you are not sure.

2. Circle the letters of the three affirmations that you feel are of primary importance for Christian faith today.

A. In the millennial kingdom, Christ will sit of the throne of David and rule the earth from Jerusalem.

B. At Christ's appearance, the church will be raptured from this earth.

C. There are already practices in our society which are suspiciously similar to what is described in the Bible as "the mark of the Beast."

D. Christ will someday return.

E. The return of Christ will mark the establishment of His universal Lordship.

F. The church must prepare to face a time of great Tribulation before the return of Christ.

G. The return of Christ will issue in a final judgment on evil.

H. The seven churches of Revelation 2-3 represent seven ages of church history.

I. God's plan for the Jews is different from God's plan for the church.

J. Israel in the Bible is always to be considered literally as the Jewish people.

K. Russia will be involved in the battle of Armageddon.

L. The situation in the Middle East today is a sure sign of the near-return of Christ.

M. The Book of Revelation is a symbolic account of the history of the church.

N. Before the return of Christ, Gabriel, the archangel, will blow his trumpet.

O. The Temple described in Ezekiel 40-48 will be built during the millennium.

P. The people of God will experience full salvation at the return of Christ.

Q. The church will not be on the earth during the time of Tribulation.

R. Satan will be released after the millennium to work deception on the people.

S. The events of the New Testament basically fulfill the prophecies of the Old Testament.

T. The signs of the times suggest that Christ will probably return in our generation.

U. We live as citizens of the world that is, and also of the world that is to come.

FOR FURTHER READING

(*An asterisk indicates a fairly nontechnical work.)

Historical Background

*C. B. Bass, *Backgrounds to Dispensationalism*. Grand Rapids: Eerdmans, 1960.

L. E. Froom, *The Prophetic Faith of Our Fathers: The Historical Development of Prophetic Interpretation*. 4 vols. Washington: Review and Herald, 1946-54.

M. Reeves, *The Influence of Prophecy in the Later Middle Ages*. Oxford and New York: Oxford University Press, 1969.

T. F. Torrance, *Kingdom and Church: A Study in the Theology of the Reformation*. Edinburgh and London: Oliver and Boyd, 1956.

Old Testament Prophecy

*H. L. Ellison, *Men Spake From God*. London: The Paternoster Press; Grand Rapids: Eerdmans, 1958.

*H. L. Ellison, *The Prophets of Israel*. Exeter: The Paternoster Press; Grand Rapids: Eerdmans, 1969.

A. B. Mickelsen, *Interpreting the Bible*. Grand Rapids: Eerdmans, 1963, chap. 13.

*P. E. Hughes, *Interpreting Prophecy*. Grand Rapids: Eerdmans, 1976.

*B. Ramm, *Protestant Biblical Interpretation*. Grand Rapids: Baker Book House, rev. ed., 1970, chap. 10.

Messianic Prophecies

W. J. Beecher, *The Prophets and the Promise*. Grand Rapids: Baker Book House, [1905] 1963.

C. A. Briggs, *Messianic Prophecy*. New York: Scribner's, 1889.

F. Delitzsch, *Messianic Prophecies*. Edinburgh: T. & T. Clark, 1880.

H. L. Ellison, *The Centrality of the Messianic Idea for the Old Testament.* London: Tyndale Press, 1953.

A. T. Hanson, *Jesus Christ in the Old Testament.* London: SPCK, 1965.

Use of the Old Testament in the New

D. L. Baker, *Two Testaments: One Bible.* Downer's Grove, IL: Inter-Varsity, 1976.

*F. F. Bruce, *This is That: The New Testament Development of Some Old Testament Themes.* Exeter: The Paternoster Press, 1968. Published in North America as *The New Testament Development of Old Testament Themes.* Grand Rapids: Eerdmans, 1968.

C. H. Dodd, *According to the Scriptures.* London: James Nisbet, 1952. Reprinted by Fontana/Collins, 1967.

E. E. Ellis, *Paul's Use of the Old Testament.* London and Edinburgh: Oliver and Boyd; Grand Rapids: Eerdmans, 1957.

R. T. France, *Jesus and the Old Testament.* London: Tyndale Press, 1971.

R. N. Longenecker, *Biblical Exegesis in the Apostolic Period.* Grand Rapids: Eerdmans, 1975.

*H. M. Shires, *Finding the Old Testament in the New.* Philadelphia: Westminster, 1974.

On the Book of Daniel

R. K. Harrison, *Introduction to the Old Testament.* Grand Rapids: Eerdmans; London: Tyndale Press, 1969.

*L. F. Hartman, "Daniel," in *The Jerome Biblical Commentary,* ed. R. E. Brown *et al.* Englewood Cliffs, NJ: Prentice-Hall, 1968; London: G. Chapman, 1969, Old Testament section, pp. 446-460.

*H. H. Rowley, "Apocalyptic Literature," and J. Barr, "Daniel," in *Peake's Commentary on the Bible,* ed. M. Black and H. H. Rowley. London and New York: Nelson, 1962.

E. J. Young, *The Prophecy of the Book of Daniel.* Grand Rapids: Eerdmans, 1949.

*E. J. Young, "Daniel," in *The New Bible Commentary: Revised*, ed. D. Guthrie *et al.* London: Tyndale Press; Grand Rapids: Eerdmans, 1970.

On the Revelation to John

G. R. Beasley-Murray, *The Book of Revelation*. (New Century Bible). London: Oliphants; Greenwood, SC: Attic, 1974.

G. B. Caird, *A Commentary on the Revelation of St. John the Divine*. (Black/ Harper Commentaries). London: A. & C. Black; New York: Harper & Row, 1966.

G. E. Ladd, *The Revelation of St. John*. Grand Rapids: Eerdmans, 1972.

P. S. Minear, *I Saw a New Earth: An Introduction to the Visions of the Apocalypse*. Washington and Cleveland: Corpus Books, 1968.

*L. Morris, *The Revelation of St. John*. (Tyndale Commentaries). London: Tyndale Press; Grand Rapids: Eerdmans, 1969.

Schools of Prophetic Interpretation

General

L. Boettner, *The Millennium*. Philadelphia: Presbyterian & Reformed, 1958.

*R. Ludwigson, *A Survey of Bible Prophecy*. Grand Rapids: Zondervan, 1973.

Dispensational Premillennialism

*R. E. Baughman, *The Kingdom of God Visualized*. Chicago: Moody, 1972.

*W. E. Blackman, *Jesus Is Coming*. Tappan, N.J.: Revell, 1932.

*J. F. Walvoord, *The Blessed Hope and the Tribulation*. Grand Rapids: Zondervan, 1976.

Nondispensational Premillennialism

*G. E. Ladd, *The Blessed Hope*. Grand Rapids: Eerdmans, 1956.

*G. E. Ladd, *Crucial Questions About the Kingdom of God*. Grand Rapids: Eerdmans, 1954.

J. B. Payne, *The Imminent Appearing of Christ.* Grand Rapids: Eerdmans, 1962.

Amillennialism

G. C. Berkouwer, *The Return of Christ.* Grand Rapids: Eerdmans, 1952.

*F. E. Hamilton, *The Basis of Millennial Faith.* Grand Rapids: Eerdmans, 1952.

*G. Murray, *Millennial Studies.* Grand Rapids: Eerdmans, 1948.

Postmillennialism

*J. M. Kik, *The Eschatology of Victory.* Philadelphia: Presbyterian & Reformed, 1971.

*J. H. Snowden, *The Coming of the Lord: Will It Be Premillennial?* New York: Macmillan, 1919.

The Kingdom of God

*G. E. Ladd, *The Gospel of the Kingdom.* Grand Rapids: Eerdmans; Exeter: The Paternoster Press, 1959.

G. E. Ladd, *Jesus and the Kingdom.* New York: Harper & Row; London: SPCK, 1964. (Revised edition published under the title *The Presence of the Future.* Grand Rapids: Eerdmans, 1974.)

H. N. Ridderbos, *The Coming of the Kingdom.* Philadelphia: Presbyterian & Reformed, 1962.

R. Schnackenburg, *God's Rule and Kingdom.* New York: Herder; London: Nelson, 1963.

The Return of Christ

G. C. Berkouwer, *The Return of Christ.* Grand Rapids: Eerdmans, 1972.

C. Brown *et al.*, *The New International Dictionary of New Testament Theology*, 3 vols. Exeter: The Paternoster Press; Grand Rapids: Zondervan, 1975-77, articles on "Eschatology" and related topics.

G. E. Ladd, *A Theology of the New Testament.* Grand Rapids: Eerdmans, 1974; London: Lutterworth, 1975.

278

*G. T. Manley, *The Return of Jesus Christ.* London: Inter-Varsity Press; Downers Grove, IL: Inter-Varsity Press, 1960.

The Problem of "Imminency"

G. R. Beasley-Murray, *Jesus and the Future.* London: Macmillan; New York: St. Martin's Press, 1954.

A. L. Moore, *The Parousia in the New Testament.* (Supplements to *Novum Testamentum* 13). Leiden, The Netherlands: E. J. Brill, 1966.

J. B. Payne, *The Imminent Appearing of Christ.* Grand Rapids: Eerdmans, 1962.

*S. Travis, *The Jesus Hope.* London: Word Books, 1974.

The Millennium

In addition to the works mentioned in the footnotes of chapter 12, see the sections on Revelation 20 in the commentaries by Beasley-Murray, Caird, and Morris (mentioned above).

The Last Judgment

Articles related to the Greek words *krisis, hēmera, eschatos,* and *aiōn* in *Theological Dictionary of the New Testament,* ed. G. Kittel and G. Friedrich, 9 vols. Grand Rapids: Eerdmans, 1964-74.

Articles related to the same words in *The New International Dictionary of New Testament Theology,* ed. Colin Brown, 3 vols. Exeter: The Paternoster Press; Grand Rapids: Zondervan, 1975–77.

J. P. Martin, *The Last Judgment in Protestant Orthodoxy to Ritschl.* London and Edinburgh: Oliver & Boyd; Grand Rapids: Eerdmans, 1963.

L. Morris, *The Biblical Doctrine of Judgment.* London: Tyndale Press; Grand Rapids: Eerdmans, 1960.

D. S. Russell, *The Method and Message of Jewish Apocalyptic.* London: SCM Press; Philadelphia: Westminster, 1964.

G. Vos, *The Pauline Eschatology.* Grand Rapids: Eerdmans, 1952.

Israel and the Church

O. T. Allis, *Prophecy and the Church.* Philadelphia: Presbyterian & Reformed, 1942.

*M. Barth, *The Broken Wall: A Study of the Epistle to the Ephesians.* London: Collins; Chicago: Judson, 1959.

*C. B. Bass, *Backgrounds to Dispensationalism.* Grand Rapids: Eerdmans, 1960.

*R. Campbell, *Israel and the New Covenant.* Philadelphia: Presbyterian & Reformed, 1954.

*H. L. Ellison, *The Mystery of Israel.* Exeter: The Paternoster Press; Grand Rapids: Eerdmans, 1968.

P. Richardson, *Israel in the Apostolic Church.* Cambridge and New York: Cambridge University Press, 1969.

*C. C. Ryrie, *Dispensationalism Today.* Chicago: Moody, 1973.

Eschatology and Ethics

C. F. H. Henry, *Personal Christian Ethics.* Grand Rapids: Eerdmans, 1957, pp. 278-326.

*G. E. Ladd, "Eschatology and Ethics," in *Baker's Dictionary of Christian Ethics,* ed. C. F. H. Henry. Grand Rapids: Baker Book House; Glasgow: Pickering & Inglis, 1973.

J. Moltmann, *Theology of Hope: On the Ground and the Implications of a Christian Eschatology.* London: SCM Press, 1967.

Index to Scripture References

Page numbers in italics indicate references found in footnotes.